ECONOMICS EXPLAINED

EVERYTHING YOU NEED TO KNOW ABOUT HOW THE ECONOMY WORKS AND WHERE IT'S GOING

Robert Heilbroner and Lester Thurow

REVISED AND UPDATED

A TOUCHSTONE BOOK
Published by Simon & Schuster
New York   London   Toronto   Sydney   Tokyo   Singapore

TOUCHSTONE
Rockefeller Center
1230 Avenue of the Americas
New York, New York 10020

Copyright © 1982, 1987, 1994 by Robert Heilbroner and Lester Thurow

Designed by Irving Perkins Associates, Inc.
Manufactured in the United States of America

10 9 8 7 6 5 4 3 2 1

Library of Congress Cataloging-in-Publication Data

Heilbroner, Robert
    Economics explained: everything you need to know about how the economy
works and where it's going / Robert Heilbroner and Lester Thurow.—revised
and updated.
        p.   cm.
    "A Touchstone book."
    Includes bibliographical references and index.
    1. Economics.   2. United States—Economic conditions—1945–
I. Thurow, Lester C.   II. Title.
HB171.H479 1994
330—dc20   93-21329
                                                      CIP

    ISBN 0-671-88422-0

The boxed material in this book and the Appendix on banking are taken directly
from Robert Heilbroner and Lester Thurow, *The Economic Problem*, 6th ed.,
Prentice-Hall, 1980

Introduction

Books on economics abound. Most of them have two purposes. They tell you how to make a great deal of money—in the stock market, in real estate, in gold; or they tout some kind of economic salvation—less government or more government, less regulation or more regulation, less capitalism, more capitalism.

There is one overwhelming problem with both kinds of books. They don't work. The books about money do not make you money— if they did, the United States would be crawling with millionaires. And the books about economic salvation do not set your mind at ease. They just make you feel better for a moment.

Then why do people go on buying these books? At bottom, we believe it is because they are in search of something more serious than instant riches or saving the world. *They want to understand the nature of the economic forces that are upsetting their lives.* They want to know the meaning of the incomprehensible vocabulary they read every morning in the newspapers and hear every night on TV—the "money supply" and "gross national product" and "government deficits" that are somehow connected with their personal and public woes and misfortunes. Is it not the truth that we simply do not understand the very words that are supposed to tell us what is the matter?

That explains the purpose of this book. To say it as directly as possible, we have written a book based on our conviction that a great many people seriously want to know what economics is all about. Thereafter, if they still want advice on getting rich, or a tract for our times, fine. At least they will then understand the words the author is using.

Our belief in an audience that wants to learn about economics comes from personal experience. We are the authors of college texts that have gone through many editions. But increasingly it has dawned on us that the people who are most eager to understand economics are not only students who want to pass a course, but men and women in the real world, including students, who need to make their way intelligently through life. This is the economics they ought to know—not to get rich, and not to have a particular point of view, but simply to be effective investors, educated persons, informed workers or just good citizens.

Now a word about the book itself. It is, of course, meant to be read straight through, and it will present a coherent story about economics if you do so. But it is also designed to fit different needs. Someone who wants to know about international economics, for instance, can turn to Part IV. Readers who can't wait to find out what we have to say about inflation can begin with Chapter Twelve. Needless to say, later chapters will mean more if you have read the earlier ones, but the book can be used selectively—skipped over, dipped into, read from back to front if you want. One final word about statistics. Almost all of them come from the *United States Statistical Abstract,* 1992 edition. But numbers change. It's always wise—and often educational—to look them up in the latest *Abstract.*

Economics Explained is very different from the text from which it derived its original inspiration. But two resemblances remain— we hope. First, it is a book of teaching, not preaching. There are plenty of controversial opinions in the book, but they are always labeled as such, never slipped across as The Truth. Second, the test of a textbook is whether a student sells it back to the college bookstore at the end of the year or keeps it around because, who knows, it's the kind of book he or she might want to look into again someday. We would like this to be that kind of book for you.

Robert Heilbroner
Lester Thurow

Contents

III Microeconomics—The Anatomy of the Market System

IV The Rest of the World

I

THE ECONOMIC
BACKGROUND

ONE

Capitalism: Where Do We Come From?

We live in a capitalist economic system. Politicians constantly talk about capitalism, or if they don't like the word, about the free-enterprise system. We are constantly being told that capitalism is the wave of the future, or would be the wave of the future if only it were left alone, or sometimes that capitalism is in decline and will fall of its own weight, like the Roman Empire.

Perhaps there is no more important economic question than the future of capitalism, none that affects more deeply our private destinies and those of our children. As we will see in our next chapter, the great economists of the past were vitally concerned with this issue. Modern economists are wiser or blinder, depending on how you look at it, and say relatively little about our long-term prospects. Nonetheless, we feel that it is impossible to understand capitalism without at least some understanding of its roots. So we are going to begin the study of our economic system rather the way a doctor begins to become acquainted with a patient—by taking its history.

Many people speak about capitalism as if it were as old as the hills, as ancient as the Bible, implying that there is something about the system that accords with human nature. Yet, on reflection, this is clearly not the case. Nobody ever called the Egyptian pharaohs capitalists. The Greeks about whom Homer wrote did not comprise a business society, even though there were merchants and traders in Greece. Medieval Europe was certainly not capitalist. Nor would anyone have used the word to describe the brilliant civilizations of India and China about which Marco Polo wrote, or the great empires of ancient Africa, or the Islamic societies of which we catch glimpses in *The Arabian Nights*.

What made these societies noncapitalist was not anything they possessed in common, for they were as different as civilizations could be, but rather, some things they *lacked* in common. To become aware of these lacks will give us a sharp sense of the uniqueness and special characteristics of capitalism itself.

To begin with, all these noncapitalist societies lacked the institution of private property. Of course, all of them recognized the right of some individuals to own wealth, often vast wealth. But none of them legally accorded the right of ownership to all persons. Land, for instance, was rarely owned by the peasants who worked it. Slaves, who were a common feature of most precapitalist systems, were only rarely permitted to own property—indeed, they *were* property. The idea that a person's property was inviolate was as unacknowledged as that his person was inviolate. The Tudor monarchs, for example, relatively enlightened as sixteenth-century monarchies went, could and did strip many a person or religious order of their possessions.

Second, none of these variegated societies possessed a central attribute of capitalism—a market system. To be sure, all of them had markets where spices, gold, slaves, cloth, pottery, and foodstuffs were offered for sale. But when we look over the expanses of ancient Asia, Africa, or the Egyptian and Roman empires, we can see nothing like the great web of transactions that binds our own economy together. Most production and most distribution took place by following the dictates of tradition or the orders of a lord. In general, only the small leftovers found their way to the market stalls. Even more important, there was no organized market at all to buy and sell land, or to hire labor, or to lend money. Markets were the ornaments of society, tradition and command its iron structure.

Under such conditions, the idea of economic freedom was held in little regard. When peasants were not free to move as they wished, when artisans were bound to their trades for life, when the relations of field-workers to their masters were that of serf to lord, who could worry about the right of contract or the right to withhold one's labor? The distinction is crucial in separating capitalism from what came before: a capitalist employee has the legal right to work or not work as he or she chooses; and whereas this right may seem to count for little under conditions of Dickensian poverty, it must be compared with the near-slavery of the serf legally bound to his lord's land and to the work his lord assigned him.

In such a setting, moneymaking itself was not much esteemed. Ambitious persons from the better walks of life sought fame and fortune in military exploits, in the service of the court, or in the hierarchies of religion. In this regard, it is interesting to reflect how twisted and grasping are the faces of merchants depicted by medieval artists, in contrast to the noble mien of soldiers and courtiers. Moneymaking was generally considered to be beneath a person of noble blood; indeed, in Christendom it was a pursuit uncomfortably close to sin. Usury—lending at interest—*was* a sin—in fact, a mortal sin.

As a consequence of all this, society's wealth was not owned by "the rich"—that is, by those whose main efforts were directly aimed at moneymaking—but rather by the powerful, who seized it in the struggle for lands and privileges. Of course, the winners in this struggle became rich, sometimes unimaginably rich, but their riches flowed from their power, not the other way around. Julius Caesar, for example, became rich only because he was appointed governor of Spain, from which he profited fabulously, as all provincial governors were supposed to do and did.

Last, and in some ways most significant, economic life was stable. It may not have seemed so to the peasants and merchants whose lives were constantly disrupted by war, famine, merciless taxation, and brigandage. But it was very stable compared to the tenor of economic life in our own time. The basic rhythms and techniques of economic existence were steady and repetitive. Men and women sowed and reaped, potters and metalworkers turned and hammered, weavers spun and wove—all using much the same kinds of equipment for decades, generations, sometimes centuries. How similar are the clothes and utensils, the materials of buildings, the means of conveyance that we see in the background of a Renaissance picture to those that we can make out on a Greek vase! How little material progress took place over a thousand years! That gives us a sense of how vast a change capitalism would bring when it finally burst upon the historic scene.

MARKET SOCIETY EMERGES

Thus we see that far from representing an eternal "human nature," capitalism comes as a volcanic disruption to time-honored routines of life. We begin to understand the immense inertia that prevented capitalism from developing in most earlier societies. From one of these societies to another, of course, different obstacles and barriers stood in the way of creating an economic way of life built on principles utterly alien to those that existed. But in all these societies, perhaps no barrier was more difficult to breach than the hold of tradition and command as the means of organizing economic life, and the need to substitute a market system in their place.

What is a market system? Essentially, it is one in which economic activities are left to men and women freely responding to the opportunities and discouragements of the marketplace, not to the established routines of tradition or the dictates of someone's command. Thus, in a market system most individuals are not only free to seek work where they wish, but must shop around for a job; by way of contrast, serfs or tradition-bound artisans were born to their employ and could only with great difficulty quit it for another. In a market system anyone is free to buy up land or to sell it: a farm can become a shopping center. By way of contrast again, land in most precapitalist societies was no more for sale than are the counties of our states.

Finally, a market in capital means that there is a regular flow of wealth into production—a flow of savings and investment—organized through banks and other financial companies, where borrowers pay interest as the reward for having the use of the wealth of the lenders. There was nothing like this before capitalism, except in the very small and disreputable capital markets personified in the despised moneylender.

The services of labor, land, and capital that are hired or fired in a market society are called the *factors of production,* and a great deal of economics is about how the market combines their essential contributions to production. Because they *are* essential, a question must be answered. How were the factors of production put to use prior to the market system? The answer comes as something of a shock, but it tells us a great deal.

There were no factors of production before capitalism. Of course, human labor, nature's gift of land and natural resources, and the artifacts of society have always existed. But labor, land, and capital were not commodities for sale. Labor was performed as part of the social duties of serfs or slaves, who were not paid for doing their work. Indeed, the serf paid fees to his lord for the use of the lord's equipment, and never expected to be remunerated when he turned over a portion of his crop as the lord's due. So, too, land was regarded as the basis for military power or civil administration, just as a county or state is regarded today—not as real estate to be bought and sold. And capital was thought of as treasure or as the necessary equipment of an artisan, not as an abstract sum of wealth with a market value. The idea of liquid, fluid capital would have been as strange in medieval life as would be the thought today of stocks and bonds as heirlooms never to be sold.

How did wageless labor, unrentable land, and private treasures become factors of production; that is, commodities to be bought and sold like so many yards of cloth or bushels of wheat? The answer is that a vast revolution undermined the world of tradition and command and brought into being the market relationships of the modern world. Beginning roughly in the sixteenth century— although with roots that can be traced much further back—a process of change, sometimes gradual, sometimes violent, broke the bonds and customs of the medieval world of Europe and ushered in the market society we know.

We can only touch on that long, tortuous, and sometimes bloody process here. In England the process bore with particular severity on the peasants who were expelled from their lands through the enclosure of common grazing lands. This enclosure took place to make private pasturage for the lord's sheep, whose wool had become a profitable commodity. As late as 1820 the Duchess of Sutherland evicted 15,000 tenants from 794,000 acres, replacing them with 131,000 sheep. The tenants, deprived of their traditional access to the fields, drifted into the towns, where they were forced to sell their services as a factor of production: labor.

In France the creation of factors of production bore painfully on landed property. When gold flowed into sixteenth-century Europe from the New World, prices began to rise and feudal lords found themselves in a vise. Like everything in medieval life, the rents and dues they received from their serfs were fixed and unchangeable.

But the prices of merchandise were not fixed. Although more and more of the serfs' obligations were changed from kind (that is, so many dozen eggs or ells of cloth or days of labor) to cash, prices kept rising so fast that the feudal lords found it impossible to meet their bills.

Hence we begin to find a new economic individual, the *impoverished* aristocrat. In the year 1530, in the Gévaudan region of France, the richest manorial lord had an income of five thousand livres; but in towns, some merchants had incomes of sixty-five thousand livres. Thus the balance of power turned against the landed aristocracy, reducing many to shabby gentility. Meanwhile, the upstart merchants lost no time in acquiring lands that they soon came to regard not as ancestral estates but as potential capital.

This brief glance at economic history brings home an important point. The factors of production, without which a market society could not exist, are not eternal attributes of a natural order. They are the creations of a process of historic change, a change that divorced labor from social life, that created real estate out of ancestral land, and that made treasure into capital. Capitalism is the outcome of a revolutionary change—a change in laws, attitudes, and social relationships as deep and far-reaching as any in history.*

The revolutionary aspect of capitalism lies in the fact that an older, feudal way of life had to be dismantled before the market system could come into being. This brings us to think again about the element of economic freedom that plays such an important role in our definition of capitalism. For we can see that economic freedom did not arise just because men and women directly sought to shake off the bonds of custom and command. It was also thrust upon them, often as a very painful and unwelcome change.

For European feudalism, with all its cruelties and injustices, did

---

*One of the many fascinating questions that surround the origins of capitalism is why it arose only in Europe, and never in any other part of the world. One part of the reason is that the collapse of the Roman Empire left many towns without an allegiance to anyone. In time these towns, which were naturally centers of trading and artisan work, grew powerful and managed to bargain for privileges with kings and lords. Capitalism thus grew up in the interstices of the medieval system. A similar opportunity and stimulus did not present itself elsewhere. A controversial but important recent work on the rise of capitalism is Immanuel Wallerstein's *The Modern World System*, Academic Press, three vols., 1974, 1980, 1989. See also Fernand Braudel, *Capitalism and Civilization*, Harper and Row, three vols., 1981, 1982, 1984.

provide a modicum of economic security. However mean a serf's life, at least he knew that in bad times he was guaranteed a small dole from his lord's granary. However exploited a journeyman, he knew that he could not be summarily thrown out of work under the rules of his master's guild. However squeezed a lord, he too knew that his rents and dues were secured by law and custom and would be coming in, weather permitting. Elsewhere, in China, India, and Japan, variants of this combination of tradition and command also provided an underpinning of security for economic life.

The eruption of the market system—better, the centuries-long earthquake that broke the hold of tradition and command in England and France and the Lowlands—destroyed that social underpinning. Thus the economic freedom of capitalism came as a two-edged sword. On the one hand, its new freedoms were precious achievements for those individuals who had formerly been deprived of the right to enter into legal contracts. For the up-and-coming bourgeois merchants, it was the passport to a new status in life. Even for some of the poorest classes, the freedom of economic contract was a chance to rise from a station in life from which, in earlier times, there had been almost no exit. But economic freedom also had a harsher side. This was the necessity to stay afloat by one's own efforts in rough waters where all were struggling to survive. Many a merchant and many, many a jobless worker simply disappeared from view.

The market system was thus the cause of unrest, insecurity, and individual suffering, just as it was also the cause of progress, opportunity, and fulfillment. In this contest between the costs and benefits of economic freedom lies a theme that is still a crucial issue for capitalism.

THE UNLEASHING OF TECHNOLOGY

The creation of a market society also paved the way for a change of profound significance in bringing about modern economic life. This was the incorporation of science and technology into the very midst of daily existence.

Technology is not, of course, a modern phenomenon. The gigantic stones that form prehistoric Stonehenge; the precision and delicacy of the monumental Egyptian pyramids; the Incan stone walls, fitted so exactly that a knife blade cannot be put between adjoining blocks; the Chinese Great Wall; and the Mayan observatories—all attest to mankind's long possession of the ability to transport and hoist staggering weights, to cut and shape hard surfaces, and to calculate complex problems. Indeed, many of these works would challenge our present-day engineering capabilities.

Nonetheless, although precapitalist technology reached great heights, it had a very restricted base. We have already noted that the basic tools of agriculture and artisan crafts remained little changed over millennia. Improvements came very slowly. So simple an invention as a horse collar shaped to prevent a straining animal from pressing against its windpipe did not appear during all the glories of Greece and triumphs of Rome. Not until the Middle Ages was there a switch from the ox to the draft horse as a plowing animal (a change that improved efficiency by an estimated 30 percent), or was the traditional two-field system of crop rotation improved by adopting a three-field system. (See box on page 19.) Thus precapitalist technology was lavished on the needs of rulers, priests, warriors. Its application to common, everyday work was virtually ignored.

There were, of course, good reasons why the technology of daily life was ignored. The primary effect of technological change in daily activity is to increase output, to enhance the productivity of the working person. But in a society still regulated by tradition and command, where production was mainly carried on by serfs and slaves and custom-bound artisans, there was little incentive to look for increases in output. The bulk of any increase in agricultural yields would only go to the lord in higher rents, not to the serf or the slave who produced them. Although a lord would benefit greatly from increases in agricultural output, how could a great noble be expected to know about, or to concern himself with, the dirty business of sowing and reaping? So, too, any artisan who altered the techniques of his trade would be expected, as a matter of course, to share these advances with his brethren. And how could his brethren, accustomed over the years to disposing of a certain quantity of pots or pans or cloth in the village market, expect to find buyers for more output? Would not the extra production simply go begging?

Thus productive technology in precapitalist societies slumbered because there was little incentive to search for change. Indeed,

THE DIFFERENCE TECHNOLOGY MAKES: THREE FIELDS VERSUS TWO

Until the Middle Ages, the prevailing system of cultivation was to plant half a lord's arable land in a winter crop, leaving the other half fallow. The second year, the two fields simply changed functions.

Under the three-field plan, the arable land was divided into thirds. One section was planted with a winter crop, one section with a summer crop, and one was left fallow. The second year, the first section was put into summer crops, the second section left fallow, and the third put into winter grains. In the third year, the first field was left fallow, the second used for winter crops, the third for spring planting.

Therefore, under the three-field system, only one third—not one half—of the arable land was fallow in any year. Suppose that the field as a whole yielded six hundred bushels of output. Under the two-field system, it would give an annual crop of three hundred bushels. Under the three-field system the annual crop would be two thirds of the area, or four hundred bushels— an increase of one third. Further, in those days it was customary to plow fallow land twice, and cultivated land only once. By cutting down the ratio of fallow to cultivated land, plowing time was reduced, and peasant productivity even more significantly improved. For more on this and other fascinating advances in precapitalist technology, see Lynn White, *Medieval Technology and Social Change* (Oxford: Clarendon Press, 1962).

powerful social forces were ranged against technological change, which could only introduce an unsettling element into the world. A society whose whole way of life rested on the reproduction of established patterns of life could not imagine a world where the technology of production was constantly in flux, and where limits were no longer recognized in any endeavor.

These inhibiting forces were ruthlessly swept away by the currents of the emerging markets for labor, land, and capital. Serfs were uprooted to become workers forced to sell their labor power; aristocratic landlords were rudely shouldered aside by money-minded parvenus; guild masters and artisans watched commercial enterprises take away their accustomed livelihood. A new sense of necessity, of urgency, infused economic life. What had been a more or less dependable round of life became increasingly a scramble for existence. The feeling that one's economic interests were best served by following in the footsteps of one's forebears gave way to the knowledge that economic life was shot through with insecurity, and was at worst a race for survival in which each had to fend for himself or herself.

The growing importance of the market, with its impersonal pressures, radically altered the place of technology, especially in the small workshops and minuscule factories that were the staging areas of the capitalist revolution. Here the free-for-all brought a need to find toeholds in the struggle for a livelihood. And one toehold available to any aspiring capitalist with an inquiring mind and a knowledge of the actual processes of production was technology itself— some invention or improvement that would lower costs or change a product to give it an edge on its competitors.

Thus in the late eighteenth and early nineteenth centuries capitalism raised a crop of technology-minded entrepreneurs, a wholly new social group in economic history. For example, there was John Wilkinson, son of an iron producer, who became a driving force for technical change in his trade. Wilkinson insisted that everything be built of iron—pipes and bridges, bellows and cylinders (one of which powered the newfangled steam engine of John Watt). He even constructed a much-derided iron ship—later much admired! There was Richard Arkwright, barber by trade, who made his fortune by inventing (or perhaps by stealing) the first effective spinning machine, becoming in time a great mill owner. There were Peter Onions, an obscure foreman who originated the puddling process for making wrought iron; Benjamin Huntsman, a clockmaker who improved the method of making steel; and a score more. A few, like Sir Jethro Tull, a pioneer in the technology of agriculture, were great gentlemen, but on the whole the technological leaders in industry were men of humble origin.

THE INDUSTRIAL REVOLUTION

The new dynamism gave rise to the Industrial Revolution, the first chapter of a still unfinished period of history in which startling and continuous changes revolutionized both the techniques of production and the texture of daily life.

A few figures tell the story. Between 1701 and 1802, as the technology of spinning and weaving was gradually perfected, the use of cotton in England expanded by 6,000 percent. Between 1788 and 1839, when the process of iron manufacture passed through its first technological upheaval, the output of pig iron jumped from 68,000 to 1,347,000 tons. In France, in the thirty years after 1815, iron output quintupled, coal output grew sevenfold, and transportation tonnage mounted ten times.

But these figures do not convey a sense of the effect of technology on daily life. *Things* became more common—and more commonplace. As late as the seventeenth century, what we would consider the most ordinary possesions were scarce. A peasant counted his worldly wealth in terms of a few utensils, a table, perhaps one complete change of clothes. In his will, Shakespeare left Anne Hathaway his "second-best bed." Iron nails were so scarce that pioneers in America burned down their cottages to retrieve them. In the wilder parts of Scotland in Adam Smith's time, nails even served as money.

Technology brought a widening, deepening, ever-faster-flowing river of things. Shoes, coats, paper, window glass, chairs, buckles—objects of solicitous respect in precapitalist times for all but the privileged few—became everyday articles. Gradually capitalism gave rise to what we call a rising standard of living—a steady, regular, systematic increase in the number, variety, and quality of material goods enjoyed by the great bulk of society. No such process had ever occurred before.

A second change wrought by technology was a striking increase in the sheer size of society's industrial apparatus. The increase began with the enlargement of the equipment used in production—an enlargement that stemmed mostly from advances in the technology of iron and, later, steel. The typical furnace used in extracting iron ore increased from ten feet in height in the 1770s to over one hundred feet a century later; during the same period the crucibles in which steel was made grew from cauldrons hardly larger than an oversized jug to converters literally as big as a house. The looms used by weavers expanded from small machines that fitted into the cottages of artisan-weavers to monstrous mechanisms housed in mills that still impress us by their size.

Equally remarkable was the expansion in the social scale of production. The new technology almost immediately outstripped the administrative capability of the small-sized business establishment. As the apparatus of production increased in size, it also increased in speed. As outputs grew from rivulets to rivers, a much larger organization was needed to manage production—to arrange for the steady arrival of raw materials, to supervise the work process, and not least, to find a market for its end product.

Thus, we find the size of the typical business enterprise steadily increasing as its technological basis became more complex. In the last quarter of the eighteenth century a factory of ten persons was worthy of note by Adam Smith, as we shall see in our next chapter. By the first quarter of the nineteenth century an ordinary textile mill employed several hundred men and women. Fifty years later many railways employed as many individuals as constituted the armies of respectable monarchs in Adam Smith's time. And in still another fifty years, by the 1920s, large manufacturing companies had almost as many employees as the populations of eighteenth-century cities.

Technology also played a decisive role in changing the nature of that most basic of all human activities, work. It did so by breaking down the complicated tasks of productive activity into much smaller subtasks, many of which could then be duplicated, or at least greatly assisted, by mechanical contrivances. This process was called the division of labor. Adam Smith was soon to explain, as we shall see, that the division of labor was mainly responsible for the increase in productivity of the average worker.

The division of labor altered social life in other ways as well. Work became more fragmented, monotonous, tedious, alienated. And the self-sufficiency of individuals was greatly curtailed. In precapitalist days most people either directly produced their own subsistence or made some article that could be exchanged for subsistence: peasants grew crops; artisans produced cloth, shoes, implements. But as work became more and more finely divided, the products of work became ever smaller pieces in the total jigsaw puzzle. Individuals did not spin thread or weave cloth, but manipulated levers and fed the machinery that did the actual spinning or weaving. A worker in a shoe plant made uppers or lowers or heels, but not shoes. No one of these jobs, performed by itself, would have sustained its performer for a single day; and no one of these products could have been exchanged for another product except through the complicated market network. Technology freed men and women from much material want, but it bound them to the workings of the market mechanism.

Not least of the mighty impacts of technology was its exposure of men and women to an unprecedented degree of change. Some of this was welcome, for change literally opened new horizons of material life: travel, for instance, once the prerogative of the wealthy, became a possibility for the masses, as the flood of nineteenth-century immigration to the United States revealed.

However, the changes introduced by technology had their negative side as well. Already buffeted by market forces that could mysteriously dry up the need for work or just as mysteriously create it, society now discovered that entire occupations, skills acquired over a lifetime, companies laboriously built up over generations, age-old industries could be threatened by the appearance of technological change. Increasingly, productive machinery appeared as the enemy, rather than the ally, of humankind. By the early nineteenth century the textile weavers, whose cottage industry was gradually destroyed by competition from the mills, were banding together to burn down the hated buildings.

These aspects of change do not begin to exhaust the ways in which technology, coupled with the market system, altered the very meaning of existence. But in considering them, we see how profound and how wrenching was the revolution that capitalism introduced. Technology was a genie that capitalism let out of the bottle; it has ever since refused to go back in.

THE POLITICAL DIMENSION

The disturbing, upsetting, revolutionary nature of the market and technology sets the stage for one last aspect of capitalism that we want to note: the political currents of change that capitalism brought, as much a part of the history of capitalism as the emergence of the market or the dismantling of the barriers against technical change.

One of these political currents was the rise of democratic, or parliamentary, institutions. Democratic political institutions far predate capitalism, as the history of ancient Athens or the Icelandic medieval parliamentary system shows. Nonetheless, the rise of the mercantile classes was closely tied to the struggle against the privileges and legal institutions of European feudalism. The historic movement that eventually swept aside the precapitalist economic order also swept aside its political order. Along with the emergence of the market system we find a parallel and supporting emergence of more open, libertarian political ways of life.

We must resist the temptation of claiming that capitalism either guarantees, or is necessary for, political freedom. We have seen some capitalist nations, such as pre-Hitler Germany, descend into totalitarian dictatorship. We have seen other nations, such as Sweden, move toward a kind of social-minded capitalism without impairing democratic liberties. Moreover, the exercise of political democracy was very limited in early capitalism: Adam Smith, for example, although comfortably off, did not possess enough property to allow him to vote.

It is true nonetheless that political liberties do not exist or scarcely existed in communist nations that have deliberately sought to remove the market system. This suggests, although it does not prove, that some vital connection exists between democratic privileges as we know them and an open society of economic contract, whether it be formally capitalist or not.

Because of the economic freedom on which the market system rested, the basic philosophy of capitalism from Adam Smith's day forward has been laissez-faire—leaving things alone.* As we study economics further, we will be tracing the evolution of that idea— the idea of leaving the market alone—as well as investigating what

---

*It is said that a group of merchants called on the great Colbert, French finance minister from 1661 to 1683, who congratulated them on their contribution to the French economy and asked what he could do for them. The answer was *"Laissez-nous faire"*—leave us alone. Since Colbert was a strong proponent of the complex regulations and red tape that tied up industry in France at this time, we can imagine how gladly he received this advice.

has happened to the system, both when it was left alone and when it wasn't.

It is much too early to take up that controversy here. Suffice it to say that if capitalism brought a strong impetus for laissez-faire, it also brought a strong impetus for economic intervention. The very democratic liberties and political equalities that were encouraged by the rise of capitalism became powerful forces that sought to curb or change the manner in which the economic system worked. Indeed, within a few years of Adam Smith's time, the idea of leaving things alone was aleady breached by the English Factory Act of 1833, establishing a system of inspectors to prevent child and female labor from being abused. In our own day that same political desire to correct the unhampered workings of laissez-faire capitalism has given rise to the Social Security system, which provides a social floor beneath the market, and to the environmental legislation that limits the market's operation in certain areas.

Thus, from the beginning, capitalism has been characterized by a tension between laissez-faire and intervention—laissez-faire representing the expression of its economic drive, intervention its democratic political orientation. That tension continues today, a deeply imbedded part of the historic character of the capitalist system.

TWO

Three Great Economists

A look back over economic history has taught us something about capitalism, the social system with which economics is mainly concerned. But we have not yet gained a sense of what economics itself is about. Perhaps we can see, however, that economics is mainly "about" capitalism—that it is an effort to explain how a society knit together by the market rather than by tradition or command, powered by a restive technology rather than by inertia, could hang together, how it would work.

There is no better way of grasping this basic purpose of economics than to look at the work of the three greatest economists—Adam Smith, Karl Marx, and John Maynard Keynes. Needless to say, these three names raise blood pressures differently, depending on whether one is a conservative, a radical, or a liberal. That's a matter for a different kind of book than this one. We want to explain what Smith, Marx, and Keynes *saw* when they looked at capitalism, for their visions still define the field of economics for everyone, right and left alike.

ADAM SMITH (1723–1790)

Adam Smith is the patron saint of our discipline and a figure of towering intellectual stature. His fame resides in his masterpiece, which everyone has heard of and almost no one has read, *The Wealth of Nations,* published in 1776, the year of the Declaration of Independence. All things considered, it is not easy to say which document is of greater historic importance. The Declaration sounded a new call for society dedicated to "Life, Liberty, and the pursuit of Happiness." The *Wealth* explained how such a society worked.

Here Smith begins by addressing a perplexing question. The actors in the market, as we know, are all driven by the desire to make money for themselves—to "better their condition," as Smith puts it. The question is obvious. How does a market society prevent self-interested, profit-hungry individuals from holding up their fellow citizens for ransom? How can a socially workable arrangement arise from such a dangerously unsocial motivation as self-betterment?

The answer introduces us to a central mechanism of a market system, the mechanism of competition. Each person out for self-betterment, with no thought of others, is faced with a host of similarly motivated persons. As a result, each market actor, in buying or selling, is forced to meet the prices offered by competitors.

In the kind of competition that Smith assumes, a manufacturer who tries to charge more than other manufacturers will not be able to find any buyers. A job seeker who asks more than the going wage will not be able to find work. And an employer who tries to pay less than competitors pay will not find workers to fill the jobs. In this way, the market mechanism imposes a discipline on its participants—buyers must bid against other buyers and therefore cannot gang up against sellers. Sellers must contend against other sellers and therefore cannot impose their will on buyers.

But the market has a second, equally important function. Smith shows that the market will arrange for the production of the goods that society wants, in the quantities society wants—without anyone ever issuing an order of any kind. Suppose that consumers want more pots and fewer pans than are being turned out. The public will buy up the existing stock of pots, and as a result their prices will rise. Contrariwise, the pan business will be dull; as pan makers try to get rid of their inventories, pan prices will fall.

Now a restorative force comes into play. As pot prices rise, so will profits in the pot business; and as pan prices fall, so will profits in that business. Once again, the drive for self-betterment will go

PORTRAIT OF AN ABSENTMINDED PROFESSOR

"I am a beau in nothing but my books" was the way that Adam Smith once described himself. Indeed, a famous medallion profile shows us a homely face. In addition, Smith had a curious stumbling gait that one friend called vermicular and was given to notorious fits of absentmindedness. On one occasion, absorbed in discussion, he fell into a tanning pit.

Few other adventures befell Smith in the course of his scholarly, rather retiring life. Perhaps the high point was reached at age four when he was kidnapped by a band of gypsies passing near Kirkaidy, his native hamlet in Scotland. His captors held him only a few hours; they may have sensed what a biographer later wrote: "He would have made, I fear, a poor gypsy."

Marked out early as a student of promise, at sixteen Smith won a scholarship that sent him to Oxford. But Oxford was not then the center of learning that it is today. Little or no systematic teaching took place, the students being free to educate themselves, provided they did not read dangerous books. Smith was nearly expelled for owning a copy of David Hume's *Treatise of Human Nature,* a work we now regard as one of the philosophic masterpieces of the eighteenth century.

After Oxford, Smith returned to Scotland, where he obtained an appointment as professor of moral philosophy at the University of Glasgow. Moral philosophy covered a large territory in Smith's time. We have notes of his lectures in which he talked about jurisprudence, military organization, taxation, and "police"—the last word meaning the administration of domestic affairs that we would call economic policy.

In 1759 Smith published *The Theory of Moral Sentiments,* a remarkable inquiry into morality and psychology. The book attracted widespread attention and brought Smith to the notice of Lord Townshend, one day to be the Chancellor of the Exchequer, responsible for the notorious tax on American tea. Townshend engaged Smith to serve as tutor to his stepson, and Smith resigned his professional post to set off on the grand tour with his charge. In France he met Voltaire, Rousseau, and François Quesnay, the brilliant doctor who had originated the ideas of physiocracy, a pioneering attempt to explain how the economic system functioned. Smith would have dedicated *The Wealth of Nations* to him, had Quesnay not died.

Returning to Scotland in 1766, Smith lived out the remainder of his life largely in scholarly retirement. It was during these years that the *Wealth* was slowly and carefully composed. When it was done, Smith sent a copy to David Hume, by then his dear friend. Hume wrote: "Euge!* Belle! Dear Mr. Smith: I am much pleased with your Performance. . . ." Hume knew, as did virtually everyone who read the book, that Smith had written a work that would permanently change society's understanding of itself.

---

*"Well done!"

to work. Employers in the favored pot business will seek to expand, hiring more factors of production—more workers, more space, more capital equipment; and employers in the disfavored pan business will reduce their use of the factors of production, letting workers go, giving up leases on space, cutting down on their capital investment.

Hence the output of pots will rise and that of pans will fall. And this is what the public wanted in the first place. The pressures of the marketplace direct the selfish activities of individuals as if by an Invisible Hand (to use Smith's wonderful phrase) into socially responsible paths. Thus the workings of the competitive system transmute self-regarding behavior into socially useful outcomes. The Invisible Hand—the words that describe the overall process—keeps society on track, assuring that it produces the goods and services it needs.

Smith's demonstration of how a market performs this extraordinary feat has never ceased to be of interest. Much of economics, as we shall see in closer detail later, is concerned with scrutinizing carefully how the Invisible Hand works. Not that it always does work. There are areas of economic life where the Invisible Hand does not exert its influence at all. In every market system, for instance, tradition continues to play a role in nonmarket methods of remuneration such as tipping. So, too, command is always in evidence within businesses, for example, or in the exercise of government powers such as taxation. Further, the market system has no way of providing certain public goods—goods that cannot be privately marketed, such as national defense or public law and order. Smith knew about these and recognized that such goods would have to be supplied by the government. Then, too, the market does not always meet the ethical or aesthetic criteria of society, or it may produce goods that are profitable to make, but harmful to consume. We shall look into these problems in due course. At this juncture, however, we had better stand in considerable awe of Smith's basic insight, for he showed his generation and all succeeding ones that a market system is a powerful force for orderly social provisioning.

He also showed that it was self-regulating. The beautiful consequence of the market is that it is its own guardian. If anyone's prices, wages, or profits stray from levels that are set for everyone, the force of competition will drive them back. Thus a curious paradox exists. The market, which is the acme of economic freedom, turns out to be the strictest of economic taskmasters. One can always appeal to a king for a special dispensation. There is no appeal to the market.

Because the market is its own regulator, Smith was opposed to government intervention that would interfere with the workings of self-interest and competition. Therefore laissez-faire became his fundamental philosophy, as it remains the fundamental philosophy of conservative-minded economists today. His commitment to the Invisible Hand did not make Smith a conventional conservative, however. He is cautious about, not dead set against, government intervention. Moreover, *The Wealth of Nations* is shot through with biting remarks about the "mean and rapacious" ways of the manufacturing class, and openly sympathetic with the lot of the workingman, hardly a popular position in Smith's day. What ultimately makes Smith a conservative—and here he *is* in accord with modern views—is his belief that the system of "natural liberty" founded on economic freedom would ultimately benefit the general public.

Needless to say, that is a question to which we will return many times. But we are not yet done with Adam Smith. For matching his remarkable vision of an internally coherent market system was an equally new and remarkable vision of another kind. Smith saw that the system of "natural liberty"—the market system, left to its own devices—would grow, that the wealth of such a nation would steadily increase.

What brought about this growth? As before, the motive force was the drive for self-betterment, the thirst for profits, the wish to make money. This meant that every employer was constantly seeking to accumulate more capital, to expand the wealth of the enterprise; in turn, this led each employer to seek to increase sales in the hope of gaining a larger profit.

But how to enlarge sales in a day long before advertising existed as we know it? Smith's answer was to improve productivity: Increase the output of the work force. And the road to increasing productivity was very clear: Improve the division of labor.

In Smith's conception of the growing wealth (we would say the growing *production*) of nations, the division of labor therefore plays a central role, as this famous description of a pin factory makes unforgettably clear:

> One man draws out the wire, another straits it, a third cuts it, a fourth points it, a fifth grinds it at the top for receiving the head; to make the head requires two or three distinct operations; to put it on is a peculiar business; to whiten it another; it is even a trade by itself to put them into paper. . . .
>
> I have seen a small manufactory of this kind where ten men only were employed and where some of them consequently performed two or three distinct operations. But though they were poor, and therefore but indifferently accommodated with the necessary machinery, they could when they exerted themselves make among them about twelve pounds of pins in a day. There are in a pound upwards of four thousand pins of middling size. These ten persons, therefore, could make among them upwards of forty-eight thousand pins in a day. . . . But if they had all wrought separately and independently . . . they could certainly not each of them make twenty, perhaps not one pin in a day.*

How is the division of labor to be enhanced? Smith places principal importance on the manner already announced in his description of the process of making pins: Machinery is the key. The division of labor—and therefore the productivity of labor—is increased

*Adam Smith, *The Wealth of Nations* (New York: Modern Library, 1937), pp. 4, 5.

when the tasks of production can be taken over, or aided and assisted, by the capacities of machinery. In this way each firm seeking to expand is naturally led to introduce more machinery as a way of improving the productivity of its workers. *Thereby the market system becomes an immense force for the accumulation of capital, mainly in the form of machinery and equipment.*

Moreover, Smith showed something remarkable about the self-regulating properties of the market system as a growth-producing institution. We recall that growth occurred because employers installed machinery that improved the division of labor. But as they thereupon added to their work force, would it not follow that wages would rise as all employers competed to hire labor? And would that not squeeze profits and dry up the funds with which machinery could be bought?

Once again, however, the market was its own regulator. For Smith showed that the increased *demand* for labor would be matched by an increased *supply* of labor, so that wages would not rise or would rise only moderately. The reason was plausible. In Smith's day, infant and child mortality rates were horrendous: "It is not uncommon," wrote Smith, ". . . in the Highlands of Scotland for a mother who has borne twenty children not to have two alive." As wages rose and better food was provided for the household, infant and child mortality would decline. Soon there would be a larger work force available for hire: ten was the working age in Smith's day. The larger work force would hold back the rise in wages—and so the accumulation of capital could go on. Just as the system assured its short-term viability by self-regulating the output of pots and pans, so it assured its long-term viability by self-regulating its steady growth.

Of course, Smith wrote about a world that is long since vanished—a world in which a factory of ten people, although small, was still significant enough to mention; in which remnants of mercantilist, and even feudal, restrictions determined how many apprentices an employer could hire in many trades; in which labor unions were largely illegal; in which almost no social legislation existed; and above all, where the great majority of people were very poor.

Yet Smith saw two essential attributes in the economic system that was not yet fully born at that time: first, that a society of competitive, profit-seeking individuals can assure its orderly material provisioning through the self-regulating market mechanism; and second, that such a society tends to accumulate capital, and in so doing, to enhance its productivity and wealth. These insights are not the last word. We have already mentioned that the market mechanism does not always work successfully, and our next two economists will demonstrate that the growth process is not without serious defects. But the insights themselves are still germane. What is surprising after two centuries is not how mistaken Smith was, but how deeply he saw. In a real sense, as economists we are still his pupils.

KARL MARX (1818–1883)

To most Americans, Karl Marx's name conjures up revolutionary images. To a certain extent, that is perfectly correct (see box on page 34). But for our purposes, Marx is much more than a political activist. He was a profoundly penetrative economic thinker, perhaps the most remarkable analyst of capitalism's dynamics who ever lived. So we will spend no time at all defending or assailing his political philosophy. What interests us is what he saw in capitalism that was different from Smith.

Adam Smith was the architect of capitalism's orderliness and progress; Marx was the diagnostician of its disorders and eventual demise. Their differences are rooted in the fundamentally opposite way that each saw history. In Smith's view, history was a succession of stages through which humankind traveled, climbing from the "early and rude" society of hunters and fisherfolk to the final stage of commercial society. Marx saw history as a continuing struggle among social classes, ruling classes contending with ruled classes in every era.

Moreover, Smith believed that commercial society would bring about a harmonious, mutually acceptable solution to the problem of individual interest in a social setting that would go on forever— or at least for a very long time. Marx saw tension and antagonism as the outcome of the class struggle, and the setting of capitalist society as anything but permanent. Indeed, the class struggle itself, expressed as the contest over wages and profits, would be the main force for changing capitalism and eventually undoing it.

PROFILE OF A REVOLUTIONARY

A great, bearded, dark-complected man, Karl Marx was the picture of a revolutionary. And he was one—engaged, mind and heart, in the effort to overthrow the system of capitalism that he spent his whole life studying. As a political revolutionary, Marx was not very successful, although with his lifelong friend Friedrich Engels, he formed an international working class "movement" that frightened a good many conservative governments. But as an intellectual revolutionary Marx was probably the most successful disturber of thought who ever lived. The only persons who rival his influence are the great religious leaders, Christ, Mohammed, and Buddha.

Marx led as turbulent and active a life as Smith's was secluded and academic. Born to middle-class parents in Trier, Germany, Marx was early marked as a student of prodigious abilities, but not temperamentally cut out to be a professor. Soon after getting his doctoral degree (in philosophy) Marx became editor of a crusading, but not communist, newspaper, which rapidly earned the distrust of the reactionary Prussian government. It closed down the paper. Typically, Marx printed the last edition in red. With his wife, Jenny (and Jenny's family maid, Lenchen, who remained with them, unpaid, all her life), Marx thereupon began life as a political exile in Paris, Brussels, and finally in London. There, in 1848, together with Engels, he published the pamphlet that was to become his best known, but certainly not most important work: *The Communist Manifesto*.

The remainder of Marx's life was lived in London. Terribly poor, largely as a consequence of his hopeless inability to manage his own finances, Marx's life was spent in the reading room of the British Museum, laboriously composing the great, never-finished opus, *Capital*. No economist has ever read so widely or so deeply as Marx. Before even beginning *Capital*, he wrote a profound three-volume commentary on all the existing economists, eventually published as *Theories of Surplus Value*, and filled thirty-seven notebooks on subjects that would be included in *Capital*—these notes, published as the *Grundrisse* (Foundations) did not appear in print until 1953.

Capital itself was written backwards, first Volumes II and III, in very rough draft form, then Volume I, the only part of the great opus that appeared in Marx's lifetime, in 1867.

Marx was assuredly a genius, a man who altered every aspect of thinking about society—historical and sociological as well as economic—as decisively as Plato altered the cast of philosophic thought, or Freud that of psychology. Very few economists today work their way through the immense body of Marx's work; but in one way or another his influence affects most of us, even if we are unaware of it. We owe to Marx the basic idea that capitalism is an *evolving* system, deriving from a specific historic past and moving slowly and irregularly toward a dimly discernible, different form of society. That is an idea accepted by many social scientists who may or may not approve of socialism, and who are on the whole vehemently "anti-Marxist."

A great deal of interest in Marx's work focuses on that revolutionary perspective and purpose. But Marx the economist interests us for a different reason: Marx also saw the market as a powerful force in the accumulation of capital and wealth. From his conflict-laden point of view, however, he traces out the process—mainly in Volume II of *Capital*—quite differently than Smith does. As we have seen, Smith's conception of the growth process stressed its self-regulatory nature, its steady, hitch-free path. Marx's conception is just the opposite. To him, growth is a process full of pitfalls, a process in which crisis or malfunction lurks at every turn.

Marx starts with a view of the accumulation process that is much like that of a businessman. The problem is how to make a given sum of capital—money sitting in a bank or invested in a firm—yield a profit. As Marx puts it, how does M (a sum of money) become M′, a *larger* sum?

Marx's answer begins with capitalists using their money to buy commodities and labor power. Thereby they make ready the process of production, obtaining needed raw or semifinished materials, and hiring the working capabilities of a labor force. Here the possibility for crisis lies in the difficulty that capitalists may have in getting their materials or their labor force at the right price. If that should happen—if labor is too expensive, for instance—M stays put and the accumulation process never gets started at all.

But suppose the first stage of accumulation takes place smoothly. Now money capital has been transformed into a hired work force and a stock of physical goods. These have next to be combined in the labor process; that is, actual work must be expended on the materials, and the raw or semifinished goods transformed into their next stage of production.

It is here, on the factory floor, that Marx sees the genesis of profit. In his view, profit lies in the ability of capitalists to pay less for labor power—for the working abilities of their work force—than the actual value workers will impart to the commodities they help to produce. Thus, profit—the difference between M and M'—essentially resides in unpaid labor. This theory of *surplus value* as the source of profit is very important in Marx's analysis of capitalism, but it is not central to our purpose here. Instead, we stop only to note that the labor process is another place where accumulation can be disrupted. If there is a strike, or if production encounters snags, the money capital (M) that is invested in goods and labor power will not move along toward its objective, a larger sum of money capital (M').

But once again suppose that all goes well and workers transform steel sheets, rubber casings, and bolts of cloth into automobiles. The automobiles are not yet money. They have to be sold—and here, of course, lie the familiar problems of the marketplace: bad guesses as to the public's taste; mismatches between supply and demand; recessions that diminish the spending power of society.

If all goes well, the commodities *will* be sold—and sold for M', which is bigger than M. In that case, the circuit of accumulation is complete, and the capitalists will have a new sum M', which they will want to send on another round, hoping to win M''. But unlike Adam Smith's smooth-growth model, we can see that Marx's conception of accumulation is riddled with pitfalls and dangers. Crisis is possible at every stage. Indeed, in the complex theory that Marx unfolds in *Capital*, the inherent tendency of the system is to generate crisis, not to avoid it.

We will not trace Marx's theory of capitalism further except to note that at its core lies a complicated analysis of the manner in which surplus value (the unpaid labor that is the source of profit) is squeezed out through mechanization. Someone who wants to learn about Marx's analysis must turn to other books, of which there are many.*

Our interest lies in Marx as the first theorist to stress the instability of capitalism. Adam Smith originated the idea that growth is an inherent characteristic of capitalism; but to Marx we owe the idea that that growth is wavering and uncertain, far from the cybernetic, assured process Smith described. Marx makes it clear that capital accumulation must overcome the uncertainty inherent in the market system and the tension of the opposing demands of labor and capital. The accumulation of wealth, although always the objective of business, may not always be within its power to achieve.

In *Capital*, Marx sees instability increasing until finally the system comes tumbling down. His reasoning involves two further, very important prognoses for the system. The first is that *the size of business firms will steadily increase as the consequence of the recurrent crises that rack the economy.* With each crisis, small firms go bankrupt and their assets are bought up by surviving firms. A trend toward big business is therefore an integral part of capitalism.

Second, *Marx expects an intensification of the class struggle as the result of the "proletarianization" of the labor force.* More and more small business people and independent artisans will be squeezed out in the crisis-ridden process of growth. Thus the social structure will be reduced to two classes—a small group of capitalist magnates and a large mass of proletarianized (i.e., propertyless), embittered workers.

In the end, this situation proves impossible to maintain. In Marx's words:

> Along with the constant decrease in the number of capitalist magnates, who usurp and monopolize all the advantages of this process of transformation, the mass of misery, oppression, slavery, degradation and exploitation grows; but with this there also grows the revolt of the working class, a class constantly increasing in numbers, and trained, united and organized by the very mechanism of the capitalist process

*At the risk of appearing self-serving, a useful introduction is R. L. Heilbroner, *Marxism: For and Against* (New York: Norton, 1980).

of production. The monopoly of capital becomes a fetter upon the mode of production which has flourished alongside and under it. The centralization of the means of production and the socialization of labour reach a point at which they become incompatible with their capitalist integument. This integument is burst asunder. The knell of capitalist private property sounds. The expropriators are expropriated.*

Much of the economic controversy that Marx generated has been focused on the questions: Will capitalism ultimately undo itself? Will its internal tensions, its "contradictions," as Marx calls them, finally become too much for its market mechanism to handle?

There are no simple answers to these questions. Critics of Marx vehemently insist that capitalism has *not* collapsed, that the working class has *not* become more and more miserable, and that a number of predictions Marx made, such as that the rate of profit would tend to decline, have not been verified.

Supporters of Marx argue the opposite case. They stress that capitalism almost did collapse in the 1930s. They note that more and more people have been reduced to a "proletarian" status, working for a capitalist firm rather than for themselves; in 1800, for example, 80 percent of Americans were self-employed; today the figure is 10 percent. They stress that the size of business has constantly grown, and that Marx did correctly foresee that the capitalist system itself would expand, pushing into noncapitalist Asia, South America, and Africa.

It is doubtful that Marx's contribution as a social analyst will ultimately be determined by this kind of score card. Certainly he made many remarkably penetrating statements; equally certainly, he said things about the prospects for capitalism that seem to have been wrong. Most economists do not accept Marx's diagnosis of class struggle as the great motor of change in capitalist and precapitalist societies or his prognosis of a trend toward socialism. But what Marx's reputation ultimately rests on is something else. It rests on his vision of capitalism as a system under tension, and in a process of continuous evolution as a consequence of that tension. Few would deny the validity of that vision.

*Karl Marx, *Capital*, Vol. I (New York: Vintage, 1977), p. 929.

• • •

There is much more to Marx than the few economic ideas sketched here. Indeed, Marx should not be thought of primarily as an economist, but as a pioneer in a new kind of critical social thought: It is significant that the subtitle of *Capital* is *A Critique of Political Economy*.

In the gallery of the world's great thinkers, where Marx unquestionably belongs, his proper place is with historians rather than economists. Most appropriately, his statue would be centrally placed, overlooking many corridors of thought—sociological analysis, philosophic inquiry, and of course, economics.

For Marx's lasting contribution was a penetration of the *appearances* of our social system and of the ways in which we think about that system, in an effort to arrive at buried essences deep below the surface. That most searching aspect of Marx's work is not one we will pursue here, but bear it in mind, because it accounts for the persisting interest of Marx's thought.

Finally, what about the relation of Marx to present-day communism? That is a subject for a book about the politics, not the economics, of Marxism. Marx himself was a fervent democrat—but a very intolerant man. More important, his system of ideas has also been intolerant, and may thereby have encouraged intolerance in revolutionary parties that have based their ideas on his thought. Marx himself died long before Soviet communism rose and fell. We cannot know what he would have made of it—probably he would have been horrified at its excesses but still hopeful for some kind of democratic socialism in the future.

JOHN MAYNARD KEYNES* (1883–1946)

Marx was the intellectual prophet of capitalism as a self-destructive system; John Maynard Keynes was the engineer of capitalism repaired. Today, that is not an uncontested statement. To some people, Keynes's doctrines are as dangerous and subversive as those of Marx—a curious irony, since Keynes himself was totally opposed

---

*This is probably the most mispronounced name in economics. It should be pronounced "canes," not "keens."

to Marxist thought and wholly in favor of sustaining and improving the capitalist system.

The reason for the continuing distrust of Keynes is that more than any other economist, he is the father of the idea of a "mixed economy" in which the government plays a crucial role. To many people these days, all government activities are suspicious at best and downright injurious at worst. Thus, in some quarters Keynes's name is under a cloud. Nonetheless, he remains one of the great innovators of our discipline, a mind to be ranked with Smith and Marx as one of the most influential our profession has brought forth. As Nobelist Milton Friedman, an avowed conservative, has declared: "We are all Keynesians now."

The great economists were all products of their times: Smith, the voice of optimistic, nascent capitalism; Marx, the spokesman for the victims of its bleakest industrial period; Keynes, the product of a still later time, the Great Depression.

PORTRAIT OF A MANY-SIDED ENGLISHMAN

Keynes was certainly a man of many talents. Unlike Smith or Marx, he was at home in the world of business affairs, a shrewd dealer and financier. Every morning, abed, he would scan the newspaper and make his commitments for the day on the most treacherous of all markets, foreign exchange. An hour or so a day sufficed to make him a very rich man; only the great English economist David Ricardo (1772–1823) could match him in financial acumen. Like Ricardo, Keynes was a speculator by temperament. During World War I, when he was at the Treasury office running England's foreign currency operations, he reported with glee to his chief that he had got together a fair amount of Spanish pesetas. The chief was relieved that England had a supply of *that* currency for a while. "Oh no," said Keynes. "I've sold them all. I'm going to break the market." And he did. Later during the war, when the Germans were shelling Paris, he went to France to negotiate for the English government; on the side, he bought some marvelous French masterpieces at much reduced prices for the National Gallery—along with a Cézanne for himself.

More than an economist and speculator, he was a brilliant mathematician; a businessman who very successfully ran a great investment trust; a ballet lover who married a famous ballerina; a superb stylist and an editor of consummate skill; a man of huge kindness when he wanted to exert it, and of ferocious wit when (more often) he chose to exert that. On one occasion, banker Sir Harry Goshen criticized Keynes for not "letting things take their natural course." "Is it more appropriate to smile or rage at these artless sentiments?" wrote Keynes. "Best, perhaps, to let Sir Harry take *his* natural course."

Keynes's greatest fame lay in his economic inventiveness. He came by this talent naturally enough as the son of a distinguished economist, John Neville Keynes. As an undergraduate, Keynes had already attracted the attention of Alfred Marshall, the commanding figure at Cambridge University for three decades. After graduation, Keynes soon won notice with a brilliant little book on Indian finance; he then became an adviser to the English government in the negotiations at the end of World War I. Dismayed and disheartened by the vengeful terms of the Versailles Treaty, Keynes wrote a brilliant polemic, *The Economic Consequences of the Peace,* which won him international renown.

Almost thirty years later, Keynes would himself be a chief negotiator for the English government, first in securing the necessary loans during World War II, then as one of the architects of the Bretton Woods agreement that opened a new system of international currency relations after that war. On his return home from one trip to Washington, reporters crowded around to ask if England had been sold out and would soon be another American state. Keynes's reply was succinct: "No such luck."

The Depression hit America like a typhoon. One half the value of all production simply disappeared. One quarter of the working force lost its jobs. Over a million urban families found their mortgages foreclosed, their houses lost to them. Nine million savings accounts went down the drain when banks closed, many for good.

Against this terrible reality of joblessness and loss of income, the economics profession, like the business world or government advisers, had nothing to offer. Fundamentally, economists were as perplexed at the behavior of the economy as were the American people themselves. In many ways the situation reminds us of the uncertainty that the public and the economics profession have shared in the face of inflation in modern times.

It was against this setting of dismay and near-panic that Keynes's great book appeared: *The General Theory of Employment, Interest and Money*. A complicated book—much more technical than *The Wealth of Nations* or *Capital*—the *General Theory* nevertheless had a central message that was simple enough to grasp. The overall level of economic activity in a capitalist system, said Keynes (and Marx and Adam Smith would have agreed with him) was determined by the willingness of its entrepreneurs to make capital investments. From time to time this willingness was blocked by considerations that made capital accumulation difficult or impossible: In Smith's model we saw the possibility of wages rising too fast, and Marx's theory pointed out difficulties at every stage of the process.

But all the previous economists—even Marx, to a certain extent—believed that a failure to accumulate capital would be a temporary, self-curing setback. In Smith's scheme, the rising supply of young workers would keep wages in check. In Marx's conception, each crisis (up to the last) would present the surviving entrepreneurs with fresh opportunities to resume their quest for profits. For Keynes, however, the diagnosis was more severe. He showed that a market system could reach a position of "under-employment equilibrium"—a kind of steady, stagnant state—despite the presence of unemployed workers and unused industrial equipment. *The revolutionary import of Keynes's theory was that there was no self-correcting property in the market system to keep capitalism growing.*

We will understand the nature of Keynes's diagnosis better after we have studied a little more economics, but we can easily see the conclusion to which his diagnosis drove him. If there was nothing that would automatically provide for capital accumulation, a badly depressed economy could remain in the doldrums unless some substitute were found for business capital spending. And there was only one such possible source of stimulation. This was the government. The crux of Keynes's message was therefore that government spending might be an essential economic policy for a depressed capitalism trying to recover its vitality.

Whether or not Keynes's remedy works and what consequences government spending may have for a market system have become major topics for contemporary economics—topics we will deal with later at length. But we can see the significance of Keynes's work in changing the very conception of the economic system in which we live. Adam Smith's view of the market system led to the philosophy of laissez-faire, allowing the system to generate its own natural propensity for growth and internal order. Marx stressed a very different view, in which instability and crisis lurked at every stage, but of course Marx was not interested in policies to maintain capitalism. Keynes propounded a philosophy as far removed from Marx as from Smith. For if Keynes was right, laissez-faire was not the appropriate policy for capitalism—certainly not for capitalism in depression. And if Keynes was right about his remedy, the gloomy prognostications of Marx were also incorrect—or at least could be rendered incorrect.

But was Keynes right? Was Smith right? Was Marx right? To a very large degree these questions frame the subject matter of economics today. That is why, even if their theories are part of our history, the "worldly philosophers" are also contemporary. A young writer once remarked impatiently to T. S. Eliot that it seemed so pointless to study the thinkers of the past, because we know so much more than they. "Yes," replied Eliot. "They are what we know."

THREE

A Bird's-Eye View of the Economy

We are almost, but not quite, ready to begin to learn modern economics. The trouble is that we can't begin to study economics without knowing something about the economy. But what is "the economy"? When we turn to the economics section of *Time* or *Newsweek* or pick up a business magazine, a jumble of things meets the eye: stock market ups and downs, reports on company fortunes and mishaps, accounts of incomprehensible "fluctuations in the exchange market," columns by business pundits, stories about unemployment or inflation.

How much of this is relevant? How are we to make our way through this barrage of reporting to something that we can identify as the economy?

THE TWO WORLDS OF BUSINESS

Of course, we know where to start. Business enterprise is the very heart of an economic system of private property and market relationships. Let us begin, then, with a look at the world of business.

The following table makes one thing immediately clear: There are at least two worlds of business. One of them, mainly proprietorships (businesses owned by a single person) and partnerships, is the world of very small business—businesses that gross less than $100,000 a year. Of course there are tiny corporations, too, and

DIMENSIONS OF BUSINESS, 1988*

	Total number of firms (000's omitted)	Total sales (billions)	Average sales per firm
Proprietorships (non-farm)	13,679	$ 672	$ 49,126
Partnerships	1,654	454	280,530
Corporations	3,563	9,801	2,757,558

*This and nearly all subsequent data from *Statistical Abstract of the United States*, Dept. of Commerce, Washington, D.C., 1992, p. 519.

there are some very big proprietorships and partnerships. But the main thing is the smallness. Here we find the bulk of the firms that fill the Yellow Pages of the phone book, the great preponderance of the country's farms, myriad mom-and-pop stores, restaurants, motels, movie houses, dry cleaners, druggists, retailers—in short, over 80 percent of all the business firms in the nation.

Small business is the part of the business world with which we are all most familiar. We understand how a hardware store is run, whereas we have only vague ideas about how General Motors operates. But the world of small business warrants our attention for two other reasons. First, small business is the employer of a substantial fraction—about a third—of the nation's labor force. Second, because the small-business proprietary point of view directly expresses the socioeconomic position of about one married household out of every five, the world of small business is the source of much middle-class opinion.

Meanwhile, we have already glimpsed another business world, mainly to be found in the corporate enterprises of the nation. Compare the average size of the sales of corporations with those of proprietorships and partnerships: the ratio is well over 50 to 1 for proprietorships; and almost 10 to 1 for partnerships. But even these figures hide the extraordinary difference between very big business and small business. *Within* the world of corporations 83 percent do less than $1 million worth of business a year. But the 17 percent that do more than $1 million worth take in 93 percent of the receipts of all corporations.

Thus, counterposed to a world of very numerous small businesses, there is the world of much-less-numerous big businesses. How large a world is it? Suppose we count as a big business any corporation with assets worth more than $250 million. There are roughly three thousand such businesses in America. Over half of them are in finance, mainly insurance and banking. About one fifth are in manufacturing. The rest are to be found in transportation, utilities, communication, trade. Just to get an idea of scale, the "richest" enterprise in the nation in 1991 was probably Citicorp, with assets of $216 billion.

The largest *industrial* firm was General Motors with assets of over $180 billion and sales of $124 billion. *These two firms together probably commanded as much wealth (assets) as all the 13 million proprietorships of the nation.* The firms change from time to time— GM and IBM have both had mighty falls—but the size pattern remains.*

Big business is to be found in all sectors, but its special place is the industrial sector, shown below:

THE INDUSTRIAL SECTOR, 1991

	$ billion
Total sales of all industrial corporations	3,010
Total sales of the 500 biggest industrial corporations	2,263

The figures show once again the twofold division of the business world. The top five hundred firms—fewer than one tenth of one percent of the total number—account for almost 80 percent of all sales. *Indeed, if we take only the biggest one hundred firms, we find that they are the source of almost half the sales of the entire industrial sector.*

---

*There is no official designation of a "big" business. We have used the *Fortune* magazine list of the top 500 industrial firms, plus their list of the top 50 firms in banking, insurance, finance, transportation, utilities, and retailing. Rule of thumb: To make it into the Fortune 500 in the 1990s, you need around $500 million in sales or about $100 million in assets.

A PARADE OF BUSINESS FIRMS

We shall have a good deal to investigate in later chapters about the world of big business. But it might be useful to end this initial survey with a dramatization of the problem. The figures are derived from statistics of a few years back, but the visual impression is still there.

Suppose we lined up our roughly 19 million businesses in order of size, starting with the smallest, along an imaginary road from San Francisco to New York. There will be 5,500 businesses to the mile, or about one per foot. Suppose further that we planted a flag for each business. The height of the flagpole represents the volume of sales: each $10,000 in sales is shown by one foot of pole.

The line of flagpoles is a very interesting sight. From San Francisco to about Reno, Nevada, it is almost unnoticeable, a row of poles only a foot or two high. From Reno eastward the poles increase in height until, near Columbus, Ohio—about four fifths of the way across the nation—flags fly about 10 feet in the air, symbolizing $100,000 in sales. Looking backward from Columbus, we can see almost two thirds of all firms have sales of less than that amount.

But as we approach the eastern terminus, the poles suddenly begin to mount. There are about one million firms in the country with sales over $500,000. These corporations occupy the last 75 miles of the 3,000-mile road. There are 700,000 firms with sales of over $1 million. They occupy the last 50 miles of the road, with poles at least 100 feet high. Then there are 2,300 firms with sales of $50,000,000 or more. They take up the last quarter mile before the city limits, flags flying at cloud heights, 5,000 feet up.

But this is still not the climax. At the very gates of New York, on the last 100 feet of the last mile, we find the 100 largest industrial firms. They have sales of at least $5 billion, so that their flags are already miles high, above the clouds. Along the last 10 feet of the road, there are the ten largest companies. Their sales are roughly $40 billion and up: Their flags fly literally in the sky.

As we said, the figures refer to dollar values a few years earlier. The flags would all fly about twice as high today—two feet off the ground from San Francisco to Reno; stratospheric in New York. But the flagpole parade would look about the same.

BIGNESS IN WORLD PERSPECTIVE

Finally—and a very important finally—we have to put the American picture into a world context. Capitalism everywhere is big business capitalism. Moreover, the size of firms has been growing more rapidly in Europe and Japan than here, so that U.S. firms are actually smaller than they used to be, compared to world GNP and to their foreign competitors. Among the fifty largest firms in the world, ranked by sales, 17 are American, 10 are Japanese, 6 are German, and 5 are British. None of the twenty biggest banks are American!

HOUSEHOLDS AND INCOMES

The two worlds of business give us a sense of the economic structure of things. But there is obviously more than business firms in the economy. Another major element in the landscape is households— the sixty-six million families and twenty-seven million single-dwelling individuals or non-family households who were the people in the economic picture in 1991.

What is it about households that interests economists? One thing is that households are the source of our labor force, a matter we'll be looking into later. But more striking in this first survey of the economy is that households give us an overview of the distribution of income in the economy. Looking at the panorama of the nation's families and single dwellers gives us an essential picture of its riches and poverty.

There are many ways of describing income distribution. We will use a method that will divide the country into five equal layers, like a great cake. The layers will help us give dollars-and-cents definitions of what we usually have in mind when we speak of the poor, the working class, the middle class, and so on. As we will see, the amounts are not at all what most of us imagine.

We begin with the bottom layer, the poor. By our definition, this will include all the households in the bottom 20 percent of the nation. From data gathered by the Census Bureau, we know that the highest income of a family in this bottom slice of the five-layered cake was under $17,000 in 1990. For purposes of comparison, the level of income designated by the Department of Commerce as "near-poverty" for a four-person family was $13,000 for that year. Thus we exaggerate, but not too much, in thinking of the bottom fifth of the nation as mainly poor, or near-poor.

The box headed "Poverty" on page 50 shows some of the characteristics of poor families, but there are two additional facts about poverty that we should note. First, not all families who are counted as poor in any given census remain poor in the next census. About one seventh of all poor households are young people just starting their careers. Some of these low-income beginners will escape from poverty. In addition, about a third of the members of the poverty class are older people. Many of these were not poor in an earlier, more productive stage of their economic lives. At the same time, this also means that some families that are not poor when a census is taken will fall into poverty at a later stage of their lives. The moral of this is that poverty is not entirely static. At any moment, some families are escaping from poverty, some entering it. What counts, of course, is whether the net movement is in or out. As we will see in our next chapter, it has recently been slowly in.

A second characteristic also deserves to be noted. Seventy-five percent of the families below the poverty line have at least one wage earner in the labor force. Thus their poverty reflects inadequate earnings. A considerable amount of poverty, in other words, reflects the fact that some jobs do not pay enough to lift a jobholder above the low-income level. In some regions, certain jobs are so low-paying that even two jobholders in a family (especially if one works only seasonally) will not suffice to bring the family out of poverty. This is often the case, for example, with migrant farm workers, or with immigrants who must seek employment in the least desirable jobs.

We usually define the working class in terms of certain occupations. We call a factory worker—but not a salesclerk—working class, even though the factory employee may make more than a salesclerk.

For our purposes, however, we will just take the next two layers

POVERTY

Thirty-six million Americans live below income levels that are officially designated as "poverty." What characteristics distinguish poor families? Here are some from the very early 1990s:

Old Age: Eleven percent of the poor are retirees.

Youth: A poor household is more likely to be headed by someone under 25 than by a person aged 25–64.

Color: About 30 percent of poor persons are black. About one third of black families are poor. Half of all black children are poor.

Sex: A poor family is three times as likely to be headed by a female as by a male.

Schooling: The heads of almost half of all poor families did not graduate from high school.

Of course many characteristics overlap and reinforce one another: poor families are often old, black, and uneducated. No one characteristic is decisive in "making" a family poor. For instance, families are poor not just because they have no schooling, but they have no schooling because they are poor. Poverty breeds poverty.

---

of the income cake and call them working class. This will include the 40 percent of the population that is above the poor. We choose this method to find out how large an income a family can make and still remain in the working class, as we have defined it. The answer is up to $36,000. To put it differently, 40 percent of the families in the country in 1990 earned between $17,000 and $36,000 a year.

With the bottom three fifths of the nation tagged—roughly one fifth poor, two fifths working class—we are ready to look into the income levels of upper echelons. First, the rich. Where do riches begin? The realistic answer does not deal with incomes, but with wealth—the assets people own, whether in stocks and bonds, real estate, or whatever. We'll come to that shortly.

Under the rich are a considerably larger group that we will call the upper class. We shall count the upper 5 percent of the nation in this class. It comprises such occupations as successful doctors and lawyers and businessmen, top airline pilots, upper-middle management, even a few professors. How much income does it take to get into the top 5 percent? In 1990 the boundary line was crossed at $105,000 for all families.

This leaves us with the middle class—the class to which we all think we belong. By our method of cutting the cake, the middle class includes 35 percent of the nation—everyone between the $36,000 working-class top income and the $100,000-plus upper-class lowest income. In 1990 an average white married couple, both working, earned a little over $43,000, enough to enter middle-class economic territory. No wonder a middle-class feeling pervades American society, regardless of the occupation or social milieu from which families come.*

It is obvious that there are great extremes of income distribution in the United States. Some years ago Paul Samuelson, perhaps the nation's most famous economist, made the observation that if we built an income pyramid out of children's blocks, with each layer representing $1,000 of income, the peak would be far higher than the Eiffel Tower, but most of us would be within a yard of the ground.

Even more striking than the inequality of income, however, is the inequality of wealth, illustrated in the table on page 52.

As we can see, a fourth of all households had virtually no wealth at all. This obviously includes the lowest fifth ("the poor") and the lower portion of the group we have designated the working class. The next 30 percent have modest assets—largely comprising the net value of their homes, cars, savings accounts, etc. This takes us

---

*Maybe you wonder how an "average white married couple" could enter an income group that we have defined as being not average. The answer is that not every household in our national layer cake was white or married with both husband and wife working. For a look at the numbers, see the *Statistical Abstract* (1992), Tables 704 and 706.

DISTRIBUTION OF FAMILIES BY NET WORTH, 1988

Percentage of families	Net worth
Lowest 25 percent	Less than $5,000
Next 30 percent	$5,000 to $50,000
Next 35 pecent	$50,000 to $250,000
Top 10 percent	Over $250,000

through the layers of working-class families, to the doorstep of the middle class. Here assets begin to amount to something, and by the time we have reached the threshold of the upper class, a typical household measures its net worth at a quarter of a million dollars— a substantial home, some insurance and other savings. Here is where stocks and bonds also enter: about 20 percent of Americans own securities.

Recent figures tell us something additional about the distribution of wealth at the very top. In 1988 there were 940,000 families with a net worth of $1 million or more—about 2 percent of all families. These assets included the value of the homes or private business enterprises owned by these families. If we count up only the families with $1 million or more in financial assets, such as stocks and bonds and insurance, the number falls sharply to about 250,000 families— one half of 1 percent of all family units. By the 1990s, this figure was larger, perhaps 1 percent.

How much wealth do millionaires own in all? We are not sure. Estimates for the 1960s indicated that millionaire families owned half to three quarters of the value of all stocks and bonds and private real estate. These figures can change as inflation waxes and wanes or as the stock market fluctuates. All during the late 1960s and 1970s, as inflation was gathering momentum, the level of stock prices was virtually unchanged. As a result, a family with an average port-folio of stocks suffered a very substantial loss of its real wealth during these years. Indeed, a person with a $1 million portfolio in 1972 would have lost half his or her purchasing power by 1981. Starting that year, however, stocks began to rise, and in 1985 and 1986 we saw a boom in which stock prices doubled, followed by another boom that doubled them again by 1992. So if the 1972 millionaire

A PARADE OF INCOMES

Suppose that like our parade of flags across the nation representing the sales of business firms, we lined up the population in order of its income. Assume the height of the middle household to be 6 feet, representing a median income of $31,000 in 1988. This will be our height, as observers. What would our parade look like?*

It would begin with a few families *below* the ground, for there are some households with negative incomes; that is, they report losses for the year. Mainly these are families with business losses, and their negative incomes are not matched by general poverty. Following close on their heels comes a long line of grotesque dwarfs who make up about one fifth of all families, people less than three feet tall. Some are shorter than one foot.

Only after the parade is half over do we reach people whose faces are at our level. Then come the giants. When we reach the last 5 percent of the parade—incomes above $100,000— people are twenty feet tall. At the end of the parade, people tower six hundred to six thousand feet into the air—one hundred to one thousand times as tall as the middle height. What is the largest income in the country? We do not know: Probably our 60-odd billionaires have incomes of over $100 million.

*Adapted from the brilliant description of an "income parade" in Jan Pen, *Income Distribution*, trans. Trevor S. Preston (New York: Praeger, 1971), pp. 48–59.

had hung in until that date, his or her portfolio would have made up all its lost value—and then some!

GOVERNMENT

We have almost completed our first overview of the economy, but there remains one last institution with which we must gain an acquaintance: the government. How shall we size up so vast and complex an organization? There is no simple or single way. Only as we proceed along will the government sector come into clearer focus. Just the same, we have to begin somewhere. These figures will start us off:

PUBLIC AND PRIVATE SECTORS, 1992 (est.)

	Public	Private
Total GNP ($ billion)	1,120	4,890
Total employees (million)	17.6	89.7

The figures show that, measured in ordinary economic terms, by the size of income or the number of employees, the private sector is much larger than the public. But clearly that understates the size and wealth of government. What dollar figure should we put on the nation's land, one third of which is owned by the federal government? What is the economic value of the national defense establishment? What is the value of the government's exclusive right to print money? When we begin to ask such questions, the idea of comparing the relative sizes of business and government falls apart.

Nevertheless, there are two points worth making strongly as we try to take an initial reading on the place of government within the economy. The first is that "government" does not just mean the federal government. As we shall see, the federal government has a crucial role to play in the economy at many levels. But we should not lose sight of the fact that state and local governments are much more important than the federal government as a source of employment—roughly four to five times as many people work for states and counties and cities as for Washington.

In addition, state and local governments produce much more public output than does the federal government in many important areas. Public output is part of GNP. If we take away defense as a special case, state and local government is therefore a much larger contributor to public output than is the federal government.* The

*Welfare expenditures are not part of public output (or GNP). These originate mainly with the federal government. This makes Washington a bigger *spender* than the states and localities, but not a bigger *producer*. More on this when we turn to a consideration of GNP in the chapters ahead.

table below is worth looking at from that point of view, for it reminds us of the range of nonfederal activities that "government" includes, a range much wider than the bureaucratic paper-pushing the word often evokes.

Second, the variety of public outputs reminds us that government is not just a dead weight on the economy, as so many tend to think. Anyone who has ever gone to a public school, been treated in a public hospital, traveled on a public road, or flown in a plane guided by a public beacon system has been the recipient of government production and knows how vital public output can be. Even those who emphasize the maddening bureaucracy and the inefficiency that can come from government activity (although government has no monopoly on either) should reflect that the system of private enterprise itself depends on the invisible output of law enforcement on which this economy, like all economies, rests.

FEDERAL VERSUS STATE AND LOCAL EXPENDITURES, 1992

	Federal $ billion	State and Local $ billion
National defense	298	0
Education	45	310
Highways	33	65
Health	175	100
Housing & utilities	10	25
Natural resources	20	9

FOUR

The Trend of Things

In our last chapter we took a kind of snapshot of the economy to look at its structure and dimensions. Now we want something more dynamic—a movie rather than a still. The purpose of this chapter is to project such a movie, to give a feeling of the main currents of the past half century or so, currents that are still carrying us into the future.

There is no doubt about the first impression. It is a sense of growth. Everything has been getting larger. Business firms have been growing in size; labor unions are bigger; there are more households and each household is richer; government is much larger. And underlying all this, the extent of the market system itself—the great circular flow of transactions—has been steadily increasing in size.

Growth is not, of course, the only thing we notice. Businesses are different as well as bigger when we compare the early 1900s with today. There are far more corporations now than in the old days, far more diversified businesses, fewer family farms. Households are different because almost half of all married women work away from home. Labor unions are no longer mainly craft unions, limited by one occupation. Government is not only bigger, but has a different philosophy.

ECONOMIC GROWTH

Nevertheless, it is growth that first commands our attention. The camera vision of the economy gives us a picture that requires an ever-larger screen. The screen has to widen because it must encompass an ever-widening river of output. Hence the first thing we must do is examine this phenomenal rise in the dollar value of total output, represented in the following table. We call this value of output, which includes all the goods and services produced by the public sector as well as those produced by the private sector, our *gross national product,* abbreviated as GNP. In our next chapter we will define GNP more carefully. Here we want to talk about its startling rise from 1900 to 1980. We will examine the years after 1980 shortly.

As we can see, the dollar value of all output over that earlier span rose by a factor of about one hundred. But undoubtedly a cautionary

VALUE OF GNP, 1900-1980

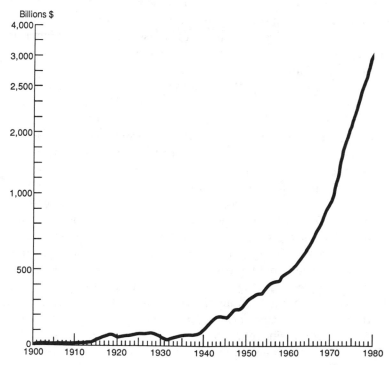

thought has already crossed your mind. If we measure the growth of output by comparing the dollar value of production over time, what seems to be a growth in actual economic activity may be no more than a rise in prices.

That cautionary thought is absolutely right. Suppose an economy produces only wheat, and suppose that wheat sold for a dollar in 1900 and four dollars in 1980. Now imagine that the actual output of wheat is unchanged, one million tons in both years. If we compute the GNP for 1900 we get one million dollars (a million tons at one dollar each), but if we compute the GNP for 1980, GNP is four million dollars! So we have to wring the inflation out of these figures. The way we do so is to use *the same prices* in computing the value of output in both years. Obviously, whatever price we use in our example, GNP will not rise.

If we calculate the value of GNP by using the different prices of the years in which the output was produced, we call the dollar total *current* or *nominal* GNP. But if we compute the values of GNP over several years, using the price of *only one year,* we call the result *real* GNP. It is real in the sense that we have pretty well eliminated the change in the value of output that is just the result of higher or lower prices; so that our results measure actual changes in production, not just changes in selling prices.

In the chart on the top of page 59 we show what happens to the upward swooping curve of nominal GNP from 1900 to 1980, when we use the prices of a single year—in this case 1972—to calculate the value of output (GNP) in each and every year. The result is still impressive—a rise of about tenfold. But clearly this is much less dramatic than the rise before we adjusted for inflation.

There remains a last adjustment to be made. Not only has output increased, but so also has population. In 1900, United States population was 76 million; in 1980 it was about 225 million. To bring our real GNP down to life size, we have to divide it by population to get GNP per person or per capita. When we do so, we get a quite astonishing result. Looking back not just to the early 1900s, but as far as we can piece together statistics, we find that the pace of real per capita growth has been amazingly steady. There are swings up and down, some of them serious. But most of the swings are within ten percent of a main trend line.

The trend itself comes to about 1.5 percent a year in real terms

REAL GNP, 1900–1980

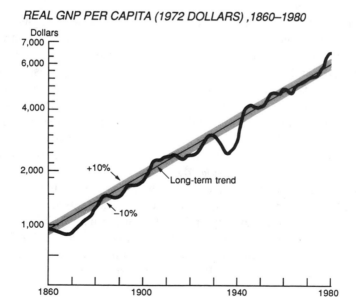

REAL GNP PER CAPITA (1972 DOLLARS) , 1860–1980

per capita. Although 1.5 percent a year may not sound like much, this figure allows us to double our real per capita living standards every forty-seven years. This is Adam Smith's growth model come to life!

How do we explain this long, steady upward trend? Essentially there are two reasons. First, the *quantity* of inputs going into the economic process increased. In 1900 our labor force was 27 million. In 1980 it was 108 million. Obviously, larger inputs of labor produce larger outputs of goods and services. Our quantity of capital inputs increased as well. For instance, in 1900 the total horsepower energy delivered by "prime movers"—engines of all kinds, work animals, ships, trains, and so forth—was 65 million horsepower. In 1980 it was almost 30 *billion*.

Second, the *quality* of inputs improved. The population working in 1980 was not only more numerous than in 1900, it was better trained and better schooled. One overall gauge of this is the amount of education stored up in the work force. In 1900, when only 6.4 percent of the working population had gone beyond grade school, there were 223 million man-years of schooling embodied in the population. In 1980, when two thirds of the population had finished high school, the stock of education embodied in the population had grown to over a billion man-years.

The quality of capital has also increased, along with its quantity. As an indication of the importance of the changing quality of capital, consider the contribution made to our output by the availability of surfaced roads. In 1900 there were about 150,000 miles of such roads. In 1980 there were 4,000,000 miles. That is an increase in the quantity of roads of over twenty-five times. But that increase does not begin to measure the difference in the transport capability of the two road systems, one of them graveled, narrow, built for traffic that averaged ten to twenty miles per hour; the other concrete or asphalt, multilane, fast-paced.

There are still other sources of growth, such as shifts in occupations and efficiencies of large-scale operation, but the main ones are the increase in the quantity and quality of inputs. Of the two, *improvements in the quality of inputs—in human skills, in improved designs of capital equipment—have been far more important than mere increases in quantity.* Better skills and technology enable the labor force to increase its productivity, the amount of goods and services it can turn out in a given time.

TURNABOUT IN THE 1980s

Readers will note that we have talked about growth only up to the 1980s. There is reason for that. For when we turn to the 1980s, we find a change in the trend.

At first glance, nothing seems awry. GNP was $3,052 billion in 1981; just over $6,000 billion in 1993. After correcting for inflation, GNP in rose by about 30 percent over the period. Even when we take into account the growth of population—up from 227 million to almost 255 million over the period—we find we still have a rise in per capita real income of over 12 percent from 1980 to 1993. It is this rise that was the basis for the frequently heard claim that the Reagan years were a continuation of the longest peacetime boom in U.S. history.

Now come the reasons for considering this period apart from the earlier long-run trend. One reason is that the rate of growth was considerably slower than over the past. During the 1970s and 1980s, GNP grew at only about half the rate of the 1940s, 1950s, and 1960s. That fall, in itself, points to problems concerning U.S. productivity, to which we will turn as we go along. But at this juncture there is a more immediate and distressing aspect of the 1980s. It is that the years were a period of unprecedented redistribution of income toward the topmost income groups. During the decade of the '80s, the average real income of the top 5 percent rose from $120,253 to $148,438, while the corresponding income of the bottom 20 percent *fell* from $9,990 to $9,431. Perhaps more shocking is the finding of the Congressional Budget Office that the top 20 percent of families took more than 100 percent of the total growth in family income. How could this be? Because the share of the lower 80 percent shrank.* No wonder that by the end of the decade the top 20 percent of Americans had the largest, and the bottom 20 percent the smallest shares in total national income in our history.† Thus, for most fam-

*New York Times, April 19, 1992, E 10.
†Lester Thurow, Head to Head (New York: Morrow and Co., 1992), p. 164.

ilies, the 1980s were not growth years at all. They were years of what economist Wallace Peterson has called a "silent depression."

BEHIND THE INCOME SHIFT

What were the reasons for this startling shift? We can clearly identify one. It was a change in the tax laws that openly and unabashedly favored the rich. From 1977 to 1990, Congress passed seven important tax bills. Their net effect was to raise the proportion of incomes that were paid in taxes by nine out of ten families. This was almost entirely the consequence of a boost in Social Security taxes, which constitute a larger source of taxation for most working families than income taxes.

At the same time, income taxes were substantially reduced for families in the upper tax brackets. The tax burden on the highest 1 percent of all families dropped by over a third. Over the 1980s, the average income of $314,859 of the top 1 percent rose by 115 percent before taxes, but by 165 percent after taxes.* Yet, the redistributional aspect of the problem is not the most disturbing aspect of the 1980s, because it is the most easily remediable one. We could, after all, restore the degree of tax fairness that prevailed during the 1960s and 1970s, when we enjoyed what has often been called our Golden Age. This is, in fact, one aim of the Clinton Administration.

What is not so easily remedied is the first cause of the break in the trend—the fact that negative growth for many families may reflect a deterioration in our basic economic situation—our possession of the requisite skills and knowledge, our managerial techniques, our government policies and institutions. To the extent these are the problems, the remedies will be much more difficult to formulate and realize, for they are likely to require many changes: from the length of the school year to school curricula; from corporate relations with labor unions to labor union relations with minorities; from Congressional budget procedures, through international negotiations on trade and production. It is too soon to get involved in these issues that underlie America's capacity to produce effectively in the emerging world market, but we will come back to them as we go along.

*Robert McIntyre, *Challenge,* Nov.–Dec. 1991, p. 24f.

A WORD ON POVERTY

The richer get richer, goes the popular adage, and the poor get poorer. What has happened to poverty during the last fifteen years bears out the adage. We can see this in the table below:

THE TREND IN POVERTY

	1959	1969	1979	1989	1991
Persons below low-income level (millions)	39.5	24.1	25.3	31.5	35.7
Percent of population	22.4	12.1	11.4	12.8	14.2

We see poverty declining sharply during the sixties, more slowly in the 1970s, then rising during the 1980s and into the 1990s. This is true even though the threshold defined as a "poverty level income" has been steadily adjusted upward to allow for inflation. A two-parent, two-child family was in poverty with an income of $4,880 in 1970; by 1989 it took an income of $11,660 to bring such a family out of poverty. The figures above do not take into account cash and noncash payments to the poor, such as food stamps and welfare aid, but these too were considerably reduced during the 1980s.

What is the reason for the melting away of poverty, followed by its resurgence? The melting away is probably the consequence of two trends during the period 1959–1979. The first of these was relatively strong growth, which offered employment opportunities to the unskilled and older unemployed who make up a large fraction of the poor. The second reason was a sharp increase in welfare assistance during those years, rescuing many from destitution.

The upturn in poverty in recent years is a complex matter. At bottom it testifies to a slowdown in growth. An important contributing factor was a cutback and a redirection in welfare spending: the largest single group in our population affected by poverty today is the children. Poverty in the 1990s thereby begins to look more and more like the symptom of an economy that failed to maintain its momentum and neglected the social obligations thrust upon it by this failure.

But there are still more reasons. The wages of ordinary workers have been falling at about 1 percent a year since 1973, despite the overall growth in GNP. Why? Probably because of the encroachment of third-world competition, into which we'll be looking later on. As a consequence of falling real wages, the proportion of year-round, full-time workers with a family of three who could not get over the poverty line doubled, from 20 to 40 percent. Some of this decline in income was made up by wives who worked more hours per week, but the increase wasn't great because the wives were working heavy schedules to begin with.

THE TREND TO BIG BUSINESS

Now let us turn to business. Here one change immediately strikes the eye. There is a marked decline of the independent, small business—with its self-employed worker—as a main form of enterprise.

In 1900 there were about 8 million independent enterprises, including 5.7 million farms. By the early 1990s, as we saw in our last chapter, the number of proprietorships had grown to over 14 million, including 2.1 million farms. Meanwhile, the labor force itself more than tripled. Thus *as a percentage of all persons working, the proportion of self-employed has fallen from about 30 percent in 1900 to around 10 percent today.*

With the decline of the self-employed worker has come the rise of the giant firm. Back in 1900 the giant corporation was just arriving on the scene. In 1901 financier J. P. Morgan created the first billion-dollar company when he formed the United States Steel Corporation out of a dozen smaller enterprises. In that year the total capitalization of all corporations valued at more than $1 million was $5 billion. By 1904 it was $20 billion. In 1985 it was about $10 *trillion.*

It hardly comes as a surprise that the main trend of the past eighty years has been the emergence of big business. More interesting is the question of whether big business is continuing to grow. This is a more difficult question to answer, for it depends on what we mean by growth.

Certainly the place of the biggest companies within the world of corporations has been rising, as our next table shows. Marx was right in predicting this trend.

LARGEST MANUFACTURERS' SHARE OF ASSETS (%)

	1948	1960	1970	1975	1983	1991 (est.)
100 largest corporations	40.2	46.4	48.5	45.0	48.3	69.5
200 largest corporations	48.2	56.3	60.4	57.5	60.8	88.7

We can see that the top one hundred companies held approximately half again as large a share of total corporate wealth in the 1980s as did the top *two hundred* companies in 1948. This growing concentration of assets in the hands of the mightiest companies is not the same thing, however, as an increase in monopolization, as we usually define that term. Monopolization refers to the share of a company within a given market, such as GM's share of the auto industry. Within the preponderance of markets in the economy, the share of giant firms has *not* markedly risen, and has often fallen, even though the total wealth of the corporate world has been steadily drifting into their hands.

Can we explain the long-term trend toward the concentration of business assets, as we did the trend toward growth in GNP? By and large, economists would stress three main reasons for the appearance of giant enterprise. The first reason is that advances in technology have made possible the mass production of goods or services at falling costs. The rise of bigness in business is very much a result of technology. Without the steam engine, the lathe, the railroad, it is difficult to imagine how big business would have emerged in the first place.

But technology went on to do more than make large-scale production possible. Typically it also brought an economic effect that we call *economies of scale*. That is, technology not only enlarged, it also cheapened the process of production. Costs per unit fell as output rose. The process is perfectly exemplified in the huge reduction of cost in producing automobiles on an assembly line rather than one car at a time (see box on page 67).

Economies of scale provided further powerful impetus toward a growth in size. The firm that pioneered in the introduction of mass-production technology usually secured a competitive selling advantage over its competitors, enabling it to grow in size and thereby to increase its advantage still further. These cost-reducing advantages were important causes of the initial emergence of giant companies in many industries. Similarly, the absence of such technologies explains why corporate giants did not emerge in all fields.

Second, business concentration is also a result of corporate mergers. Ever since J. P. Morgan assembled U.S. Steel, mergers have been a major source of corporate growth. At the very end of the nineteenth century there was the first great merger wave, out of which came the first huge companies, including U.S. Steel. In 1890 most industries were competitive, without a single company dominating the field. By 1904 one or two giant firms, usually created by mergers, had arisen to control at least half the output in seventy-eight different industries.

Again, between 1951 and 1960 one fifth of the top one thousand corporations disappeared—not because they failed, but because they were bought up by other corporations. In all, mergers have accounted for about two fifths of the increase in concentration between 1950 and 1970; internal growth accounts for the rest.

Finally, concentration is accelerated by the business cycle. Depressions or recessions plunge many smaller firms into bankruptcy and make it possible for larger, more financially secure firms to buy them up very cheaply. This is once more as Marx anticipated. When industries are threatened, the weak producers go under; the stronger ones emerge relatively stronger than before. Consider, for example, that three once-prominent American automobile producers—Studebaker, Packard, and Kaiser Motors—succumbed to the mild recessions of the 1950s and 1960s, and to the pressure of foreign competition. In 1980 Chrysler skirted bankruptcy.

MERGER MANIA

Has the trend to bigness leveled off? Only a few years ago it seemed that the trend was winding down. But the 1980s witnessed another vast merger wave—indeed, the largest such wave in history. In 1984 some three thousand giant mergers took place, involving $124 billion in assets. In 1985 the total was even higher. In that year there were at least five mergers, *each of which was larger than the total value of all the mergers of the pre-merger decade.* Just as examples, General Electric bought RCA for $6.3 billion; Philip Morris bought General Foods for $5.8 billion; and General Motors bought Hughes Aircraft

FROM PIN FACTORY TO ASSEMBLY LINE

We recall Adam Smith's pin factory (Chapter Two). Here is a later version of that division of labor, in the early Ford assembly lines:

"Just how were the main assembly lines and lines of component production and supply kept in harmony? For the chassis alone, from 1,000 to 4,000 pieces of each component had to be furnished each day at just the right point and right minute: a single failure, and the whole mechanism would come to a jarring standstill. . . . Superintendents had to know every hour just how many components were being produced and how many were in stock. Whenever danger of shortage appeared, the shortage chaser—a familiar figure in all automobile factories—flung himself into the breach. Counters and checkers reported to him. Verifying in person any ominous news, he mobilized the foreman concerned to repair deficiencies. Three times a day he made typed reports in manifold to the factory clearinghouse, at the same time chalking on blackboards in the clearinghouse office a statement of results in each factory-production department and each assembling department."[*]

Such systematizing in itself resulted in astonishing increases in productivity. With each operation analyzed and subdivided into its simplest components, with a steady stream of work passing before stationary men, with a relentless but manageable pace of work, the total time required to assemble a car dropped astonishingly. Within a single year, the time required to assemble a motor fell from 600 minutes to 226 minutes: to build a chassis, from 12 hours and 28 minutes to 1 hour and 33 minutes. A stopwatch man was told to observe a 3-minute assembly in which men assembled rods and pistons, a simple operation. The job was divided into three jobs, and half the men turned out the same output as before.

---

[*]Allan Nevins, *Ford, the Times, the Man, the Company* (New York: Scribner's, 1954), p. 1,507.

for $5.1 billion. The trend continued through 1989, when another 4,000-odd mergers amounted in themselves to $254 billion.

That this vast spree of amalgamation will change the corporate scene is evident. That it will change it for the better is not so evident. Its supporters say that the survivors will be better able to hold their own in a world of fierce international competition. Its detractors say that the mergers have saddled the survivors with a heavy layer of expense—most of the mergers were paid for by issuing new bonds whose interest payments must be met, come hell or high water. As of now, the detractors seem to have the better of the argument. The great merger mania more and more resembles the irrational speculative crazes of the past, like the "tulip mania" of seventeenth-century Holland, when vast fortunes were made and lost on tulip bulbs, for what reasons no one could afterward say.

A few prospects seem less fanciful. If the 1980s were years of extraordinary fattening for "winning" corporations, the 1990s seem likely to be years in which the winners will be notable for their ability to slim down. One after another, giant firms that appeared to be unassailable because of their very size have turned out to be economic dinosaurs, unable to hold their own in the high-tech, quick turnaround, just-in-time production patterns of the 1990s. General Motors, International Business Machines, Sears Roebuck have all started on major downsizings, trying to regain a capacity for flexibility and efficiency that they lost as a consequence of growth for growth's sake alone.

As we saw in our last chapter, megasize is a worldwide, not just an American phenomenon. But there is a difference. Abroad, the movement has been one of deliberate consolidation, often with government consent and even encouragement, not a hell-for-leather bidding contest. As a result, Europe and Japan have created giant firms that have largely avoided the financial problems and organizational topheaviness that have been the great weaknesses of America's winners. It is not the trend to bigness that seems to be the problem so much as the way the movement is carried out. The American way does not seem to be the answer. We will come back to this matter more than once before we are done.

THE ROLLER COASTER IN LABOR

In their formative years, labor unions grew in strength roughly as a counterpart to the growth of big business. Unions were, after all, largely a social response to the pressures exerted by massive enterprises on their work forces. Thus the numbers of men and women in unions increased from less than a half million in 1897 to just over 3.5 million in 1929. Thereafter membership remained static until the passage of the National Labor Relations Act of 1935, which legitimized industrial as well as craft unionization. That green light soon doubled union membership, and this number grew still further in the postwar years, until by the mid-1950s some 18 million workers—31 percent of the labor force—belonged to either a craft or an industrial labor organization.

There has been a dramatic decline since then, as the percentage of unionized labor in the national labor force has been cut in half. What lies behind this extraordinary fall? There is more than one answer. The decline begins with the swelling of employment in the service sector during the 1950s and 1960s—a sector populated by small businesses and a heavy preponderance of female workers, both relatively difficult to unionize. At the same time, the decline reflects a growing inertia on the part of top labor leadership in the 1960s, content with its comfortable bargains with management. The decline gains further momentum in the 1970s when management turns more aggressively against unions, under the duress of shrinking profit margins. Finally, government completes the decline during the Reagan years with an increasingly open antiunion stance.

Perhaps more significant than this roller-coaster profile of labor union strength is the inability of the United States to accord a legitimacy to unions comparable to that found in Canada and in virtually all European nations. There has been nothing like the decline of union strength abroad that we have seen here, and the strongly adversarial position of both government and management toward unions in our country has to be compared with very different attitudes abroad. In Germany, for example, union leaders sit on large corporation boards by law. If this labor-management accord works, as it is supposed to, both to moderate inflationary wage demands and to enhance managerial efficiency, it will give our European competitors a substantial competitive edge. For the moment, however, such a way of dealing with the "labor problem" does not seem to be within the American imagination.

BIG GOVERNMENT EMERGES

We pass now to the last great trend of the economy, a trend whose end result has been the emergence of that large government apparatus we noted in our previous chapter.

There are three quite different ways of measuring the rise of the public sector. The first is to examine the proportion of GNP that government directly produces or purchases. This might be regarded as a rough indication of the degree to which we have become a nationalized economy.

A second way is to inquire into the extent to which the government reallocates incomes by taxing some persons and giving others "transfer payments" such as Social Security benefits or welfare or unemployment insurance. This might be regarded as an index of the degree to which we have become a welfare state.

Last is the extent to which government interferes in the working of the economy by regulating various aspects of economic life or by exercising its economic powers in other ways. By far the most difficult to measure exactly, this might be thought of as an indication of the extent to which we have moved in the direction of a guided or controlled capitalism.

No one will be surprised to learn that all three indicators are up over the long run. Take the trend of direct government production or purchases. In 1929 government bought less than 10 percent of total output; in 1992 it bought about 20 percent. Most of this increase, it ought to be noted, comes from two sources: a very large rise in federal spending for defense and a very substantial growth of state and local spending on education and roads. Defense aside, the federal government is not a big buyer of goods and services, impressions to the contrary notwithstanding. Moreover, the percentage of federal government buying of GNP has been stable for 25 years.

But certainly the federal government is a big spender of money. This brings us to the second indication of the growth of government, its welfare function. Back in 1929 less than 1 percent of GNP was redistributed as a transfer payment by government. In 1992 transfer payments amounted to roughly 14 percent of GNP. The bulk of this was federal expenditures for Social Security, Medicare, and other "safety net" purposes. It is the growth in government transfers, not the growth in government purchasing, that accounts for the real bulge in public spending. The two combined streams now come to about one third of GNP. We'll be talking about the implications of this as we go along. Here we only want to call attention to the fact that this is a worldwide trend, and that most European capitalisms spend or transfer a considerably larger fraction of their GNPs through government hands than we do.

Last, there is the third measure of government size—the extent of its intervention, the bulk of its sheer presence as a supervisor or regulator of the system.

Because of its varied nature, and because the importance of government intervention is not always shown by the amount of money that an agency spends or the number of personnel it employs, this is a trend that defies easy measurement. Much of the spending that we have noted, for example, is carried out through established departments of the executive branch of government, especially Health and Welfare, from which Social Security checks flow, and the Defense Department, source of military spending.

But we ought to have at least some indication, however impressionistic and incomplete, of the widening reach of government concern within various areas of the economic system. The following list gives us some inkling of the variety and importance of these functions:

Federal Aviation Administration *regulates air safety*
Environmental Protection Agency *administers antipollution legislation*
Federal Reserve Board *regulates banks*
Federal Communications Commission *assigns airwave frequencies to stations*
Federal Trade Commission *polices business activities in restraint of trade*
Interstate Commerce Commission *regulates rail, canal, and truck industry*
National Labor Relations Board *supervises union elections*
National Science Foundation *supports scientific research*
Tariff Commission *holds hearings on tariff matters*
Office of Economic Opportunity *oversees employment practices*

Some of these regulatory agencies, such as the Tariff Commission, are almost a hundred years old. Others, like the Environmental Protection Agency, are relatively new. But obviously the range and reach of government intervention into the economy has increased enormously, whether we look back a century or only a relatively short time. Perhaps now, with the Clinton administration, that long trend may come to a halt or may even be permanently reversed. That is a matter to be considered as we go along. But first we must seek to understand the reasons for the long-run upward trend in all indicators: government buying, government transfers, government intervention.

There is, of course, no simple or even irrefutable answer. But a backward glance over history suggests these causes:

The growing size of business itself has evoked a need for government intervention. As business firms have increased in size, private decisions have become fraught with social consequences. The decisions of big business have widespread repercussions. Building or not building a plant may spell prosperity or decline for a town, even a state. Cutthroat competition can spell ruin for an industry. Polluting a river can ruin a region. Much government effort, at the local and state as well as federal level, represents attempts to prevent big business from creating social or economic problems, or to cope with problems it has created.

Technology has brought a need for public supervision. An impressive amount of government effort goes into the regulation of problem-creating technologies. Examples: the network of state and local highway and police authorities that deal with the automobile; the panoply of agencies designed to cope with airplanes, television and radio, atomic energy, new drugs, and weaponry. As long as technology increases its power to affect our social and natural environment, it is likely that public supervision will also increase.

Urbanization has created a need for centralized administration. City life has its appeals, but it also has its perils. Men and women cannot live in crowded quarters without police, public health, traffic, sanitation, and educational facilities far more complex than those needed in a rural setting. Government is, and always has been, concentrated in cities. As a nation urbanizes, it requires more government.

Unification of the economy has given us additional problems. Industrialization knits an economy together into a kind of vast, interlocked machinery. An unindustrialized, localized economy is like a pile of sand: if you poke a finger into one side of it, some businesses and individuals will be affected, but those on the other side of the pile will remain undisturbed. The growing scale and specialization of industrial operations unify the sandpile. You poke one side of it, and the entire pile shakes. Problems can no longer be localized. The difficulties of the economy grow in extent: there is a need for a national, not a local, energy program, for national transportation, urban, and educational programs. Government—largely federal government—is the principal means by which such problems are handled.

Economic malfunction has brought public intervention. Fifty or seventy-five years ago the prevailing attitude toward the economy was a kind of awed respect. People felt that the economy was best left alone, that it was fruitless as well as ill-advised to try to change its normal workings. That attitude changed once and for all with the advent of the Great Depression. In the ensuing collapse, the role of government was greatly enlarged, to restore the economy to working order. The trauma of the Depression and the determination to prevent its recurrence were a watershed in the trend of government spending and government intervention. Keynes's thinking played a very important part in this transition to a mixed economy; and not even the most conservative government today has any intention of returning to a pure laissez-faire system. That is no longer possible.

Last, but not least, we no longer live in a society in which old-age retirement, medical expenses, and income during periods of unemployment are felt to be properly the responsibility of the individuals concerned. For better or worse, these and similar responsibilities have been gradually assumed by governments in all capitalist nations. In fact, the United States is a laggard in these matters compared with many European capitalist states. Here lie crucial reasons for the swelling volume of state, local, and federal production and purchase that have steadily enlarged the place of government within the economy.

No doubt there are other causes that could be added to this list.

Bureaucracies have ways of feeding on themselves. But the overall conclusion is already evident. In modern capitalism, government is a major factor in the economic system. More and more, we *make* our history, rather than just waiting for it to happen. How well government fulfills this function, and to what extent it realizes the hopes that have been thrust upon it, are themes that will constantly occupy us as we continue along.

II

MACROECONOMICS— THE ANALYSIS OF PROSPERITY AND RECESSION

FIVE

The GNP

One of the reasons for the mystification that obscures economics is the vocabulary it employs. Not only does it use common, ordinary words, such as *saving* or *investing,* in ways that are not exactly the way we use them in everyday talk, but it leans on barbarous and intimidating terms like *macroeconomics* or *gross national product*— nowadays also known as *gross domestic product.* (We'll explain the difference below.)

It would be nice if we could purge economics of its jargon, but that would be like asking doctors to tell us about our troubles in plain English. Instead, we must learn to speak a certain amount of economics—that is, to become familiar with, and easy about, some of the basic terms in which economists tell about our economic condition.

One of these is that odd word "macroeconomics." It comes from the Greek *macro,* meaning big, and the implication is that macroeconomics therefore grapples with very big problems. It does, including such problems as inflation and recession and unemployment and economic growth. But that is not what distinguishes macro from its brother, microeconomics, whom we will meet later. Rather, macroeconomics refers to a perspective, a vantage point, that throws into high relief certain aspects of the economic system.

What does the economy look like from the macro perspective? The view is not unlike that which we have gained in the chapters just past. We look down on the economy, as from a plane, to see it as a vast landscape populated by business firms, households, government agencies. Later, when we take up the micro perspective, we will examine the selfsame landscape from a worm's-eye, rather than a bird's-eye view, with surprising changes in the features of the landscape that spring into sharp focus.

The purpose of looking down on the economy from the macro vantage point is that it allows us to see, more clearly than from ground level, a process of crucial and central importance. This is the ceaseless activity of production on a national scale, the never-ending creation and re-creation of the wealth by which the country replenishes and renews and expands its material life. This great central flow, on which we all depend, is called the *gross national product,* often abbreviated as GNP. When TV newscasters say that GNP has gone up or down, what they mean is that the river of output has gotten larger or smaller, that we are producing more or less. Learning about *why* production varies is the first task of macroeconomics.

WHAT GNP IS MADE UP OF

We start to unravel the question by looking more closely at the river itself. One thing is immediately clear. The flow of output arises from the cooperation of the factors of production—from the efforts of the labor force mustered from the nation's households, working with capital and land mainly owned by the nation's businesses, under the rules and laws established by the government. We can literally see the flow of production originating in ten million farms and factories, offices and agencies, over which we fly. It is from these wellsprings that the river of national output is formed.

As we look down on it, the river seems at first to be made up of an unclassifiable collection of outputs. There are hundreds of thousands, perhaps millions, of kinds of goods and services in the stream of production—foods of every conceivable kind, spectrums of clothing, catalogs of machinery, jumbles of junk. But at second look, we can see that this vast and variegated output can be divided into two basic sorts of production. One of them consists of goods and services that will be bought by households for their personal use: cars, haircuts, jewelry, meat. We call this branch of the river of production *consumption,* and the various goods and services in it *consumers' goods.*

The consumption branch of our production process is familiar to us. But looking again from our macro vantage point, we can see that there are goods and services that never end up in any consumer's possession. Here is a stream of outputs such as machines, roads, office buildings, bridges, not to mention smaller objects such as office furniture and office typewriters. These goods are also obviously part of our gross national product, but they are not consumers' goods. We give them a special name—*investment goods* or *capital goods*—and we will soon see that they play a vital role in determining our economic well-being.

The macro view also enables us to see a rather surprising thing about the two branches of output. It is that each stream supports a different part of the economy. The flow of consumers' goods obviously goes to restore the working strength and well-being of the nation's households. Without it, we would perish in a few weeks. But the investment flow of output also plays a restorative function. Investment output replenishes and renews the capital wealth of the nation, mainly owned by its firms and, to a smaller extent, by the government. The flow of investment output terminates in repairs to and extensions of our system of dams and roads, assembly lines and warehouses, lathes and drill presses, farm equipment and apartment houses. If that stream of output dried up, we would not perish as quickly as if consumer output disappeared, but our productive strength would soon wither, and by degrees we would be forced back to the level of an underdeveloped, then of a primitive, society.

GDP, then, consists of two main kinds of output—consumption goods and investment goods. The roughly $6 trillion that gross national product amounted to in 1993, for instance, is nothing but the total sales value of these two basic kinds of output. It may help to think of the river of production as passing through the checkout counters of an immense supermarket. The sales ticket on each item is rung up on a cash register. After a year of ringing up the checkouts, a total is taken of the tapes. That's GDP for the year.*

*Here's an important footnote: What's the difference between gross national product and gross domestic product? It is that GNP includes the value of all production by U.S. citizens or companies, even if they are located abroad, whereas GDP counts

• • •

A few things ought to be noticed about this GNP. One of them is that the flow of output through the checkout counter is comprised of both public and private goods and services. Take the flow of consumption, for example. Consumption goods or services, as the words indicate, are goods that we consume or use up, usually in a fairly short period. Most consumption goods are bought by private households for their personal use—food or clothing, for instance, or services such as movie admissions or legal advice. But some consumption outputs are bought by local or state or federal governments. Teachers' or firefighters' services, for example, resemble the professional services of lawyers or oil-well firefighters, but they are part of public consumption, not private. This is true even though households in the end get the benefit of teachers' or firefighters' performances: the "person" who pays the bill for their services is the state.

The same division into private and public can be observed if we look at investment. Investment goods typically last a long time and are replaced when they wear out, as is the case with a factory. But this is also true of a road or a dam or a city-owned incinerator plant. These are investment goods, too, but they are public, not private.

While we are concerning ourselves about public output, one further thing should be noted. It is that very large and important flow of government spending, mainly federal, called *transfer payments*. As we know, this is a stream of payments mainly for "safety net" purposes: Social Security payments, unemployment compensation, help for the disabled or disadvantaged, plus subsidies of various

---

the value of production within the country, regardless of whether it was produced by U.S. citizens or companies or not. A Honda assembly plant in California isn't included in the tally of our GNP, but it is included in our GDP. A Pepsi plant located in Mexico does not contribute to our GDP (it contributes to Mexico's), whereas it would contribute to our GNP because it is an American producer. The actual difference between the two measures is not large, usually less than 1 percent of difference, sometimes in favor of one measure, sometimes the other. Because most countries want to know the value of output within their own boundaries (where the money is paid out), gross domestic product has become the main statistical measuring rod, and the United States has also recently adopted it. But GNP is deeply ingrained in our vocabulary—one hears it on TV when the economy is being discussed—so for this edition, at least, we'll continue to speak of GNP, with occasional references or comparisons to GDP.

kinds. Federal transfers came to almost $800 billion in 1992, or about 17 percent of GNP.

Yet when we add up GNP, we do not include any transfer payments in it! This is because transfers, as the name indicates, are payments made for social purposes, not because the recipients perform a useful service. Here is the difference: when we pay our cleaning bill, we transfer money to someone who has done work for us. So too, when we pay taxes to help finance schools or fire departments or even armies, we also pay individuals who perform services on our behalf. But the portion of the taxes we pay that is used to provide income to individuals who cannot find work, or are too infirm to support themselves, or who have reached the age of retirement, is not a reward for effort. It is a pure transfer payment—a form of institutionalized social responsibility that has become part of every advanced nation. It is, in fact, the public equivalent of private charity. *But because no production takes place in exchange for a transfer payment, such as a Social Security check, transfers are simply left out when we calculate GNP.* * The same is true for gambling outlays, or the buying of stocks and bonds, or disaster relief. These are all large and important flows of spending, but they do not reflect the activity of production that GNP sets out to measure.

When GNP is actually calculated by Commerce Department statisticians, the river of output is imagined to pass through not one, but four checkout lines. One of them rings up the total of personal consumption expenditures, all of them made by private households. A second register totals up all the private domestic investment output of the country, mainly business plant and equipment and new homes for families. A third checkout line keeps track of all public output, whether for consumption or investment purposes. There is really no reason why we do not separate public output into a consumption and an investment stream, as we do with private output, and it might help us better understand the government's place in the economy if we did. But we don't, so school lunch programs and

---

*Another way of looking at it is that a transfer payment takes money from some Americans and transfers it to others—for example, from taxpayers to Social Security recipients or the unemployed. *But government itself does not "spend" the money, unlike the case with government spending that enters GNP, such as road-building or military expenditures.*

new subway trackage are put together in one government output figure.

Finally, there is a fourth counter, where we ring up all the U.S. production that is sold abroad and where we subtract all the foreign production that is bought here. If we sell more abroad than we buy, there is a positive "export balance" as part of GNP. If, as in recent years, we buy more abroad than we sell there, there is a negative export balance—a net stream of purchasing power that wends its way abroad.

Thus the GNP figure we read about is the sum of four separate tallies (involving hundreds and hundreds of detailed reports and estimates) of our national output. In 1992, for example, the four tallies were:

GNP: 1992	$ billion
Personal consumption expenditure	4,094
Private domestic investment outlays	776
Government purchases	1,115
Export balance	− 60
Total Gross National Product	5,995*

There is one last matter. In adding up our GNP, government statisticians do not record the value of every good that it produced, each time it is sold. If they did, they would have to add up the value of a bushel of wheat to a grain elevator, the grain sold to a miller, the flour sold to a baker, the bread sold to a supermarket, and, finally, the loaf to a consumer. This would be a much bigger figure than the value of the final loaf, and yet the value of the loaf clearly contains the payments that have been previously made to the baker, the miller, the grain elevator, and the farmer.

Following along this line, statisticians only keep track of *final* goods, not of intermediate ones. As we would imagine, each of the checkout counters tots up one category of these final goods: consumers' goods, investment goods, government output, and net exports.

*For purposes of comparison, Gross Domestic Product for 1992 came to $5,951 billion.

WHAT DOES GNP TELL US?

It should be pretty clear by now what GNP consists of. What is not yet so clear is how important it is. Does the size of GNP tell us accurately if we are better off or not? Is it good if GNP goes up, and bad if it goes down?

The answer is yes and no. The yes part is easy to understand. When the value of production rises, more people are likely to be employed. When the value of total output increases, more incomes are sure to be received. So there is an evident connection between the size of GNP and the level of employment and of national incomes. The size of GNP also serves as a general measure of the amount of goods and services that we can buy, individually and collectively. That is why, all things considered, a rising GNP is always welcome, and a falling one unwelcome.

Yet GNP is also a flawed and deceiving measure of our well-being, and we should understand the weaknesses as well as the strengths of this most important single economic indicator.

To begin with, GNP deals in dollar values, not in physical units. Therefore we have to correct it for inflation. As we know from our last chapter, trouble arises when we compare the GNP of one year with that of another to determine whether or not the nation is better off. If prices in the second year are higher, GNP will appear higher even though the actual volume of output is unchanged or even lower. Thus, GNP is an accurate indicator of well-being only if we can accurately take out the inflation factor in comparing one year with another. Can we? Well, partly, but not perfectly. There is always a margin of uncertainty in comparing the "real" GNP of today with that of yesterday.

A second weakness of GNP also involves its inaccuracy as an indicator of "real" trends over time. The difficulty revolves around changes in the quality of goods and services. In a technologically advanced society, goods are usually improved over time, and new goods are constantly being introduced. At the same time, in an increasingly high-density society, the quality of other goods may be lessened: an airplane trip today is certainly preferable to one of thirty years ago, but a subway ride is not. Government statisticians try to adjust GNP statistics for such changes in quality, but obviously there is a margin of uncertainty here too.

A third difficulty with GNP lies in its blindness to the ultimate use of production. If in one year GNP rises by a billion dollars, owing to an increase in expenditure on education, and in another year it rises by the same amount because of a rise in cigarette production, the figures in each case show the same amount of growth. Even output that turns out to be wide of the mark or totally wasteful—such as the famous Edsel car that no one wanted or military weapons that are obsolete from the moment they appear—all are counted as GNP.

The problem of environmental deterioration adds another difficulty. Some types of GNP growth directly contribute to pollution—cars, paper or steel production, for example. Other types of GNP growth are necessary to stop pollution—sewage disposal plants or the production of a clean internal-combustion engine.

Our conventional measure of GNP makes no distinction among such outputs. For instance, the cleaning bills we pay to undo damage caused by smoke from the neighborhood factory became part of GNP, although cleaning our clothes does not increase our well-being but only brings it back to what it was in the first place. These problems also cloud the meaning of GNP.

Finally, GNP does not indicate anything about the distribution of goods and services among the population. Societies differ widely in how they allocate goods and services among their populations: compare Sweden and Mexico, whose total GNPs are roughly the same; or Sweden and the U.S., whose per capita GNPs are much alike. Thus to know the size of GNP or the level of GNP per capita is to know nothing about the social consequences of that GNP. A rich country may have lots of poverty which it is indifferent to, or perhaps impotent to correct. A poor country can produce a few millionaire families: some Indian princes used to receive their weight in gold from their peoples each year.

All these doubts and reservations (and some others we've left unmentioned) should instill in us a caution against using GNP as if it were a clear-cut measure of social contentment or happiness. Economist Edward Denison once remarked that perhaps nothing affects national economic welfare so much as the weather, which certainly does not get into the GNP accounts! Hence, although the U.S. may have a GNP per capita that is higher than that of, say, Japan, it does not mean that life is better here. It may be worse. In fact, by the indices of health care or incidence of crime, it probably is worse.

Yet, with all its shortcomings, GNP is still the simplest way we possess of summarizing the overall level of activity of the economy. If we want to examine its welfare, we had better turn to specific social indicators of how long we live, how healthy we are, how cheaply we provide good medical care, how varied and abundant is our diet, and so forth—none of which we can tell from GNP figures alone. But we are not always interested in welfare, partly because it is too complex to be summed up in a single measure. For instance, the indices of health care or crime are better in Japan than in the United States, but not the index of living space per person. There are lots of other data that could be consulted. GNP has the great value of being at everyone's fingertips, and of being, for better or worse, the yardstick that has become accepted by most nations in the world. It will remain a central theme in the economic lexicon for a long time to come.

SIX

Saving and Investing

Why does GNP fluctuate? Accidents of weather or natural disasters aside, why does the river of production run fast one year and slow the next? The question begins to take us into the real purpose of macroeconomic inquiry. Now that we know what GNP is, we want to know why it behaves the way it does.

A good way to begin is to look once again at the flow of output—this time paying heed not to the actual production of goods and services that get tallied by the Commerce Department statisticians, but at the buyers standing at those checkout counters to take delivery of the nation's production. As we would expect, the nation's households are gathered at the consumption counter, its business firms cluster around the investment counter, government agencies make up the buyers at the government counter, and foreign firms and individuals and governments wait at the last counter.

Looking at GNP from this perspective, we see it not so much as a stream of goods, but as a flow of buying, of expenditure, of demand. Each and every good that moves along the river of output is drawn by someone's expenditure for it. Money makes goods move. As Adam Smith said, "Money is the great wheel of circulation."

Switching our attention from production to buying brings us much closer to an answer for why the level of GNP fluctuates. Output fluctuates because the demand for it rises and falls. This is not the *only* reason why production varies—droughts and earthquakes, stiikes and technical hang-ups, government regulations may also alter the level of production. Later in this chapter we will take a first look at "supply side" economics, which emphasizes the adverse effects of taxation on the incentive to produce. But even the most determined supply sider will agree that demand—the willingness and ability to buy goods—is essential for the river of production to flow. Thus the way to begin our investigation is by examining where demand comes from and what makes it rise or fall.

HOUSEHOLD SAVING, BUSINESS SPENDING

We turn to the first checkout counter, where the nation's households are queuing up to buy the national output of consumers' goods and services. Where does the flow of household spending come from?

The answer is that it comes in the main from household earnings— from the wages, salaries, rents, dividends, profits, or whatever other payments householders have received from the work they have performed. It also comes from transfer payments, such as Social Security checks. The flow of spending can be augmented, at least for a while, if households actually draw down their savings accounts or liquidate stocks or bonds, but people rarely do that to buy ordinary consumers' goods. Finally, the flow can be also augmented by borrowing, so that in any one year some households will spend more than their current incomes—often the case when there is an expensive purchase such as a car.

Just the same, when we look at the sum total of all household incomes and compare it with the total of all household expenditures for consumers' goods, we discover that households as a whole (as a "sector," economists say) regularly save some portion of their incomes.* Year in and year out, the fraction is about 5 percent. That is, even *after* households have borrowed, used their credit cards and charge accounts and all the rest, they still take in more money than they lay out.

Hence there is no difficulty in understanding where the demand comes for the part of GNP that is made up of consumers' goods. All of it comes directly out of the earnings and transfer incomes of

---

*This includes household spending for autos, but not for houses. They are counted as *investment* goods, not as consumer goods.

households, supplemented by their borrowings. In fact, looking at GNP from the macro viewpoint, the question that occurs to us is not where consumer demand comes from, but what happens to the 5 percent of household earnings that do *not* get returned to the economy, but are instead saved.

That question turns our attention to the next checkout counter, where investment goods are bought by private business. Just as the household sector buys its everyday consumption goods mainly out of its earnings, so the business sector buys its ordinary day-to-day requirements from the money it regularly takes in from its sales. We can picture the nation's business as a gigantic household, buying its needed services of labor and its inputs of raw materials or semi-finished goods from the receipts it takes in by selling its finished output.

There is, however, a critical difference between the household sector and the business sector. It is that the business sector does not normally save some portion of its receipts. *On the contrary, it spends more than it takes in through its sales.* That idea is so important that it warrants saying a second time. The normal, regular, healthy, and even necessary behavior of the business community as a whole is to lay out more money for wages, salaries, raw materials, semifinished goods, land, and capital than the total amount it takes in by selling its own output.

When we put it this way, business behavior sounds very unsafe. How can even the largest corporation afford to lay out more, year after year, than it takes in from its sales? The answer is that business does not spend all its *earnings*. Part of these it too "saves" as profits, although it may disburse these profits in whole or part as dividends or as expenditures for capital goods. But over and above its normal revenues, business takes in additional financial revenues by borrowing from banks or by selling its stocks and bonds. These additional resources—the new capital funds it raises—are also spent, not to pay the regular running expenses of firms, but to pay for their capital improvements. AT&T does not use the proceeds of its bond issues to pay the wages of its phone operators, but to pay for the additions to its phone lines, its new buildings, its satellites.

Thus the process of saving and investing goes directly to the central issue of macroeconomics. Household savings are "acquired" by the business sector to finance the building of new capital goods. In turn, this becomes a primary means by which we increase our productivity and thereby cause GNP to increase. Here is the first explanation of how GNP grows and why it fluctuates. The explanation is important enough to set apart:

1. Gross national product grows because savings are converted into capital equipment.*
2. The savings that originate in the household sector are invested by the business sector.
3. GNP fluctuates because the process of transforming savings into investment is not always smooth or steady.

HOW THE SECTORS INTERLOCK

These critical relationships may come as something of an anticlimax, because everyone knows that savings and investing lie at the heart of economic growth, even if the process is not often described so precisely. But there are aspects of the saving and investing process that everyone does not know, and it is these to which we could now turn.

Let's begin with saving. We think of saving as putting money in a bank or in a financial institution of some other kind. What we do not often realize is that saving has two quite distinct meanings. The first of these is indeed putting money aside—not spending it. The second is letting go of resources. As we shall see, the two aspects have quite different consequences: the first bad, the second good.

Putting money in a bank or in a new insurance policy or a new issue of stock has the *immediate* effect of creating a gap or a shortfall in demand. The gap arises because some of the earnings that house-holders have received from firms or government will not be returned to circulation as part of the consumption flow. In a word, saving means not consuming. As we have just seen, this doesn't mean that those savings remain permanently removed from circulation. We can picture householders on the consumption queue, lending or

---

*Capital equipment, such as machinery or plant, is the largest, and usually most important component of investment. But more and more attention is being directed to such activities as research and development, or education, as strategic forms of growth-promoting expenditure. In other words, the category called "investment" is losing its exclusively nuts-and-bolts character.

otherwise transferring their savings to the businessmen standing at the investment queue. But until the transfer is actually made, through the banking system or the stock market or the purchase of life insur ance, saving means only that householders have taken some of their earnings and decided not to use it for buying consumption goods.

We'll return in a moment to the question of getting the money into the hands of the business queue. Meanwhile, however, we must also understand that saving is more than just a financial matter. It is also an action that frees labor and resources from the production of consumers' goods and thereby makes them available for producing other goods.

An illustration may help us see this. Suppose, for example, that businessmen decided to double their investment spending, in anticipation of a boom. Or suppose that the government wanted to double its military spending, in anticipation of a war. It is obvious that such an increase in the spending of the business or government sectors would send the price of labor and of other materials shooting upward, as business and government struggled to get their hands on the labor force and the materials they needed. That would result in higher costs, and could start an inflationary scramble.

In fact, there is only one way in which a large increase in investment or government spending can possibly be undertaken without such a scramble: the resources and labor they need must be made available to them. One way in which this can be done is by taxing— simply taking away spending power from households and giving it to government. But industry has no taxing power. For business, the *only* way that resources can be made available on a large scale is for them to be voluntarily relinquished by the household sector. We call that process of voluntary relinquishment *saving*. (Of course householders may be tempted to give up their spending by all sorts of inducements from banks or other institutions, but it is a voluntary, not a forced act nonetheless.)

Thus the really constructive aspect of saving is not so much its financial side, which merely creates a gap in spending, but its "real" side—giving up a claim on land and labor and capital for the immediate enjoyments they could produce.

This leads to the last vital link in the chain. The released resources must now be taken up and put to use by the business sector. If they are not put to use, the shortfall in demand created by the financial act of saving will simply hurt consumer sales without any compensation in the sales of other goods, and the labor and other resources released by households will stand idle. Thus the last, most active and creative part of the whole process lies in the decisions of the business sector to undertake the act of capital formation. As we will see in our next chapter, this is inherently a risky and uneven process.

So saving and investment have implications and meanings less familiar to us than the general recognition that there is a saving-and-investing process at work. Indeed, there is one unfamiliar aspect that we can now see is the key to how the macro system works. It is that *economic growth takes place through the coordination and cooperation of the sectors.*

As ordinary participants in the economy, we never think of co-ordinating our activity with that of anyone else, much less that of a sector. Nor does any businessman think of cooperating with the household or any other sector when he undertakes plans for an addition to his establishment. Nevertheless, it is by such a continuous coordination and cooperation that the system grows—and it is by imperfections in the interplay of the sectors that it falters.

The interplay can be very simply stated:

1. A gap in demand, in any sector, must be offset by additional demand in another sector. If this act of coordination does not take place, there will be a fall in demand, a decline in GNP, unemployment, and trouble.

2. An increase in investment or in government spending, assuming there is reasonably full employment, requires that resources be made available to the expanding sector. This can only be accomplished by taxing or by voluntary saving.

3. If expanding sectors spend more than the savings made available to them, there will be an upward pressure on the system, and the possibility of inflation. If the active sectors spend less than the flow of savings, there will be a downward pressure on the system, and the possibility of a recession.

Of course this is not the whole story of boom and bust, inflation and recession. We have not touched on such critical matters as money, producitivity, or the role of government. But a first *structural* understanding of the economy has begun to emerge. We can see that growth does not just happen, but comes about from a mutually supportive interaction of the sectors of the system. How that interaction is brought about and how it can be corrected when it fails to achieve the right result are the problems that will occupy us over many pages to come.

THE GOVERNMENT ENTERS

But we are not yet done with the checkout counter. We have seen how demand for GNP arises because households spend most of their earnings and businesses spend most of their own revenues plus the savings they have acquired from the household sector. But we have not yet observed what happens at the government checkout station or at the counter where foreigners line up.

Government first. At first glimpse there is an immediate resemblance between the government sector and the sector of business or of private households. Considering government as a collection of local, state, and federal purchasing agencies, we can see that the sector buys its goods and services with its everyday receipts—its tax revenues—just as businesses and families spend their normal receipts. In an important way, however, the receipts of government are different from those of households and businesses. With rare exceptions, government does not sell its outputs, however useful they may be. Toll roads or the fees for landing at an airport are exceptions to the general rule that government distributes its services without charge. Therefore it has to assure its income by some other means, and so the government simply commandeers a portion of household or business income. The word *commandeer* may seem extreme, but we must recognize that taxes are not like ordinary charges. A household or a business may refuse to purchase the output of another household or business, but they cannot refuse to purchase the output of government. Taxes are a compulsory payment.

On the other hand, it is well to bear in mind that taxes are also the expression of the will of the electorate, however clumsily that will may be expressed. Moreover, we should bear in mind that government provides one absolutely essential service in exchange for its taxes—a service without which no household or business could earn a cent. That is the service of the maintenance of law and order and the protection of property rights. "It is only under the shelter of the civil magistrate," wrote Adam Smith, "that the owner of . . . valuable property . . . can sleep a single night in security."*

Thus there is a profound difference between the political roles of the public and private sectors. But we must also recognize that there is a striking resemblance between the sectors with regard to their economic cooperation and coordination. Suppose, for example, that the household sector creates a demand gap by making its normal savings, and that the business sector, for whatever reason, fails to offset that gap by borrowing or gathering the savings through new stock issues and the like. *Could not the government borrow these unused savings and close the demand gap by spending them for public purposes, such as public investment?*

The answer, of course, is that it can. If there is a demand gap that must be "closed" by investment spending, what difference does it make if the investment is for a communications satellite owned by AT&T or one owned by the government, or a rail line owned by Santa Fe or owned by Amtrak, or a private utility plant or a public one, a private factory or a public dam? There is no difference. What is essential is that the savings of one sector be spent by another, or that the investment spending of one sector be saved by another.

Of course this is not an end to the matter. There is room for a great deal of controversy as to which activities the government should pursue and which it should not. There is room for debate as to whether the government can safely spend its borrowings for consumption purposes—Social Security, for instance. There is a great deal of controversy as to whether the government may inadvertently "crowd out" private enterprise when it expands its activities.

So the question of the role of government is not easily settled. What is easily settled, however, is that the government sector *can* play exactly the same investing role as the business sector. Government *can* use its borrowing powers just like business to offset a shortfall in spending elsewhere. Whether it *should* do these things is a question we will have to consider further. But it is important

*Wealth of Nations, op. cit., p. 670.

to see that the government, as a sector, can—indeed must—coordinate its activities with other sectors. No economist, conservative or radical, would deny that.

One last source of demand should be looked at quickly. This is the foreign checkout counter, where overseas buyers provide demand for U.S. output by taking delivery of grain and computers and jet planes and machinery, and where foreign sellers deliver coffee and ores and oil and Toyotas to waiting American buyers. The workings of the foreign-demand part of GNP are more complicated than those of the other sectors. We will come back to this aspect later, in Chapter Nineteen. For the time being, we can simply note its presence, while we concentrate our attention on the three domestic counters—households, business, and government.

So we have come to see that saving-and-investing—we hyphenate the process to emphasize its essential linkage—is the key to economic growth and economic fluctuation. It is the key to growth because investment is the activity by which we lay down the equipment that makes us more productive. It is by investment that Adam Smith's pin factories are built, multiplying by factors of ten and a hundred and a thousand the material goods that can be fashioned in an hour of work. Saving-and-investing is also the key to fluctuation in GNP because the process does not go on at a steady rate, but faster or slower as various factors alter the flow of saving—or more usually, as they alter the prospects for investment. That is a matter we will examine next.

Last, we can see one vitally important point. *Demand is the immediate driving force of the economy.* It is the volume of total spending—the spending of households on consumption goods, of business firms on capital goods, of government on its consumption and investment purchases, and of foreigners on net exports—that supplies the day-by-day stimulus for our gross national production. Even "supply-side" economists, who stress the importance of the incentive to produce and the dampening effects of taxes, would willingly concede this point. When demand falters for any reason, GNP falters, and with it, employment and incomes. Supply-side and demand-side economists differ, however, as to whether the demand generated by the normal investment activities of the private sector, once onerous taxes and regulations are removed, will suffice to generate sufficient growth. Supply siders say yes, demand siders believe that government will probably have to play a supportive role.

That's obviously an important question for later. But it's no use getting into discussions about supply-side economics until we understand still more deeply how the household and business and government sectors operate. That's the agenda to which we now turn.

SEVEN

Passive Consumption, Active Investment

Of all the forms of economic behavior, household spending and saving are the most familiar. Who has not fretted about adding to a savings account or life insurance or investments? Who has not experienced the tug-of-war between the desire to live it up—"buy now, pay later"—and the desire to provide for the proverbial rainy day or college education or retirement or whatever?

These small dramas of deciding between spending and saving are played out each year in millions of households, each of which is convinced that its circumstances are unique. In fact, when we take the household sector as an entirety, the dramas come to an astonishingly predictable collective conclusion. As we have already noted in our last chapter, households altogether regularly spend about ninety-five cents of every dollar they receive and save about five cents. This makes American families spendthrifts compared with West Germans, who save about 15 percent of their incomes, or Japanese, who save up to 20 percent. Later on, when we investigate the question of productivity, we will come back to these differences in national savings rates.

THE PROPENSITY TO CONSUME

Right now, while we are still concentrating on the dynamics of GNP, the thing to bear in mind is that there *are* national savings rates—

propensities to save, economists call them—that are surprisingly stable and dependable. Among the few things that economists can predict with a high degree of certainty is the amount of consumption (or its counterpart, saving) that will be associated with any given level of household income.

Taken all together, this flow of consumption spending is about two thirds as large as GNP. That is, household buying provides the demand that brings forth two thirds of our national production. About 40 percent of this household buying is for "nondurables"— perishable items such as food and clothing and the like. A slightly larger stream of buying is for a variety of consumer services, ranging from air travel to restaurants. The remainder is for long-lasting items, such as automobiles or household appliances, called consumer durables. As we would imagine, the demand for durables is much more volatile than that for nondurables: people must eat, but they can postpone buying a TV set. Hence, even within the broad flow of household buying there are subflows that are extremely steady and others that are highly dynamic.

Just the same, *the essential characteristic of consumer spending as a whole is its dependable, predictable, passive nature.* Give an economist reason to believe that next year's GNP will be so-and-so many billions, and he or she will be able to tell you within a percentage point or two how large consumer buying will be. It's on this basis that various economic "models" permit businesses to make forecasts with regard to general market prospects.*

There are, in fact, only three circumstances in which consumer spending does not behave in this predictable, passive fashion. One of these is wartime. As we would expect, during most wars consumer spending is deliberately held back by heavy taxes to make room for swelling military expenditure. During World War II, for example, consumption was squeezed back by heavy taxes to barely more than half of GNP. Even though dollar expenditures for consumption rose all during the war, GNP itself rose so much faster that the *share* of consumption fell markedly: consumers took a smaller share of a much bigger pie. And one of the reasons why the Vietnam War

*Of course, it is one thing to forecast that total consumer spending will be so-and-so many hundred billion dollars, and another thing to predict the particular tiny eddy in which your specific product will be carried along.

seems to have lit the fuse of our subsequent inflation is that military expenses for that conflict were *not* compensated by taxes to roll back consumption.

A second circumstance in which consumption departs from its normal propensity is during extreme depressions. There are needs that must be filled to keep going; and when incomes fall because of unemployment, afflicted families may beg, borrow, and if necessary steal to keep body and soul together. Certainly, during bad times household savings are rapidly eaten up. Hence consumption tends to be a larger *proportion* of GNP, even though the actual amount of consumer spending is down: the GNP pie is smaller, but the consumption portion takes a larger share of the diminished pie.

Finally, the propensity-to-consume relationship may depart from the norm during inflationary periods. The reason is that families begin to feel the inflationary itch—the decision to buy ahead of their normal requirements in order to get things before they become more expensive. Thus inflation can give rise to a surge of buying at the expense of normal savings. During the early to mid 1980s, for example, household saving in the United States slipped to a very low level. The reasons for that slippage are not clear, but some economists believe it was a consequence of the inflationary syndrome.

Economists have spent a great deal of time investigating the propensity to consume. For our purposes, however, the dependable and predictable behavior of normal consumption has one simple but central implication. It is that consumption spending—the broad flow of household expenditure that buys up two thirds of GNP—is *not a driving force in our economy, but a driven one.* For all its size, it is not the engine of GNP. It is the caboose.

To be sure, we have to be a little careful about this assertion. We have already noted that consumer spending on durable items such as cars is much more volatile than spending for nondurables or services, and swings in durable spending can pack a substantial economic wallop. In 1974 and again in 1979, for example, consumers held back on auto purchases for fear of gasoline shortages, and each time the effect on auto sales alone had an impact on GNP.

Just the same, these are exceptions to the rule. During the normal course of things, no matter how intense their wants may be, consumers lack the spendable income to translate their wants into actions. They have desires, but demand requires more than desire: it must be backed up by available cash.

This highlights an extremely important point. Wants and appetites alone do not drive the economy upward; if they did, we should experience a more impelling demand in depressions, when people are hungry, than in booms, when they are well off. Hence the futility of those who urge the cure of depressions by suggesting that consumers should buy more! There is nothing more consumers would rather do than buy more, if only they could. Let us not forget, furthermore, that consumers are at all times being cajoled and exhorted to increase their expenditures by the multibillion-dollar pressures exerted through the advertising industry.

The trouble is, however, that consumers cannot buy more unless they have more income to buy with. Of course, for short periods they can borrow or they may temporarily sharply reduce their rate of savings; but each household's borrowing capacity or accumulated savings are limited, so that once these bursts are over, the steady habitual ways of saving and spending are apt to reassert themselves.

Thus it is clear that in considering the consumer sector we study a part of the economy that, however ultimately important, is not in itself the source of major changes in activity. Consumption mirrors changes elsewhere in the economy, but it does not initiate the greater part of our long-run economic fortunes or misfortunes.

INVESTMENT DEMAND

Consumer buying, we have seen, gives the impetus to about two thirds of GNP. Where does the rest come from? We already know that it originates in the other buying queues: businesses seeking to build more capital or to spend more on R & D; government buying various public outputs; foreigners taking American goods and services.

Investment is the queue that we need to examine next. But investment is not as familiar an activity as consumption, so we must take a moment to clarify our economic vocabulary.

What most people mean by investing is buying stocks or bonds. But that is not exactly what economists mean by the term. They mean the counterpart to the "real" act of saving. The real act of saving, we remember, was to release resources from consumption.

The real act of investment is to put these resources to work creating capital goods.

This real act of investing may or may not require the purchase of stocks or bonds. When we buy an ordinary stock or bond on the stock exchange, we usually buy it from someone who has previously owned it. Therefore our personal act of investment becomes, in the economic view of things, merely a transfer of claims without any direct bearing on the creation of new wealth. A pays B cash and takes his General Motors stock; B takes A's cash and doubtless uses it to buy stock from C; but the transactions between A and B and C in no way alter the actual amount of real capital in the economy.

Only when we buy newly issued shares or bonds, and then only when their proceeds are directly allocated to new equipment or plant, does our act of personal financial investment result in the addition of wealth to the community. In that case, A buys his stock directly (or through a broker) from General Motors itself. A's cash can now be spent by General Motors for new capital goods, as presumably it will be.

Thus, much of investment, as economists see it, is a little-known form of activity for the majority of us. This is true not only because real investment is not the same as personal financial investment, but because the real investors of the nation usually act on behalf of an institution other than the familiar one of the household. Boards of directors, chief executives, or small-business proprietors are the persons who decide whether or not to devote business cash to the construction of new facilities or to the addition of inventory; and this decision is very different in character and motivation from the decisions familiar to us as members of the household sector.

Households buy goods to satisfy their needs and wants, and we have seen how stable is their propensity to consume. But investment is not decided by personal considerations. The only relevant determination that must be made is whether adding to capital goods is expected to yield a good return. Unlike the household sector, the business sector is motivated by profit: "I'm not in business for my health" is the well-known quip.

The imperative of profits is, of course, central to capitalism—both the source of its dynamic drive and the root of many of its endemic ills. But from the viewpoint of GNP, what is important about profit is that it is always oriented to the future. A firm may be enjoying large profits on its existing plant and equipment, but if it anticipates no profits from an additional investment, the firm will make no additions to capital. Another firm may be suffering current losses, but if it anticipates a large profit from the production of a new good, it may be able to launch a considerable capital expenditure. The view is always forward, never backward.

There is a sound reason for this anticipatory quality of investment decisions. Typically, the capital goods bought by investment expenditures are expected to last for years and to pay for themselves only slowly. In addition, they are often highly specialized. If capital expenditures could be recouped in a few weeks or months, or even in a matter of a year or two, or if capital goods were easily transferred from one use to another, they would not be so risky. But it usually takes three to five years to go from the drawing board to full-steam production. That means making predictions about the nature of demand well into the future. In addition, it is characteristic of most capital goods that they are durable, with life expectancies of ten or more years, and that they tend to be limited in their alternative uses, or to have no alternative uses at all. You cannot spin cloth in a steel mill or make steel in a cotton mill.

The decision to invest is thus always forward-looking. Even when the stimulus to build is felt in the present, the calculations that determine whether or not an investment will be made necessarily concern the flow of income to the firm in the future. These expectations are inherently much more unstable than the current drives and desires that guide the consumer. Expectations, whether based on guesses or forecasts, are capable of sudden and sharp reversals of a sort rare in consumption spending.

There is a very important consequence of all this for our understanding of GNP. It is that investment is inherently volatile in a way that consumption is not. In the short run, this volatility often expresses itself in sharp swings in inventory buying. We do not ordinarily think of inventories as constituting part of our capital wealth, but they are—as we discover, for example, when we run out of stocks of coal during a coal strike. The volatility of inventory buying comes about because businesses may rapidly increase or decrease inventory purchases. When they increase them, of course they give rise to a quick upswing in the demand for goods. When they cut back on inventory purchases, there is an equally sharp letdown in demand. Just as an illustration, businesses were working off inventories at the rate of $60 billion a year during the last quarter of 1982. Five quarters later they were accumulating inventories at a rate of $92 billion per year. That was an upward swing of $152 billion in demand for GNP.

The second form of investment instability is related to the longer business cycle, with its irregular sequence of ups and downs. When the outlook for several years ahead is gloomy, investment spending can fall precipitously. During the Great Depression of the thirties, business virtually ceased all expansion and barely replaced its machinery and equipment when it wore out: from 1929 to 1933, when household consumption fell by 41 percent, investment fell by *91 percent*. In fact, at the bottom of the Depression it was estimated that one third of all unemployment in the nation was directly attributable to the catastrophic shrinkage in the demand for capital goods. Conversely, when the Depression finally turned around in 1933, consumption rose by somewhat more than half over the next seven years, but investment expanded *nine times*.

One further aspect of the investment problem is worth our notice. Investment is not only a driving and potentially destablizing force in the economy, but its impact is magnified because of what economists call the *multiplier* relation. The idea of the multiplier is simplicity itself. When a change in spending occurs, such as a new investment project, the money laid out for construction workers' wages, materials, and the like does not stop there. The recipients of the first round of investment spending will engage in additional spending of their own. And so initial bursts of spending create secondary and tertiary bursts until the effect is finally dissipated.

By and large economists estimate that the impact of the multiplier over the course of a year is about two. Thus the contraction in spending of $30 billion during 1991 gave rise to a twofold contraction in incomes throughout the nation, pulling the demand for GNP down by $60 billion. And of course when investment rises by, say $10 billion, the country will enjoy an increase of incomes of that original $10 billion plus an additional $10 billion from the multiplier.

Two final and very important conclusions follow from this. First, we can see that investment is a driving, not a driven, part of the

THE STOCK MARKET AND INVESTMENT

How does the stock market affect business investment? There are three direct effects. One is that the market has traditionally served as a general barometer of the expectations of the business-minded community as a whole. We say "business-minded" rather than "business" because the demand for, and supply of, securities mainly comes from securities dealers, stockbrokers, and the investing public, rather than from nonfinancial business enterprises themselves. When the market is buoyant, it has been a signal to business that the "business climate" is favorable, and the effect on what Keynes called the "animal spirits" of executives has been to encourage them to go ahead with expansion plans. When the market is falling, on the other hand, spirits tend to be dampened, and executives may think twice before embarking on an expansion program in the face of general pessimism.

This traditional relationship is, however, greatly lessened by the growing power of government to influence the trend of economic events. Business once looked to the market as the key signal for the future. Today it looks to Washington. Hence, during the past decade when the stock market has shown wide swings, business investment in plant and equipment has remained basically steady. This reflects the feelings of corporate managers that government policy will keep the economy growing, whatever "the market" may think of events.

A second direct effect of the stock market on investment has to do with the ease of issuing new securities. One of the ways in which investment is financed is through the issuance of new stocks or bonds whose proceeds will purchase plant and equipment. When the market is rising, it is much easier to float a new issue than when prices are falling. This is particularly true for certain businesses—public utilities, for example—that depend heavily on stock issues for new capital rather than on retained earnings.

Finally, when the market is very low, companies with large retained earnings may be tempted to buy up other companies, rather than use their funds for capital expenditure. Financial investment, in other words, may take the place of real investment. This helps successful companies grow, but does not directly provide growth for the economy as a whole.

---

economy. To be sure, as with consumption, investment spending is also influenced by the incomes that businesses receive. Some investment follows the direction of consumer buying. But the distinguishing feature of investment, taken as the critical activity of the business sector, is that it is not a caboose, but an engine. It leads the economy.

Second, there is the question of how we explain why investment spending seems to follow some sort of roughly cyclical pattern—years of boom followed by years of bust. William Stanley Jevons suggested in the 1870s that the reason was sunspots. His answer was not as foolish as it may appear. Jevons, an astronomer by training, believed that the well-known ten-year cycle of sunspot activity gave rise to changes in weather, which gave rise to changes in rainfall, which gave rise to changes in crop yields, which gave rise to variations in output. Later research killed the theory by showing that the sunspot cycle did not correspond closely enough to the weather cycle.

Many candidates have been suggested to replace sunspots—bouts of inventory accumulation led by overoptimism and followed by the inevitable periods of inventory selloff; overexpansion of bank credit followed by credit squeezes—we'll be looking into how credit is created in Chapters 10 and 11 ahead. But more recently, attention has been less focused on the pendulum-like aspect of "cycles," and more generally directed to the fundamental forces that make the rate of investment spending—the motor of growth—run now fast, now slow.

TRANSFORMATIONAL GROWTH

At the risk of some oversimplification, here is what many economists believe today:

Growth is the norm in a capitalist economy. It is the norm because every business, at least every business beyond mom-and-pop size, is constantly trying to expand—seeking new products, new markets, more efficiency, whatever. Thus, rather as Adam Smith thought, the inner tendency of a free-enterprise economy is toward expansion.

Normal expansion can be helped or hindered by a number of things, some beyond anyone's control, some not. It can certainly be helped by monetary policies that make interest rates low and thereby encourage borrowing for expansion, and it can be slowed down, or brought to a halt, by the opposite—"tight" money. Political developments undoubtedly play their encouraging or discouraging roles. Government fiscal policy can help or hinder, as we will see in our next chapter.

But when all is said and done, normal growth, with its ups and downs, is only the background against which the investment drama is played out. The most dramatic and important factor seems to be something else: technology. Looking back over the history of capitalism we find periods of great prosperity, often lasting a decade or two, followed by equally extended periods of very slow, or even zero growth—periods we call depressions.

The most convincing explanation of this phenomenon seems to be that from time to time technology opens up a whole new vista of growth opportunities. In the jargon of the profession, the "production possibility frontier" moves out. What moves it out?

Economist Edward J. Nell has given the term "transformational growth" to clusters of inventions and innovations that play this vitalizing role. One of them was certainly the industrial revolution that introduced the factory system itself in the early nineteenth century. A second was the advent of the railroads that "transformed" the economic map of every nation. A third was electrification, bringing power to remote areas, and not less important, into the home. A fourth was the automobile that brought paved highways, gas stations, garages, a whole new tempo to life. In our own time we have seen a fifth in the jet plane and the computer. The computer changed the organization of every business from dry cleaning to multinational corporations; the jet giant brought tourism, by the 1960s the largest single industry in the world.

Transformational changes have imparted immense momentum to economic life. But it is the nature of these changes that after a time the new production possibility frontier is occupied and a period of "digestion" follows that of expansion. Then we sit around and wait for a new transformational boom to come.

Will another such boom arrive? Many industries are mentioned as potential sources of another great investment Klondike: microelectronics, biotechnology, new materials such as ceramics, telecommunications, machine tools, and (as they say) much, much more. Will these give us transformational growth? We do not know. Might there be some other way? Perhaps. That is the question we will look into in our next two chapters.

EIGHT

The Economics of the Public Sector

The economics of households and business presents no special problem. But the economics of the public sector—that's a different matter. Even before they have read about it, many people *know* that they hate the public sector or love it, that government is the cause of our ruination or the source of our salvation.

We will try to cope with that state of mind by tackling the problem in two stages. First there are some things to be learned with respect to the economics of the public sector about which virtually all economists, of whatever political stripe, see eye to eye. Although these matters are not controversial, they are important and perhaps surprising. They are the aspects of the problem we will attend to in this chapter. Then there are the issues about which liberals and conservatives do not agree. These mainly have to do with government's *effectiveness* in economic affairs, rather than the manner in which the public sector fits into GNP. Here is where supply-side economics makes its appearance to debate with demand-side economics. We will present both sides of that debate in the chapter to come. But first we must clarify a few basic matters.

WHAT "GOVERNMENT" MEANS

The place to begin is by reminding ourselves of three things we have already observed. The first is that we must distinguish the role of government in the economic process as a buyer of output from its role as a spender of money. The difference, we may remember, lies in those important expenditures called transfer payments, such as Social Security. Many of the disputes about how big government is or how fast it is growing hinge on whether the arguer is talking about government as a buyer or as a spender. In 1992, for example, government bought about 20 percent of GNP. But the amount that government *spent* was over 50 percent larger, or about 40 percent of GNP, transfers accounting for the difference.

Which measure "counts"? Essentially, the answer depends on what we want to know. Government as a buyer of GNP—a purchaser of defense, postal services, transportation, and the rest, gives us some idea of the importance of public output as a component of GNP. Transfer payments tell us something quite different. However many billions they may involve, transfer payments do not add a penny to GNP. Transfers are therefore an indication of the extent of the government's role as an agency for the redistribution of income, rather than for the production of output. Probably the total of government purchases *plus* transfers provides the most useful gauge of the extent of government's impact on the economy as a whole.

The second distinction is one we have been at pains to emphasize all along—that between federal versus state or local government. Most of the buying of GNP takes place at the state and local level, not at the federal level. Most of the transfer payments emanate from the federal government, not the state and local. The box of figures on page 109 shows this clearly.

One of the reasons we should bear this division in mind is that the federal government gives a good deal of money to state and local governments. These "grants-in-aid" are, of course, transfer payments. One result is that states and localities can carry out various programs they could not otherwise afford. A second result is that the federal government incurs a deficit partly because it supports state and local activity. Erase the transfer from the federal government to cities and states and you will lessen the federal deficit by that amount. Alas, you would simultaneously put the states and localities in a terrific bind. More on that later, too.

Third, we cannot consider government without keeping somewhere in our minds the division between welfare and warfare. Here the purchases-versus-transfers distinction again helps sort out things.

Most of federal purchasing of GNP has to do with warfare—in 1992, for example, almost three quarters of the federal contribution to GNP was for military purposes. Despite the cry about an expanding federal government, the federal government buys virtually the same fraction of goods and services from the economy as it did in 1940. It is the states and localities that have vastly enlarged their purchasing, with much larger health and education and transportation programs.

Then why the outcry about the federal government? The reason lies in the tremendous growth in welfare—mainly transfer payments. When a national health program is finally put into place, these expenditures may soar still further—how much further we do not yet know.

Is there a "right" level of government spending? There is no doubt that there exists a very strong antigovernment-spending sentiment in many parts of the nation today. Much of this sentiment, it is only fair to point out, has a strong flavor of self-interest. City dwellers do not think that government spends too much on urban problems, but country dwellers do. Country dwellers do not think that government spends too much on agricultural problems, but city dwellers

---

HOW BIG IS THE PUBLIC SECTOR?

Here are the numbers that fit into various categories of the public sector.

	1992 $ billion
Total Government Purchases	1,115
Federal	447
State and Local	666
Federal Government Transfers	605
To States and Localities	169
Total Government Spending (purchase plus transfers)	2,256

do. Couples with children do not want school expenditures cut, but childless couples do. Older people want higher Social Security benefits, younger people do not.

An economist has no special expertise that enables him to solve these essentially political problems. Economists can speak with some knowledge about the effects of various kinds of welfare spending— for example, the effects of unemployment insurance in making it less costly for someone to quit a job—but they cannot really pronounce on whether the effect is good or bad. That is a matter where value judgments come into play.

THE GOVERNMENT AS A SECTOR

However one feels about what government *should* do, it is vital to understand what it *does* do. Economists who disagree sharply about the best government policy for the country can still agree in their understanding of how the public sector works.

Here the appropriate place to begin is with the difference in motivations that guide public, as contrasted with private, spending. The motivations for the household sector and the business sector are lodged in the free decisions of their respective units. Householders decide to spend or save their incomes as they wish. Similarly, business firms exercise their own judgments on their capital expenditures.

But when we turn to the expenditures of the public sector, we encounter an entirely new motivation. It is no longer fixed habit or profit that determines the rate of spending, but political decision— that is, the collective will of the people as it is formulated and expressed through their local, state, and federal legislatures and executives.

Thus the presence of an explicit political will gives to the public sector a special significance. *This is the only sector whose expenditures and receipts are open to deliberate control.* Through public action we can exert very important influences on the government of households and firms. But we cannot directly alter their economic activity in the manner that is open to us with the public sector.

The basic idea behind modern public-sector policy is simple enough. We have seen that economic recessions have their roots in a failure of the business sector to offset the savings of the economy through sufficient investment. But if a falling GNP is caused by an inadequacy of expenditures in one sector, our analysis suggests an answer. Could not the insufficiency of spending in the business sector be offset by higher spending in another sector, the public sector? Could not the public sector serve as a supplementary avenue for the transfer of savings into expenditure?*

We already know the answer. A demand gap can indeed be closed by transferring savings to the public sector and spending them. We have already seen that so far as the mechanics of the process is concerned, it makes no difference if savings are borrowed by AT&T and spent for a privately owned satellite, or borrowed by the U.S. Treasury and spent for a publicly owned satellite. The politics is different. The effect on business opinion and expectations and confidence may be very different. But speaking strictly in terms of how the sectors operate and cooperate, there is no difference at all. Although economists disagree fiercely about the implications and secondary repercussions of government spending, none would dissent from the proposition that the government's economic activities have to be analyzed as a sector, comparable to the sector of business or households.

This means that when the government increases its purchases by borrowing and spending, it adds to GNP, just as when households or businesses do the same. (When the government spends more money on transfers, it may or may not indirectly stimulate GNP, depending on whom it takes money away from and whom it gives it to.) Conversely, when government decreases its spending, the level of economic activity falls, again just like business or households. Finally, if government regularly saves money by taking in more taxes than it spends, thereby running up a budget surplus, it will create a demand gap exactly as when households save their incomes. In that case, business must invest enough to match the savings of both the household and the public sectors, if GNP is not to fall.

---

*Of course, another way of stimulating GNP would be to cut taxes in the hope of spurring investment. That is what the supply siders want to do. Here we are not arguing in favor of public spending rather than tax cutting. We are only interested in showing that there is a much closer resemblance between public spending and private investment than is usually recognized.

DEFICIT SPENDING

So it makes a difference when we see the government's activities as those of a cooperating sector, not as those of a single household or firm. And the difference becomes sharpest when we examine that most misunderstood of all government's activities—deficit spending. Deficit spending means that the government spends more than it takes in through taxes, borrowing the rest. The borrowed sums become part of the government debt, and we frequently hear admonitions about this debt that stem from the tendency to view it as if it were the debt of a single family or enterprise. "The government," we are told, "cannot borrow indefinitely, any more than a family or a firm. A government that incurs a deficit is simply living beyond its means."

Is this true? It *sounds* true. And yet even economists who strongly oppose deficit spending for other reasons would admit that the arguments that equate government with single families or firms are *not* true. Let us take the matter of the deficit. Can the government safely incur a deficit—that is, borrow as well as tax? In Chapter Five, when we first noted how the different queues bought GNP, we saw that the business sector as a whole regularly spent more than its receipts from sales. The difference, we recall, lay in the savings of the household sector that business borrowed to finance its capital outlays.

Now that kind of "excess" spending is certainly not called a deficit by any business firm. When the American Telephone and Telegraph Company or the Exxon Corporation uses the savings of the public to build a new plant and new equipment, it does not show a loss on its annual statement to stockholders, even though its total expenditures on current costs and on capital equipment may have been greater than sales. Instead, expenditures are divided into two kinds: one relating current costs to current income, and the other relegating expenditures on capital goods to an entirely separate capital account. *Instead of calling the excess of expenditures a deficit, they call it investment.*

Can AT&T or Exxon afford to run "deficits" of the latter kind indefinitely? The answer is yes. To be sure, after a stated number of years, AT&T's or Exxon's bonds will come due and must be paid back. Perhaps the companies can do that out of their accumulated earnings. Usually, however, when a bond becomes due, a corporation issues new bonds equal in value to the old ones. It then sells the new bonds and uses the new money it raises to pay off its old bondholders.

Many big corporations such as Exxon or AT&T do, in fact, continuously "refund" the bond issues, paying off old bonds with new ones, and never paying back their indebtedness as a whole. AT&T, for instance, actually increased its total indebtedness almost tenfold. Between 1929 and 1991 Exxon ran up its long-term debt from $170.1 million in 1929 to over $8 billion. And the credit rating of both companies today is as good as, or better than, it was in 1929.

More important, the business sector is constantly increasing its total indebtedness. In 1975 total corporate long-term debt (debt over one year in maturity) totaled $587 billion. In 1991 it was over $2.2 trillion. Was this safe? The question brings us to a very important point. Borrowing is safe or unsafe, depending to a large degree on what the money is borrowed for. If a company's debt is originally incurred to finance the construction of new plant and equipment, and if the projects are wisely chosen, the rise in its debt is likely to be perfectly safe. The growing business debt is then simply the financial face of the company's growing stock of real tangible assets—the machines and equipment that have been purchased with the borrowed funds. As long as that physical capital is still productive and regularly replaced, why should not the bonds that were sold to pay for it—or new bonds that will replace old ones—still be perfectly sound investments for the individuals or banks or financial companies that wanted a profitable place to invest their savings?

That is why most corporate debt has, in fact, generally grown over the years in safety.* But there is also another, different answer. Suppose that corporations borrow funds not to buy capital equipment, but for speculative purposes that turn out badly. Then obviously a growing debt can become a burden on the companies that must pay interest on borrowings that have not produced more income for them—not to speak of a burden on the investors who have invested their savings in nothing.

That is, in fact, what happened during the greater merger wave

---

*To be sure, some companies go under, and their bonds lose part—once in a while all—of their value. But corporate debt as a whole is very safe. If it wasn't, the business system would long ago have collapsed.

of the 1980s. During those "go-go" years, raiding parties of investors would search out likely targets for a "takeover." The targets were usually big, but lackadaisical, companies that did not run their operations with an eye on the bottom line. The raiders would then begin to buy stock in the company, usually with the help of a hefty line of credit from a cooperative bank. As soon as a raiding group succeeded in getting enough shares to exercise a controlling voice in a company's affairs, it would install a new management to complete the coup. The new management would thereupon issue very high-interest bonds, using the proceeds to pay back their indebtedness to the bank. They would also "strip" the company of its best assets, leaving the corporate shell with massive amounts of debt that that was not backed by productive assets. These so-called "junk bonds" then became a burden both on the company and on the incautious investors who had bought them. During these merger-mania years, the total volume of corporate debt doubled, from $1 trillion to $2 trillion, so that by the beginning of the 1990s, the cost of meeting interest absorbed 90 percent of all after-tax income of American corporations.

PRIVATE V. PUBLIC DEBTS

Is there a moral in this for the federal deficit? There are two. The first is that the government sector, like the business sector, can also justify its rising debt in terms of an increasing stock of real assets—dams and roads and housing projects and the like. All through the 1980s, federal "investment-type" outlays—the analog of private investment—ran at levels roughly equal to the deficit. According to the Office of Management and Budget, such government expenditures amounted to an estimated $581 billion over the fiscal years 1984–1986, close to the total deficit of $624 billion racked up over the same period. If these growth-creating expenditures had not been lumped together with other government spending, we would have had almost no "deficit." Instead, we would have designated these expenditures as Public Investment, which is indeed what they were; and we would have thought it just as proper to finance them by borrowing as we think it proper to finance private investment by borrowing. In that case the nation would not have wasted its energies and raised its blood pressure over the misleading question of whether its deficit was too large, but would have argued over the very real and important issue of how much Public Investment we wanted, and of what kind.

The second moral is that we do not run our government affairs in this sensible way, because we do not separate government spending into an investment and a consumption category. Instead we lump all government spending into a single flow called "G" (for government), and assume that all of G is used for consumption. If we separated G into expenditures for Government Investment and Government Consumption, we would then be able to see exactly how much larger our borrowing was than the amount that could be justified by growth-promoting or other necessary purposes.* We could then indeed allow our blood pressure to rise, while we made a real effort to finance our Government Consumption spending—the "normal running expenses" of the great public household—by the means best suited to that purpose: taxes of one sort or another.

There is an even more important explanation why government as a sector can safely run a deficit. The reason is that the regular income of the public sector comes from taxes, and taxes reflect the general income of the country. Thus most of the money that the government lays out enters the general stream of GNP, where it is largely available to recapture by taxation. The government's "earning capacity" is therefore far greater than that of any single business. It is comparable only to the immense earning capacity of *all* business.

This reasoning helps us understand why federal finance is different from state and local government finance. An expenditure made by New York City or New York State is apt to be respent in many other areas of the country. Thus taxable incomes in New York will not, in all probability, rise to match local spending. As a result, state

---

*Those "other necessary purposes" may also justify some of the otherwise wasteful deficit. Probably as much as $500 billion of government debt will eventually be issued to make good the government's obligation to insure deposits in the failed Savings and Loan banks. In other words, the S&L fiasco converted a standby government pledge into an actual need for funds. But even a $500 billion issuance of debt for this purpose is by no means all waste. In the 1930s, we had no government insurance of bank accounts. When the banks went broke, they pulled their nine million depositors with them. Five hundred billion seems a modest price to avert another such catastrophe.

and local governments must look on their finances much as an individual business does. The power of full fiscal recapture belongs solely to the federal government.

This difference between the limited financial powers of a single firm and the relatively limitless powers of a national government lies at the heart of the basic difference between business and government deficit spending. It helps us understand why the government has a capacity for financial operation that is inherently of a far higher order of magnitude than that of business.

Business firms owe their debts to someone distinct from themselves—someone over whom they have no control—whether this be bondholders or the bank from which they borrowed. Therefore, to service or to pay back its debts, a business must transfer funds from its own possession into the possession of outsiders. If this transfer cannot be made, if a business does not have the funds to pay its bondholders or its bank, it will go bankrupt.

The government is in a radically different position. Most of its bondholders, banks, and other people or institutions to whom it owes its debts belong to the same community as that whence it extracts its receipts.* In other words, the government does not have to transfer its funds to an outside group to pay its bonds. It transfers them, instead, from some members of the national community over which it has legal powers (taxpayers) to other members of the same community (bondholders). The contrast is much the same as that between a family that owes a debt to another family, and a family in which the husband has borrowed money from his wife; or again between a firm that owes money to another, and a firm in which one branch has borrowed money from another. Internal debts do not drain the resources of one community into another, but merely redistribute the claims among members of the same community.

Just the same, some nagging doubts may remain. In view of the fact that our federal debt today figures out to approximately $13,000 for every man, woman, and child, it is not surprising that we frequently hear appeals to common sense, telling us how much better we would be without this debt, and how our grandchildren will groan under its weight.

---

*The exception are foreign owners of U.S. bonds. About 15 percent of our national debt is owned by foreign banks and individuals.

Is this true? Suppose we decided that we would pay off the debt. This would mean that our government bonds would be redeemed for cash. To get cash, we would have to tax ourselves (unless we wanted to roll the printing presses), so that what we would really be doing would be transferring money from taxpayers to bondholders.

Would that be a net gain for the nation? Consider the typical holder of a government bond—a family, a bank, or a corporation. It now holds the world's safest and most readily sold paper asset from which a regular income is obtained. After our debt is redeemed, our families, banks, and corporations will have two choices:

THE POWER TO PRINT MONEY

Ultimately the federal government has the power to incur an unlimited deficit because it has the power to print money. If a local government such as New York City incurs too much debt, investors lose confidence in the ability of the city to buy back its bonds when they come due. Therefore they will refuse to buy the city bonds and the municipality can go bankrupt.

This cannot happen to the federal government because by constitutional authority it has the power to create money. It could, therefore, simply print up the money needed to buy back its own obligations!

Needless to say, this is a cure that might well be worse than the disease. We hear about "rolling the printing presses" as the worst symptom of inflation. If the government actually began printing money wholesale to buy its own bonds, there would be a flight from the currency—maybe from the country!—and the specter of a runaway inflation might become a reality. We will discuss printing money again in Chapter 10. But we must recognize that the *unused* power of the printing press still reassures investors that they will never face default on a federal bond. It is odd, isn't it: The power to print money is the most important safeguard for government bonds—as long as it isn't used!

(1) They can hold cash and get no income, or (2) they can invest in other securities that are slightly less safe. Are these investors better off? As for our grandchildren, it is true that if we pay off the debt they will not have to carry its weight. But to offset that, neither will they be carried by the comfortable government bonds they would otherwise have inherited. They will also be relieved from paying taxes to meet the interest on the debt. Alas, they will be relieved as well of the pleasure of depositing the green Treasury checks for interest payments that used to arrive twice a year.

After these reassuring words, we need a sobering conclusion. A large and continuing deficit, such as we have in the 1990s, can indeed bring economic troubles in its wake. These are not the troubles of national bankruptcy, however, but the problems of careless national budgeting.

When the federal government undertakes more expenditures than can be paid for by taxes, it must borrow the difference through the issuance of Treasury bonds. Because these bonds are the safest credit instrument available, and because the Treasury will price its bonds at whatever levels are required to sell them, the federal government always has first crack at the nation's savings. All other borrowers— states and localities, businesses, households—have second crack. These borrowers may therefore be "crowded out," if the total demand for savings is greater than the supply. Federal government will get the funds it needs, but some nonfederal or private borrowers may not get the funds *they* need.*

If there were a national consensus on the top priority of federal needs, that precedence accorded to Treasury bonds would be right and proper. This is normally the case, for example, in wartime, when everyone recognizes the necessity for federal government to use as much of the national pool of savings as it needs. But in

---

*We were rescued from the possibility of crowding out in the early to mid 1980s because foreign investors—individuals and corporations alike—used tens of billions of yen, marks, francs, and other currencies to buy Treasury bonds. We are a long way from the situation of Mexico or Israel, but for the first time in this century, the nation's debt cannot be viewed as almost entirely an internal obligation. Moreover, insofar as the debt is owed to foreigners, not to ourselves, our children *will* have to pay for it by accepting a lower standard of living, because some portion of American wealth must be transferred to non-Americans to service the foreign-owned debt.

ordinary times no such priority attaches to federal projects. The scramble for funds will therefore result in using the nation's savings for projects whose only claim to getting first crack is that they are federally financed, not that they are the most productive of growth, profits, or well-being.

When we have a good deal of unused resources in the labor market or in our factories, the worries about crowding out do not apply, because additional federal spending will not come at the expense of other kinds of spending—there is room for all. *But at full employment, the federal government can increase its share of national output only at the expense of someone else.* If that share is obtained by higher taxes, there is a prima facie presumption that the electorate has decided that the government's share in total output *ought* to rise. But when the share of government is obtained only because of its superior borrowing power, there is no such presumption. Hence most economists agree that we ought to have a balanced federal budget at full-employment levels of output.

That concludes the first look at the economics of the public sector— the part about which virtually all economists agree. To repeat: government is a sector, not a single family or firm. As a sector, it has to dovetail with the household and business sectors. The activities of borrowing—running up a deficit—are different for the federal government than they are for local governments or even for very large firms. Federal spending for investment is not treated as a capital expense, the way it is in the private sector. There is a wide measure of consensus about all that.

But there is certainly anything but a consensus as to what the proper role of the government should be. Before we turn to that debate, it's important to reflect on the contents of this chapter. Much of the vociferous arguing one hears about government is based on analogies that we can now see are misleading. If the pros and cons of the public sector are to be intelligently sorted out, we must recognize that it *is* a sector and not just a large household; and that it *has* economic capabilities unlike those of other sectors. As we shall see, there is much to disagree about with respect to the economics of the public sector, but it is important to draw the line between disagreement and sheer incomprehension.

NINE

The Debate About Government

Two big questions frame the debate about government in the economy. (1) Is it inflationary? (2) Can government add to the growth of GNP? By and large, the conservative side, especially within the business community, answers yes to the first question and no to the second. The liberal side says no—or perhaps maybe—to the first, and yes to the second. Our own views tend to the liberal side, but not entirely so. There is something to be said for both sides of the debate, and we shall try to say it.

First, inflation. Does government spending produce inflation? As we will see, this is a question with question marks: no absolutely clear-cut answer is possible. But we can narrow down the area of disagreement by starting with aspects on which there is unanimity.

Everyone agrees that government spending must be inflationary under certain conditions. These conditions are described by the words "full employment," meaning an economy in which there is only a very small pool of workers available for jobs at going wages, and in which most plant and equipment is being used up to normal capacity. When you have a situation like that, additional government spending is bound to push up prices, either because the added demand for labor will send up wages or because trying to produce more goods than a plant is designed for will send up costs. Thus, no one in his right mind would ever advocate increasing government spending when the economy is already in full boom.

Nevertheless, a few comments have to be made even about this clear-cut case. The first is that full employment is a situation in which additional spending *of any kind* will produce inflation. More household spending or more business spending will bid up wages or send up costs in exactly the same way as more government spending. So it is not the fact that the additional spending originates from the government that is important, but that any kind of increased buying from any sector will bring trouble when we are at full employment.

If we are in such a state and *want* to increase government spending—say, for military preparedness or to launch a program of urban renewal—the only way to avoid inflation is to trim spending in some other sector. In full employment, you cannot have more warfare or more welfare without inflationary consequences unless you make room for the larger government portion of GNP by holding down either household or business buying, or both.

A somewhat less clear-cut case involves the situation at the other end of the economic scale, when the economy is suffering from high levels of unemployment and low levels of utilization. Can you have more government spending under such circumstances without sending up prices? The conventional wisdom of the last several decades was that you could. The presence of millions of idle workers and banks of unused machines make it plausible that you could spend more money, for whatever purpose, without bidding up prices or costs. Perhaps the most convincing illustration was the U.S. experience from 1934 to 1940, when GNP expanded by 50 percent, stimulated by higher government spending, whereas prices rose by less than 5 percent.

This conviction is not so firmly held today as it was in the Depression years. The economy is much more inflation-prone than in the past—a question we will look into again in Chapter 12. So it's not so easy to be sure today that increased government spending, even under conditions of high unemployment and considerable idle plant, might not result in higher prices, along with higher employment and output. On the other hand, the same unhappy conclusion again applies to more spending by business, or from a surge of consumer buying. If we live in an inflation-prone system, *any* increase in demand—not just government—is likely to give inflation a shove.

• • •

Here the debate between liberals and conservatives divides on two issues. The first is whether the additional output and employment that government spending may bring forth is worth the additional inflation it may also generate. By and large the liberals say yes, the conservatives no. These are questions we will consider again when we devote a chapter to unemployment.

The second issue turns on the relative effectiveness of government spending versus private spending in giving us more output. Here the conservatives argue that private spending for plant and equipment increases our capacity to produce, thereby ultimately slowing down inflation because there are more goods to buy. Public spending, on the contrary, it is claimed, adds little or nothing to salable output, and therefore pushes directly on the price level.

There is something to be said for this argument, but not the way it usually is said. When the issue is debated in terms of "public" versus "private" expenditure, we tend to get ideological fervor, not analytical insight. After all, "public" expenditure can be for bombers, which will certainly not increase salable output, or for education, which may indeed increase the output of our labor force. Private output may be concentrated in high technology or in high-rise luxury hotels. Moreover, some kinds of private spending can only be undertaken if they are accompanied, or prepared for, by public spending: we had to build highways before we could build an auto industry, and we may well have to build a public coal port before we can expand the production of coal for export. Thus our own view is that some kinds of expenditure are indeed more inflation-producing than others, but that these kinds are not *necessarily* located in the public sphere. The argument has to be examined in its particulars, not used as a bludgeon.

There is one further aspect to the question of how inflationary government spending is. This centers on the manner in which government spending is financed. Conservatives have no vehement objection to government's borrowing directly from the private sector— for instance, by floating school bonds—or simply by issuing savings bonds. Conservatives may object to the purposes for which the money is spent, but they do not claim that borrowing household or business savings is inflationary. Why should it be more inflationary for New York City to borrow money to renovate its subway system than for Consolidated Edison to borrow money to renovate its power stations?

The inflationary argument is focused on the federal government's borrowing directly from the Federal Reserve banks, by selling them its Treasury securities. This is called monetizing the debt. Monetizing the debt increases the ability of banks to lend money, which, as we shall see in the coming chapter, is the same thing as increasing the amount of money in the system. All economists agree that increasing the amount of money is usually inflationary. The bone of contention is whether money is the chief—or the only—villain. Our own belief is that selling government bonds to finance public spending may help support inflation by making credit more easily available (as we shall see later), but that is by no means the same thing as saying that it is the prime cause of inflation. We will have to be content with that unexplained answer until we go a little further into money and inflation questions up ahead.

DEMAND MANAGEMENT

We turn now to the second major bone of contention—whether government spending can actually increase GNP. Essentially, liberals say yes, conservatives no. We will present both sides of the case as we see it.

The liberal arguments are already familiar to us because they have been incorporated in our book. They hinge on two matters that should now be very familiar. The first is that government—always meaning local, state, and federal—produces a wide spectrum of outputs, and that these outputs must be examined one by one before general pronouncements can be made about them. When we look at government we see the construction of dams and sewer systems, the support of research, and the creation of soil erosion programs just as much as we see the payments of welfare checks, the proliferation of bureaucracies, and the cost overruns on nuclear submarines. So, of course, we believe that government spending can increase GNP *because it is part of GNP,* and of course we believe that government spending can increase our productivity insofar as it is spending on well-chosen public investment.

Indeed, one of the points of converging opinion between liberals and conservatives is the growing recognition that government can play a vital part in economic growth by shoring up our infrastructure. Infrastructure is a word that covers both old-fashioned public capital, such as dams and waterways and roads and the like—the Panama Canal must be the biggest infrastructure project ever undertaken—and new-fashioned growth-promoting public undertakings, such as research and development and most important of all, education.

In 1990, economist David Alan Aschauer published a research paper claiming that a decade of neglect and cutting back under the Reagan and Bush administrations had so depleted the nation's stock of public capital that a dollar invested in infrastructure would bring a larger rise in GNP than a dollar spent for private investment.* Greeted originally with widespread skepticism, research has now generally vindicated Aschuaer's position. Government spending on infrastructure fell to only half of what it was in the 1960s, after adjusting for inflation! Even before the Clinton administration made the restoration of infrastructure a prime policy target, the Bush administration had begun to recognize the necessity of shoring up public capital on many fronts as necessary precondition for achieving strong private growth.

The second issue is also well rehearsed by now. It is that government can offset gaps in the demand for GNP just as effectively as the business sector, by borrowing savings and spending them. One of the most important conceptual breakthroughs that macroeconomics gives us is a recognition of how the government sector plays a balancing role with respect to the other sectors—borrowing and spending, when the business sector fails to do so, and holding back its spending—actually running a budget surplus—when the private sectors are failing to save enough.

Thus, the liberal side of the argument stresses the role of government as a *demand manager,* taking on the responsibility for creating the volume of demand we need to get up to a satisfactory level of performance. That is not to say that demand managing is an easy objective. There was a time, not so long ago, when liberal economists talked rather glibly of "fine tuning" the economy, as if we could regulate the level of employment and output with all the

*David Alan Aschauer, *Public Investment and Private Sector Growth,* Economic Policy Institute, Washington, D.C., 1990.

precision of a hi-fi set. That easy optimism has long since vanished. We know that it is difficult to bring the economy up to high levels of performance without incurring an unacceptable degree of inflation. We know that we cannot raise or lower taxes or expenditures as if they were just numbers in an equation. The realities of public opinion, political coalitions, or structural resistances in the economy make it utopian to imagine that the government can guide the economy toward some goal like steering a ship in calm weather. The reality is more like trying to keep a compass heading against squalls and rough waves and countercurrents.

Indeed, matters are even worse than we have described. Demand management has not only had to struggle to maintain headway in very rough seas, but it has also been the cause of most modern-day business cycles. No longer can we pin the blame for recession solely on a lagging pace of private investment. To some extent, every recession since World War II can be traced to federal budgetary policies. In 1949, 1954, 1957–1958 and 1960–1961 the government cutailed its military spending without compensating for that curtailment by cutting taxes or raising civilian expenditures. In 1969–1970, 1974–1975, and 1980–1982, government deliberately *created* an economic slowdown through policies aimed at dampening inflation. Inflation was not much affected, but the economy was.

Thus it must be abundantly clear that demand management is no panacea. In its effort to stave off problems, it may create new ones, possibly equally serious. Nonetheless, in the view that we endorse, demand management remains an indispensable tool. This is because we see the economy as inherently subject to booms and busts stemming from the instability of business investment, from waves of optimism and pessimism that affect consumer buying, and from shifts in government policy itself, for instance in the amount of military spending. If we are to avoid the full effect of these shifting winds and currents, we have to use the public sector—increasing its expenditures when the private sector slows down, decreasing them when the private system revs up. Alternatively, we can regulate demand by raising and lowering taxes while keeping public expenditures unchanged. The fact that we have steered badly, sometimes even perversely, does not mean that we should jettison the rudder of federal management. The challenge, rather, is to learn how to use it better.

SUPPLY-SIDE ECONOMICS

That's the way liberal economists see it, but it is not the way conservatives see it. A new term came into economic parlance in the
early Reagan years—supply-side economics. By and large it takes
a quite opposite view from ours. Government cannot increase output, or at least not significantly. And government cannot play the
balancing role we have just described.

As the words indicate, supply-side economics is more concerned
with supply—production—than with demand or buying. Supply siders are not against regulating demand. For instance, they want to
increase private buying by cutting taxes. What is crucial is their
belief that the volume of private demand, once the public sector has
been pulled back, will be large enough to provide high employment
and vigorous growth. "Produce the goods," they say, "and the purchasing power to buy them will be created in the act of production
itself."

And will there be *enough* production, the great worry of the
demand siders? Yes, say the supply-side economists, provided that
the incentive to produce is given its due. The supply-side image of
the economy is that of a great spring, held down by the weight of
high marginal taxes and excessive spending. Take away the taxes
that discourage risk taking and expansion, roll back the government
spending that absorbs labor and resources that ought to be available
to the private sector, and the inherent dynamism in the spring will
manifest itself.

Thus the supply siders put things in a different perspective. The
additions to output that government makes are seen as often interfering with, or taking the place of, additions to output that would
be made by private enterprise if it were not so heavily taxed, regulated, and browbeaten. And the balancing role of the government
sector is played down because supply siders believe there will be
very little need for such a role if the business sector is given its head.

We've had enough experience with supply-side policies—cutting
high marginal tax rates and rolling back regulation—to allow us to
make a few judgments with respect to these questions. One thing
we know is that supply-side policies generate *some* response, but
nothing like the immense response that its most ardent supporters
expected of it. One of the rosy predictions made in the days when

the supply-side slogan was first coined was that cutting taxes would unleash such a mighty wave of investment that GNP would rise enough to generate *more* tax revenues, despite the lower tax rates. That hope proved to be a chimera—the cut in taxes did help GNP grow, but the growth was nowhere near enough to increase the government's revenue, adjusted for inflation.

On the other hand, the rollback in regulations and the tax bonanza probably did help lay the basis for the boom that began in 1983, after the Federal Reserve eased up on its stringent monetary policy. So probably there was some positive economic effect. It's hard to say what this effect might have been if the Reagan Administration had not accompanied its supply-side measures with anti-inflation tight-money measures. The combination of the two was like stepping on the accelerator and the brake at the same time.

Another thing we know is that cutting taxes and expenditures can create problems as well as alleviate them. For wealthy taxpayers, supply-side economics did indeed get the government off their backs. For beneficiaries of government expenditure programs, such as families who depended on food stamps, or government-subsidized school lunches, supply-side economics pulled the rug from under their feet. An increase in well-being at the top was thus offset by an increase in ill-being at the bottom. As part of its income distribution problem, the 1980s produced a rise in poverty—the first such rise in two generations. That was a consequence of supply-side economics, just as much as the boom.

Should one, then, declare the supply-side vision a success or a failure? As is the case with most controversies in economics, the verdict will not be awarded by a jury of economists. It will be determined in the courtroom of history. Unfortunately, in that courtroom there are no rules as to the admissibility of evidence or the veracity of witnesses, so that even after the verdict has been delivered, there is always room for argument. Still today there are some economists who doubt that the New Deal proved the case for demand-side policies during depressions, arguing that without the intervention of the government the economy would have recovered anyway, perhaps more quickly. So, too, the effects of supply-side policies, to whatever extent they will be carried out, will not provide absolutely convincing evidence as to the rightness of the diagnosis of supply-side economics.

Much hinges here on one's ultimate vision of capitalism and its historic trajectory, on the conception of the role of government in assisting or interfering with that trajectory, and on the belief in the inherent capacity of the system to resolve its problems or to succumb to them. The ideas of Adam Smith, Karl Marx, and John Maynard Keynes powerfully influence the interpretation we put on the past, as well as the anticipations we bring to the future. In some deep sense it is the political image we have of capitalism that decides the economics we believe in.

A GOVERNMENT-LED TRANSFORMATIONAL BOOM?

This brings us to the question we posed, but left answered at the end of Chapter 7—is there something we could do about conjuring up another transformational boom, except sitting around and waiting for one?

The answer is closely tied into what we believe that capitalism is, or could be, or should be. There is no doubt that government has the capability of setting into motion a very large, "transformational" boom through a program of infrastructural spending—bullet trains and research-and-development assistance to industry, aid to education and the reconstruction of the inner cities, and all the other much-needed public undertakings we have looked into. Moreover, we have seen that it would be as legitimate for government to borrow for such growth-producing purposes as for private business to borrow for its investment objectives. Then what stands in the way?

Two obstacles constitute the difficulty. The first is that a government-led transformational boom is bound sooner or later to exert inflationary pressure, exactly as would a private boom. Can we find the means of holding such an inflation in check? We have had glimpses of how complicated the problem would be. In Chapter 12 we learn why it is so difficult.

But difficult is not impossible. The second problem in generating a public sector boom involves the question of what we think capitalism should be. Are we prepared to have government assume the role of leading an economic boom? Here an anecdote sheds some light. Sociologist Seymour Martin Lipset, in *The First New Nation*, contrasts two countries whose histories have been shaped by a similar challenge—absorbing a great contiguous wilderness. The countries were, of course, Canada and the United States. Out of this common experience two national heroes spontaneously emerged in the national folklore. For the Canadians it was the scarlet-coated Northwest Mounted Police, bringing law and order into the newly won wilderness. For the United States it was the cowboy. The choice of such different heroes speaks to such a question as "Can there be a government-led boom?" The answer is more likely to be affirmative in Canada than in the United States. On such deep grounds of differences in national cultures and institutions stand much of the economic capabilities and incapabilities of all nations.

TEN

What Money Is

Economists like to complain that the single most persistent misconception against which they must do battle is that banks are warehouses stuffed full of money. What *are* they stuffed full of? That is a matter we will spend this chapter investigating.

First a word of warning is in order. Money is a genuinely perplexing and also a genuinely complex subject. In this chapter we have tried to remove the perplexity, but we have not really come to grips with the complexity. For someone who wants to know how banks *really* work, we have added an Appendix, where we hope the mysteries of money will be removed once and for all. For those who are less interested, this chapter should at least remove the mystique, if not the mysteries, surrounding money and banks and gold, enabling us to learn more about monetary theories of inflation in the chapters that follow.

CASH AND CHECKS

Let us begin by asking, What is money? Coin and currency are certainly money. But are checks money? Are the deposits from which we draw checks money? Are savings accounts money? Government bonds?

The answer is somewhat arbitrary. Basically, money is anything we can use to make purchases with. But there exists a spectrum of financial instruments that serve this purpose—a continuum that varies in liquidity, or the ease with which it can be used for purchasing. By law, coin and currency are money because they are defined as legal tender: a seller must accept them as payment. Checks do not have to be accepted (we have all seen signs in restaurants saying, WE DO NOT ACCEPT CHECKS), although in fact checks are overwhelmingly the most frequent means of payment. Today checks can often be written on savings accounts as well as on checking accounts. On occasion, government bonds are accepted as a means of payment.

Thus, a variety of things can be counted as money. By far the most important general definition is the sum of all cash in the hands of the public plus all checking accounts, which are called demand deposits (because, unlike all savings accounts, they must be paid on demand).

Of these two kinds of money, currency is the form most familiar to us. Yet there is considerable mystery even about currency. Who determines how much currency there is? How is the supply of coins or bills regulated?

We often assume that the supply of currency is set by the government that issues it. Yet when we think about it, the government does not just hand out money, and certainly not coins or bills. When the government pays people, it is nearly always by check.

Then who does fix the amount of currency in circulation? You can answer the question by asking how you yourself determine how much currency you will carry. The answer is that you cash a check when you need more currency than you have, and you put the currency back into your checking account when you have more than you need.

What you do, everyone does. The amount of cash the public holds at any time is no more and no less than the amount that it wants to hold. When it needs more—at Christmas, for instance—the public draws currency by cashing checks on its own checking accounts; when Christmas is past, shopkeepers (who have received the public's currency) return it to their checking accounts.

Thus the amount of currency we have bears an obvious, important relation to the size of our bank accounts, for we can't write checks for cash if our accounts will not cover them.

Does this mean, then, that the banks have as much currency in their vaults as the total of our checking accounts? No, it does not. But to understand that, let us follow the course of some currency that we deposit in our banks for credit to our accounts.

When you put money into a commercial bank, the bank does not hold that money for you as a pile of specially earmarked bills or as a bundle of checks made out to you from some payer. The bank takes notice of your deposit simply by crediting your "account," a computer tape recording your present balance. After the amount of the currency or check has been credited to you, the currency is put away with the bank's general store of vault cash and the checks are sent to the banks from which they came, where they will be charged against the accounts of the people who wrote them.

Thus you might search as hard as you pleased in your bank, but you would find no money that was yours other than a bookkeeping account in your name. This seems like a very unreal form of money, and yet the fact that you can present a check at the teller's window and convert your bookkeeping account into cash proves that your account must be real.

But suppose that you and all the other depositors tried to convert your accounts into cash on the same day. You would then find something shocking. There would not be nearly enough cash in the bank's till to cover the total withdrawals. In 1992, for instance, total demand or other checkable deposits in the United States amounted to about $600 billion. But the total amount of coin and currency held by the banks was under $30 billion!

At first blush, this seems like a highly dangerous state of affairs. But second thoughts are more reassuring. After all, most of us put money into a bank because we do not need it immediately, or because making payments in cash is a nuisance compared with making them by check. Yet there is always the chance—more than that, the certainty—that some depositors will want their money in currency. How much currency will the banks need then? What will be a proper reserve for them to hold?

THE FEDERAL RESERVE SYSTEM

For many years the banks themselves decided what reserve ratio constituted a safe proportion of currency to hold against their demand deposits. Today, however, most large banks are members of the Federal Reserve, a central banking system established in 1913 to strengthen the banking activities of the nation. Under the Federal Reserve System, the nation is divided into twelve districts, each with a Federal Reserve Bank owned by the member banks of its district. In turn, the twelve Reserve Banks are themselves coordinated by a seven-member Federal Reserve Board in Washington. Since the President, with the advice and consent of the Senate, appoints members of the board for fourteen-year terms, they constitute a body that has been purposely established as an independent monetary authority.

One of the most important functions of the Federal Reserve Board is to establish reserve ratios for different categories of banks, within limits set by Congress. Historically these reserve ratios have ranged between 13 and 26 percent of demand deposits for city banks, with a somewhat smaller reserve ratio for country banks. Today, reserve ratios are determined by size of bank and by kind of deposit, and they vary between 18 percent for the largest banks and 8 percent for the smallest. The Federal Reserve Board also sets reserve requirements for time deposits (the technical term for savings deposits). These range from 1 to 6 percent, depending on the ease of withdrawal.

A second vital function performed by the Federal Reserve Banks is that they serve their member banks in exactly the same way as member banks serve the public. Member banks automatically deposit in their Federal Reserve accounts all checks they get from other banks. As a result, banks are constantly clearing their checks with one another through the Federal Reserve System, because their depositors are constantly writing checks payable to someone who banks elsewhere. Meanwhile, the balance that each member bank maintains at the Federal Reserve—its "checking account" there—counts as part of its reserves against deposits, just like the currency in its tills.

Thus we see that our banks operate on what is called a fractional reserve system. That is, a certain specified fraction of all demand deposits must be kept on hand at all times in cash or at the Fed (as economists and bankers call the Federal Reserve). The size of the minimum fraction is determined by the Federal Reserve, for reasons of control that we shall learn shortly. It is not determined, as we might be tempted to think, to provide a safe backing for our bank deposits. Under any fractional system, if all depositors decided to draw out their accounts in currency and coin from all banks at the same time, the banks would be unable to meet the demand for cash and would have to close. We call this a run on the banking system. Runs have been terrifying and destructive economic phenomena. Today they no longer pose so dire a threat because the Federal Reserve Banks can supply their members with vast amounts of cash, as we shall see.

But why court the risk of runs, however small this risk may be? What is the benefit of a fractional banking system? To answer that, let us look at your bank again.

Suppose its customers have given your bank $1 million in deposits and that the Federal Reserve Board requirements are 20 percent, a simpler figure to work with than the actual one. Then we know that the bank must at all times keep $200,000 either in currency in its own till or in its demand deposit at the Federal Reserve Bank.

But having taken care of that requirement, what does the bank do with the remaining deposits? If it simply lets them sit, either as vault cash or as a deposit at the Federal Reserve, our bank will be very liquid—that is, it will have a great deal of instantly spendable cash—but it will have no way of making an income. Unless it charges a very high fee for its checking services, it will have to go out of business.

And yet there is an obvious way for the bank to make an income while performing a valuable service. The bank can use all the cash and check claims it does not need for its reserve to make loans to businesses or families or to make financial investments in corporate or government bonds. It will thereby not only earn an income, but it will assist the process of business investment and government borrowing.

Thus fractional reserve allows banks to lend or invest part of the funds that have been deposited with them. But that is not their only useful purpose. As we shall see in our next chapter, fractional reserves also give the Fed a means of regulating how much the banking system can lend or invest. In other words, fractional reserves are the lever through which the Federal Reserve authorities can control the quantity of money in the system—namely, the amount of deposits that banks are able to accept.*

PAPER MONEY AND GOLD

Our next chapter will take us into the question of how the Fed manages our money. But before we leave the question of what money is, we ought to clear up one last mystery—the mystery of where currency (coin and bills) actually comes from and where it goes. If we examine most of our paper currency, we will find that it has the words "Federal Reserve Note" on it: That is, it is paper money issued by the Federal Reserve System. We understand by now how the public gets these notes: It simply draws them from its checking accounts. When it does so, the commercial banks, finding their supplies of vault cash low, ask their Federal Reserve district banks to ship them as much new cash as they need.

And what does the Federal Reserve Bank do? It takes packets of bills (one- and five- and ten-dollar-bills) out of its vaults, where these stacks of printed paper have no monetary significance at all; charges the requisite amount against its members banks' balances; and ships the cash out by armored truck. So long as these new stacks of bills remain in the member banks' possession, they are still not money! But soon they will be passed out to the public, where they will be money. Do not forget, of course, that as a result the public will have that much *less* money left in its checking accounts.

Could this currency-issuing process go on forever? Could the Federal Reserve print as much money as it wanted to? Suppose that the authorities at the Federal Reserve decided to order a trillion dollars worth of bills from the Treasury mints. What would happen when those bills arrived at the Federal Reserve Banks? The answer is that they would simply gather dust in their vaults. There would be no way for the Federal Reserve to "issue" its money unless the public wanted cash. And the amount of cash the public could want

---

*Here is where we skip over the actual workings of the monetary system. A reader who is interested in learning how the banks actually create new deposits should turn to the Appendix, starting on page 261.

is always limited by the amount of money in its checking accounts.

Thus the specter of "rolling the printing presses" has to be looked at knowingly. In a nation such as pre-Hitler Germany, where most individuals were paid in cash, not by check, it was easier to get the actual bills into circulation than it would be in a highly developed check money system such as ours. The roads to inflation are many, but the actual printing of money is not likely to be one of them.*

Are there no limitations on this note-issuing process? Originally there were limitations imposed by Congress, requiring the Federal Reserve to hold gold certificates equal in value to at least 25 percent of all outstanding notes. (Gold certificates are a special kind of paper money issued by the U.S. Treasury and backed 100 percent by gold bullion in Fort Knox.) Soaring inflation rates and the fall in the international value of the dollar in the 1960s gradually resulted in a situation where our gold reserves could not provide the legal backing required by law. Basically there were two ways out. One would have been to change the gold cover requirements from 25 percent to, say, 10 percent. The second way was much simpler: eliminate the gold cover entirely. With very little fuss, this is what Congress did in 1967.

Does the presence or absence of a gold cover make any difference? From the economist's point of view it does not. Gold is a metal with a long and rich history of hypnotic influence, so there is undeniably a psychological usefulness in having gold behind a currency. But unless that currency is 100 percent convertible into gold, any money demands an act of faith on the part of its users. If that faith is destroyed, the money becomes valueless; so long as it is unquestioned, the money is "as good as gold."

*We have all seen pictures of German workers in the 1920s being paid their wages in wheelbarrow loads of marks. The question is this: why didn't the German authorities simply print paper money with bigger denominations, so that someone who was paid a billion marks a week could get ten 100-million-mark notes, not one thousand 1-million-mark notes? The answer is that it takes time to go through the bureaucratic process of ordering a new print run of higher denomination notes. Imagine a young economist at the finance ministry suggesting to his chief that they ought to stock up on billion-mark notes to be put into circulation six months hence. His superior would certainly be horrified. "You can't do that," he would protest. "Why, an order for billion-mark notes would be—*inflationary!*"

Thus the presence or absence of a gold backing for currency is purely a psychological problem, so far as the value of a domestic currency is concerned. But the point is worth pursuing a little further. Suppose our currency were 100 percent convertible into gold— suppose, in fact, that we used only gold coins as currency. Would that improve the operation of our economy?

Recurrently there is a flurry of interest in some kind of gold standard—although not, of course, a reliance on gold coins. But a moment's reflection should reveal that a gold standard would saddle us with a very difficult problem that our present monetary system handles rather easily. This is the problem of how we could increase the supply of money or diminish it, as the needs of the economy changed. With gold coins as money we would either have a frozen stock of money or our supply of money would be at the mercy of our luck in gold mining or the currents of international trade that funneled gold into our hands or took it away. We will look into this again in Chapter 19. And incidentally, a gold currency would not obviate inflation, as many countries have discovered when the vagaries of international trade or a fortuitous discovery of gold mines increased their holdings of gold faster than their actual output.

How then, do we explain the worldwide rush to buy gold—a rush that raised the dollar price of gold from thirty-five dollars an ounce— its official price as late as 1971—to over eight hundred dollars an ounce in 1979, before it fell again to half that level?

Once again, the economist offers no rational explanation for such a phenomenon. There is nothing in gold itself that possesses more value than silver, uranium, land, or labor. Indeed, judged strictly as a source of usable values, gold is rather low on the spectrum of human requirements. The sole reason why people want gold—rich people and poor people, sophisticated people and ignorant ones— is that gold has been for centuries a metal capable of catching and holding our fancy, and in troubled times it is natural enough that we turn to this enduring symbol of wealth as the best bet for preserving our purchasing power in the future. Right or wrong, gold has for centuries been regarded as mankind's most reliable "store of value." Will gold in fact remain valuable forever? And if so, how valuable? There is absolutely no way to answer such a question.

Money is a highly sophisticated and curious invention. At one time or another nearly everything imaginable has served as the magic symbol of money: whales' teeth, shells, feathers, bark, furs, blankets, butter, tobacco, leather, copper, silver, gold, and (in the most advanced nations) pieces of paper with pictures on them, or simply numbers on a computer printout. In fact, anything is usable as money, provided that there is a natural or enforceable scarcity of it so that men can usually come into its possession only through carefully designated ways. Behind all the symbols, however, rests the central requirement of faith. Money serves its indispensable purposes as long as we believe in it. It ceases to function the moment we do not. Money has well been called "the promises men live by."

ELEVEN

How Money Works

Every capitalist nation has a monetary system basically similar to ours. As a consequence, all have developed central banks whose duties are essentially like those of the Federal Reserve—namely, to exert control over the direction and extent of changes in the money supply.

The aim of all central banks is also the same. They want to keep their economies supplied with the "right" amount of money. If money supplies are scarce, the economy will suffer as if it were in a straitjacket—householders and businesses alike seeking in vain for credit from their banks, and householders and businesses alike contracting their economic activity as a result. If money supplies are too large, householders and businesses will find themselves with larger bank accounts than normal, and will be tempted by their liquidity, or by the low interest rates offered by their banks, to increase their spending.

This would seem to make the task of the Federal Reserve rather easy. All it has to do is to take the temperature of the economy and adjust the amount of money accordingly. If the economy is "overheated," with inflation worsening, clearly it is time to cut back on the availability of money. If the economy is in the doldrums, with unemployment rising, just the contrary must be the proper course to follow. It sounds, therefore, as if the job of the central banker is an easy one. As we shall see, it is not.

HOW THE FED WORKS

How does a central banker increase or decrease the supply of money? The key, as we saw in our last chapter, lies in the fact that we have a fractional reserve system in which banks can make loans or investments with "excess" reserves. Excess reserves are simply cash or deposits at the Fed that are greater than those required by law to back up their customers' deposits.

Essentially the Federal Reserve is a system designed to raise or lower the reserve requirements of its member banks. When it raises them, it squeezes its members, who find that they have less free reserves to lend or invest. When the Fed lowers requirements, just the opposite occurs, and member banks are able to lend or invest more of their reserves, thereby making more profit for themselves.

Actually, there are three ways in which the Fed can act. The first is by directly changing the reserve requirements themselves. Because these new reserve requirements affect all banks, changing reserve ratios is a very effective way of freeing or contracting bank credit on a large scale. But it is an instrument that sweeps across the entire banking system in an undiscriminating fashion. It is therefore used only rarely, when the Federal Reserve Board feels that the supply of money is seriously short or dangerously excessive and needs remedy on a countrywide basis.

A second means of control uses interest rates as the money-controlling device. Member banks that are short on reserves have a special privilege, if they wish to exercise it. They can borrow reserve balances from the Federal Reserve Bank itself and add them to their regular reserve account at the bank.

The Federal Reserve bank, of course, charges interest for lending reserves; this interest is called the *discount rate.* By raising or lowering this rate, the Federal Reserve can make it attractive or unattractive for member banks to borrow or augment their reserves. Thus, in contrast with changing the reserve ratio itself, changing the discount rate is a mild device that allows each bank to decide for itself whether it wishes to increase its reserves. In addition, changes in the discount rate tend to influence the whole structure of interest rates, either tightening or loosening money. When interest rates are high, we have what we call tight money. This means not only that borrowers have to pay higher rates, but that banks are stricter and more selective in judging the credit worthiness of business applications for loans. Conversely, when interest rates decline, money is called easy, meaning that it is not only cheaper but also easier to borrow.

Although changes in the discount rate can be used as a major means of controlling the money supply and are used to control it in some countries, they are not used for this purpose in the U.S. The Federal Reserve Board does not allow banks to borrow whatever they would like at the current discount rate. The discount "window" is a place where a bank can borrow small amounts of money to cover a small deficiency in its reserves, but it is not a place where banks can borrow major amounts of money to expand their lending portfolios. As a result, the discount rate serves more as a signal of what the Federal Reserve would like to see happen than as an active force in determining the total borrowing of banks.

Most frequently used, however, is a third technique called open-market operations. This technique permits the Federal Reserve banks to change the supply of reserves by buying or selling U.S. government bonds on the open market.

How does this work? Let us suppose that the Federal Reserve authorities wish to increase the reserves of member banks. They will begin to buy government securities from dealers in the bond market, and they will pay these dealers with Federal Reserve checks.

Notice something about these checks: They are not drawn on any commercial bank! They are drawn on the Federal Reserve Bank itself. The security dealer who sells the bond will, of course, deposit the Federal Reserve's check, as if it were any other check, in his or her own commercial bank; and his or her bank will send the Federal Reserve's check through for credit to its own account, as if it were any other check. As a result, the dealer's bank will have gained reserves, although no other commercial bank has lost reserves. On balance, then, the system has more lending and investing capacity than it had before. Thus by buying government bonds the Federal Reserve has, in fact, deposited money in the accounts of its members, thereby giving them the extra reserves that it set out to create. This is what is meant by monetizing the debt.

Conversely, if the monetary authorities decide that member banks' reserves are too large, they will sell securities—the U.S. Treasury notes that make up part of the assets of the Federal Reserve

Banks. Now the process works in reverse. Security dealers or other buyers of bonds will send their own checks on their own regular commercial banks to the Federal Reserve in payment for these bonds. This time the Fed will take the checks of its member banks and charge their accounts, thereby reducing their reserves. Since these checks will not find their way to another commercial bank, the system as a whole will have suffered a diminution of its reserves. By selling securities, in other words, the Federal Reserve authorities lower the Federal Reserve accounts of member banks, thereby diminishing their reserves.

Thus we see that there are three ways in which the Federal Reserve can decrease or increase the money supply. It can raise or lower bank reserves. It can raise or lower the discount rate. And it can sell or buy government bonds.

How well do these techniques work? Can the Fed accurately match the supply of money to the country's need for it? Like so many economic issues, the answer is less than crystal clear. There is no doubt that the Fed—or its counterpart central banks abroad—can change the money supply. Whether they can do it accurately, or exactly as they wish, is another question.

Essentially, the Fed faces two different kinds of problems:

1. It may not know what to do.
This certainly is not meant to impugn the intelligence or economic sophistication of the board of governors of the Federal Reserve System, with its superb technical staff. Rather, it reflects the unhappy condition of "stagflation" that has come to characterize the economy of most Western nations during the last decade or so.

Stagflation means that the economy is both inflating and stagnating at the same time. Prices may be going up in many industries, although large numbers of men and women cannot find work. This poses a cruel dilemma for the monetary authorities. If they decide that the stagnation aspect of the economy is more serious than the inflationary aspect, they will increase money supplies, but the result may well be an immediate jump in the cost of living and no dramatic improvement in the employment situation. Contrariwise, if the Fed is more worried about inflation than unemployment, it will reduce the availability of reserves. This may show up quickly in a fall in employment, especially in businesses that depend heavily on bank financing, such as the home construction business, without producing instant relief for price-conscious buyers.

We will be talking about this dilemma again in our next chapters. But we can see it poses a terrible problem for any central bank. Whatever policy it follows—anti-inflation or anti-stagnation—will be painful. Neither will produce quick cures. The danger, then, is that the central bank authorities will vacillate, first easing up on money, then tightening it, then easing up again, then tightening again. It is hardly surprising that the economy does not respond well to such treatment.

2. It may not be effective in doing what it seeks to do.
Even when the Fed knows clearly what it wishes to do, it cannot always accomplish its aim. The ability of the Fed to control the money supply is often likened to our ability to manipulate a string. It's easy to pull with a string, hard to push with it. So, too, with the Fed. It's easy to tighten money by cutting back on the reserves of member banks in various ways. But it is not so easy to increase the money supply as to reduce it. The Fed may reduce reserve ratios or monetize the debt (buy government bonds on the open market), thereby pumping reserves into the banking system. But it cannot force banks to make loans if they do not wish to do so.

Normally banks *will* wish to, but in bad times—such as the Great Depression—they may prefer to pile up unused reserves than to venture into the risky loan market. If that is the case, there is nothing the Fed can do to get the banks' reserves into the hands of the public.

In addition, the Fed's task is complicated because increases or decreases in the supply of money are not always used to finance or curtail spending for goods and services. They may also be used to add to or to reduce the public's holdings of cash, its liquidity. Suppose, for example, that the officials at the Fed expect an acceleration of inflation and decide to tighten the screws on money to make it more difficult for banks to lend. If things worked out just that way, there would be less lending and therefore less spending, and therefore less pressure on prices in the marketplace. But if the public feels the same way about the future as the Fed, individuals may decide to become less liquid, to spend their money "while it's still good." In that case, the restraining actions of the Fed can be frustrated by a rise in the spending habits of the public.

3. International developments can limit the Fed's power.
This is a new and important development. Something like an international pool of credit is today available to all industrial nations. An American firm looking for funds can borrow them in Germany or France as easily as from its home bank. And the same is true for firms located abroad. This transnational access to funds greatly limits the power of the Fed, or any central bank, to control long-term interest rates, simply because borrowers can do an end run to other countries' banks.

During the early 1990s, for example, Germany more or less set world interest rates, including our own. Why? Because the German mark was regarded as the world's strongest currency, as the dollar used to be. Therefore the German interest rate became the reference point for investors in all countries who wanted to judge relative risks. As we write these words, this situation seems to be changing. Perhaps the "leading currency" in the future will be determined by the European Community as a whole; perhaps it will revert to the United States; or perhaps it will simply remain a less certain proposition than used to be the case.

MONETARISM

This is by no means a complete list of the problems facing the Fed. But it is enough to indicate how difficult the art of monetary management must be. Indeed, it is just because the art is so difficult and the outcome of policy so often unexpected that much attention has been drawn in recent years to monetarism, a proposal for a new kind of monetary management suggested by the eminent conservative economist and Nobel prizewinner Milton Friedman. Friedman's proposal is simplicity itself. He believes that *nothing* in the system is as important as the quantity of money. Consequently he also believes that the regulation of the money supply should not be left to the judgment of the Federal Reserve authorities. With the best will in the world, he says, they will never get the supply of money right. This is partly because neither they nor anyone else knows the *real* state of the economy at any moment—it takes weeks or months to gather data and interpret it. It is partly because all authorities become "dug into" their previous policy decisions and need a great deal of time to change their minds. It is also because the data may be genuinely ambiguous, capable of justifying more than one direction of monetary management.

The result, in Friedman's view, is that the monetary authorities in all nations more often than not aggravate their countries' plights by expanding the supply of money when they ought to be reining it in, and vice versa. The right medicine, applied at the wrong time, doesn't cure the disease, it worsens it.

The cure is a bold one. Friedman advocates that *the supply of money should be expanded by an unchanging fixed percentage geared to the long-term growth of the nation's output.* * That way, he asserts, the supply of money will not only accommodate the growing need for larger payrolls and inventories and loans, but the very steadiness of its growth will serve to keep the economy on the track of growth. If we find ourselves headed into a recession, let us say because of international developments, the steady increase in money supply will add to banks' reserves, encouraging them to expand their loans and thereby to move us out of recession. On the other hand, if we experience a sudden surge of inflation, the same steady and unchanging rate of growth of bank lending capability will act as an automatic curb, holding down the banks' ability to finance the inflation-swollen demands of their customers, and thereby serving to mitigate the inflationary pressure.

Friedman's idea undoubtedly has an appeal. But it also has its problems. One of them is economic. The problem is deciding what the regular or normal rate of economic growth is or should be. Friedman's plan is based on the supposition that our capacity to produce goods and services will follow its historical trend, essentially reflecting our long-run increase in productivity. But recent years have shown that the increase in productivity is not as automatic as we might once have thought. Furthermore, even if we knew that

---

*Notice that this is not the same thing as supply-side economics. Supply-siders want to encourage growth by lowering taxes and removing regulation. Monetarists want to encourage it by a fixed and steady growth of money. The two policies can come into sharp conflict if an administration wishes to pursue an expansionary course by cutting taxes, but is not willing to relax its strict monetarist constraints on the money supply. This is exactly what got the Reagan administration into trouble in mid 1981.

"natural" forces had propelled the economy forward at about 3 percent a year in the past, can we be sure that is the appropriate rate of growth for the future? Suppose environmental constraints require us to slow up, or that stubborn unemployment indicates we ought to hurry up? It's not so sure, in other words, that we want a steady rate of growth rather than one that fits changing circumstances.

The second problem is political rather than economic. Friedman is effectively asking us to stop monkeying with the system and to let its natural dynamism assert itself. But what if the dynamism isn't there for a few years? Does this mean that we are prohibited from advancing the economic throttle, even though the economy is losing altitude? If Friedman's plan were followed, that is exactly what we would do, assuring the passengers that the natural aerodynamics of our system would ultimately give us a smoother and safer flight than allowing the pilot to override the automatic flight-control machinery.

This is probably the fatal flaw in Friedman's plan, as we see it. It mirrors our skepticism regarding supply-side economics. Right or wrong, the trend over the last century has been in the direction of increasing our intervention into the workings of the system. This is not only because many economists believe that we *can* intervene effectively, despite all the problems raised by Friedman and his fellow monetarists, but also because there has been a growing political pressure to "do something" about bad economic performance. The willingness to stand by and allow the system to work out its own destiny is largely a thing of the past. The philosophy of Adam Smith has been pushed aside by that of John Maynard Keynes. We may not be able to intervene very effectively; we may indeed bring about outcomes that are different from those we anticipated; in a word, Milton Friedman's warnings may be borne out in fact. But it seems unrealistic that we will content ourselves ever again with a passive attitude toward the economic system. "Doing nothing" sounds like a feasible policy option, but in fact it is not.

TWELVE

Inflation

For our parents and grandparents, the single most potent formative economic experience of their lives was the Great Depression. For ourselves it was the Great Inflation, the twenty-odd-year period beginning in the mid 1960s, and still not entirely over, during which prices rose by more than 300 percent. Whether the trauma of inflation is as firmly put behind us as that of depression is a question we cannot answer with assurance, because the institutional safeguards that we have erected against another bottomless depression have not been matched by safeguards that would prevent another near-runaway inflation.

As we write these words, however, inflation has receded from a rampant disease to a mild one, not only in the United States but in all capitalist nations. Therefore this seems a good time to assess the phenomenon as a whole, prior to asking what we can do to prevent its serious recurrence in the future.

THE ROOTS OF INFLATION

Let us begin from an elemental but often overlooked fact of economic life. It is that capitalist economies are always in a state of nervous tension, of actual or potential movement, of overt or latent disequilibrium. Wars, changes in political regimes, resource changes, new technologies, shifts in consumers' tastes, all constantly disturb the tenor of business life. Ask any businessman if he lives in a calm pond or a choppy lake.

It may not seem important to begin from a stress on this deep-seated vulnerability characteristic of capitalist systems. But once we place the fact stage center, a striking question immediately faces us: how does it happen that the vulnerability results in inflation, and not depression or some other malfunction? For when we think of it, it was not inflation but other kinds of dysfunction that troubled capitalism in previous periods—think of the slump of 1893: *six years* of unemployment ranging from 12 to 18 percent of the labor force; or the collapse of the 1930s. Or recall the traumatic emergence of the new giant industrial trusts in the late nineteenth century, emerging like corporate icebergs amid the floe of small enterprises of that time.

From this perspective, inflation appears as the way in which the capitalist system responds to shocks and disruptions in the institutional setting of the late twentieth century. Take, for example, the impetus given to inflation by the oil price rise of 1973. Now suppose that an exactly comparable shock had been administered a century earlier, say by the Pennsylvania coal companies banding together as a coal cartel and suddenly announcing a fourfold increase in coal prices. Would such a coal cartel have produced inflation? The question is ludicrous. It would have brought on a massive depression. Coal mines would have closed, steel mills shut down, car loadings fallen. That imaginary but unchallengeable scenario then puts the right question: *What happened between 1873 and 1973 so that the same shock—an abrupt rise in energy prices—would have produced depression in one era and did produce inflation in another?*

The question is not hard to answer. Far-reaching changes have taken place within the social and economic structure of capitalism all over the world. Of these, by far the most visible and important has been the emergence of large and powerful public sectors. In all Western capitalisms, these public sectors pump out 30 to 50 percent of all expenditures, sometimes even more. *These public expenditures provide a floor for economic activity that did not exist before.* In itself that is enough to shift a depression-prone world toward an inflation-prone one.

The floors of public expenditure do not prevent the arrival of all recessions, as we know from experience. The difference is that a market system with a core of public spending does not easily move from recession into ever-deeper depression. The downward tendency of production and employment is limited by the support of government spending such as Social Security, unemployment insurance, insurance of bank deposits, and the like. Cumulative, bottomless depressions are changed into limited, although persisting, recessions.

A second aspect of the sea change that has come over capitalism in the last century is the rise in private power. We see it in the vast organizations—the icebergs—that dominate the waters of business and labor alike.

The emergence of massive institutions of private power makes an important contribution to our inflationary propensity. A striking difference between today and yesterday is that in the past inflationary peaks were regularly followed by long deflationary periods. Prices tended irregularly *downward* over most of the last half of the nineteenth century. Why? One reason is that the economy was much more heavily agricultural in those days, and farm prices have always been more volatile, particularly downward, than the prices of manufactured goods. Hence an industrial economy, just by virtue of being dominated by manufactures, is much less likely to have price declines than a farming economy. A second reason is that the character of the manufacturing sector has also changed. In the early decades of the twentieth century, it was not unusual for big companies to announce across-the-board wage cuts when times were bad. In addition, prices declined as a result of technological advances, and as a consequence of the dog-eat-dog price wars that continually broke out among industrial competitors.

That is all part of a chapter of economic history largely written *finis*. Agriculture is now only a small part of GNP. Technology continues to lower costs, sometimes dramatically—look what has happened to the computer during the last decade!—but these lower industrial costs have been offset by a "ratchet tendency" shown by wages and prices since World War II. A ratchet tendency means that prices and wages go up, but rarely or never come down—always excepting technological revolutions or market debacles such as the chaos of the American automobile industry. In normal times and normal business, we see the ratchet at work. Concentrated business and union power, coupled with a general horror of the tactics of cutthroat competition, mean that wages and prices generally move in one direction only—up. Except when business is bad and competition gets nasty, big companies do not cut salaries. These tendencies also add to our inflationary drift.

There are still other institutional changes that have made today's system more inflation-prone than that of a hundred, or even fifty, years ago. We are a more service-oriented economy, and productivity rises less rapidly in services than in goods. We are more affluent, and therefore less willing to abide meekly by traditional pecking orders: the "lowly" cop or sanitation man or elevator operator doesn't feel so lowly any more and instructs his union negotiators accordingly. These more assertive attitudes also tilt the system in the direction of inflation.

These changes help us understand why we live in a world which, compared to that of our fathers, has become inflation-prone. We "catch" inflation the way capitalism of the late nineteenth and early twentieth centuries caught deflation.

But inflation susceptibility is one thing, its actual advent is another. Our inflationary experience has its origins in specific events that started the process off, just as did the depressions of bygone eras. In our case, inflation probably received its initial impetus from the boost to spending that resulted from the Vietnam War. A powerful stimulus to inflation in *other* countries then resulted from the manner in which the United States used its hegemonic power to force other nations to accept our dollars in lieu of gold, building up inflationary expansions of credit abroad that eventually fed back on our own price levels. And then came the famous oil shock of 1973, when the Organization of Petroleum Exporting Countries (OPEC) raised prices from three dollars to eleven dollars per barrel, and then again in 1979 when oil jumped from thirteen dollars to twenty-eight dollars in the wake of Iran's revolution.

We have already reflected on the difference between the inflation-creating effects of that oil shock and the depression-creating effects that would likely have accompanied an imaginary "coal shock" in 1873. Now we must pay heed to a very important institution that made the higher prices of the oil shock so contagious. This is the presence of *indexing arrangements* which gear payments to some index, such as the consumer cost of living, computed by the Bureau of Labor Statistics. Indexing changes the way an economy works. Higher prices no longer serve as a deterrent to buying, as they would have in 1873. Under indexing the additional income needed to cover the higher-cost items is automatically provided by COLAS (cost-of-living adjustments) or by Social Security and other indexed payments. When prices rise suddenly, as a consequence of oil shock or wage shock or any other cost increase, momentarily the economy shudders, as sales lag and employment declines. But then the higher oil or wage or other costs show up in a higher cost-of-living index number, and as the index rises so do the green checks that go to Social Security recipients, or the wage adjustments paid out on indexed contracts. All this serves the excellent purpose of short-circuiting recession. But it also greases the skids for inflation.

With this inflation-transmitting change in institutions comes an even more dangerous inflation-transmitting change in mind sets. In the old days the prevailing point of view about economic life was summed up in the adage, "What goes up must come down," so that booms and price rises typically (although not always) generated a salutary degree of caution. Nowadays attitudes have changed. When we learn that a commodity is going up, our first reaction is that it will probably continue to go up, maybe faster, so that we had better get in there while the getting is good. Thus the very expectation of higher prices becomes an inflation-sustaining mechanism, much as during the Depression, when bad times were stretched out because businesses *expected* them to go on and on. Expectations are self-fulfilling, self-generating. In the inflationary process, the widespread and unchallenged belief that "Next year will be 10 percent higher," leads to the very kind of buy now, pay later behavior that guarantees that next year will, in fact, be 10 percent higher.

All this allows us to see that many of the conventional explanations given for inflation have played some role in sustaining the chronic malfunction of our economy. Government has indeed been responsible for inflation, insofar as it has introduced floors under the economy, indexed important payments, and bolstered security to the point at which our expectations and attitudes have been much more aggressive than formerly. The massing of union and business power has also contributed to inflation through the ratcheting of wages and prices. And still other villains can be seen at work in the background or the foreground.

GETTING OUT OF INFLATION

Against all these built-in tendencies, how did we finally get out of the inflationary spiral?

Essentially two developments did the trick. One of these was sheer good luck. One of the major inflation-generating forces during the 1970s was the upward pressure of "outside" shocks (*exogenous* shocks, in economists' language). We have already seen that inflation gained a good deal of its underlying momentum from rising oil prices. Also important was a consistent upward pressure of food prices, partly the consequence of serious food shortages in the underdeveloped world, partly the result of adverse weather. A third cause was the generally rising trend of many other raw-materials prices, pulled up by the worldwide boom. All these exogenous shocks acted as a constant inflationary stimulus whose effects were spread throughout the system by indexing arrangements.

Now comes the good luck. By the 1980s, all these pressures had disappeared. The OPEC cartel had set the price of oil so high that oil production soared, while oil consumption was dramatically economized. As a result, the price of oil fell from $40 a barrel to just above $10. In the underdeveloped world, population growth finally slowed down and agricultural production finally speeded up. With good weather as a big assist, long-persisting food shortages gradually gave way to exportable food "surpluses," with the consequence of falling agricultural prices. As the boom in the developed world slowed down in the early 1980s, demand for raw materials slumped, sometimes disastrously; after correction for inflation, copper prices fell to levels below those of the Great Depression.

Taken together, these exogenous developments cut the inflationary pressure by at least half during the 1980s. But because none of these developments was within the control of American (or European) policymakers, we can only call this first reason for the decline of the inflationary spiral good luck.

A second reason was tough policy. Everyone had always known that there existed one sure cure for inflation. It was to send the economy deliberately into a really deep recession. Until the 1980s, however, no one was prepared to try the medicine, because no one was prepared to risk the political consequences of attempting such a cure.

The situation changed in the early 1980s, first under the administration of President Carter, then with redoubled intensity under that of President Reagan. Tight monetary policies pushed interest rates over 20 percent, with the *desired* consequence of a steep and prolonged business recession. At 20-percent interest rates, small businesses found themselves unable to afford the normal loans needed to provide them with working capital. Consumers were driven out of the mortgage and household-appliance markets. Even the biggest corporations were themselves caught in a devastating squeeze as interest costs mounted and as buyer demand declined.

Thus, as expected *and desired,* tight money brought on a recession. By 1982, unemployment in the United States had passed the 11-percent mark; in Europe unemployment soared even higher. As unemployment rose, wage cuts—unheard of during the previous long boom—were instituted in hard-pressed industries. And as the pressure of wage costs declined, and the easy days of ever-expanding markets gave way to hard days of stable or contracting markets, corporations were forced into strategies that many economists thought had been permanently relegated to the history books: they began to shave prices.

A final coup de grâce was administered by the pressures of foreign competition. As American interest rates soared, foreigners began to move their funds into high-yielding American bonds. The inflow of capital thereupon drove up the price of dollars as foreigners exchanged their domestic currencies for the dollars needed to buy U.S. Treasury or other securities. As the dollar rose in value, Americans went on a shopping tour for foreign merchandise that could be bought in America at bargain-basement prices. At the same time, foreigners found themselves unable to afford American goods, now priced out of sight.* Thus the pressures of foreign competition provided another source of inflation-taming competition.

Together, good luck and tough policy broke the back of the inflationary spree. Double-digit inflation petered out into single-digit

*In Chapter 18 we will see why high dollars bring cheap imports and dear exports.

inflation. By 1985, price *declines* began to show up in a few industrial sectors. Inflation almost disappeared in 1986—almost, but not quite: prices rose .6 percent that year. Since then they have resumed a yearly gain of around 3 percent. That seems to be "normal" these days.

COPING WITH INFLATION

So the Great Inflation came to an end—rather ignominiously, but an end just the same. But what about the Great Inflationary Propensity? We got out of the Great Depression through the spending generated by the advent of World War II. But not until the 1950s did we lay in the structure to prevent *another* Great Depression, mainly by a far-reaching extension of Social Security, unemployment insurance, and a welfare support system. The efficacy of those measures is shown by the fact that two back-to-back recessions in 1980 and 1981 did not bring on the cumulative collapse characteristic of the economy's behavior in the pre-support days.

We have seen that a combination of ruthless tight-money policy and good luck pulled us out of the Great Inflation. But we have not yet laid in the institutional counterpart of the support system that has prevented a replay of the depressionary experience. What could such institutional changes be?

It must be apparent that there is little or nothing that we can do to cope with the basic causes of our inflationary tendencies. Chronic inflation comes about because capitalism exerts its nervous, thrusting, expansive energy in a changed social environment. Capitalism is now government-supported capitalism, power-bloc capitalism, a capitalism of high public expectations. These structural properties are not going to change. Despite the efforts of the Reagan administration, government cannot be disengaged from our economic structure, because it is not lodged there like a great foreign body, but is woven and integrated into the fabric of society at every level. Much the same can be said of big labor and big business, neither of which could be plucked from our midst without ripping up the social cloth with horrendous results. As we shall see, international competition has lessened the power of both labor and capital, but it has not removed it. Capitalism will remain, by and large, the massive, complex entity that we know it to be—dependent on a very large degree of public intervention, support, regulation, and interference (which does not mean, of course, that some programs cannot be trimmed back or even eliminated). As a result, capitalism will continue to respond to outside shocks like OPEC or to inside ones like high wage settlements in ways that send prices up rather than production down. An inflationary tendency is the manner in which the modern capitalist mechanism reacts to its own strains and stresses, just as depressions were the way in which it reacted in a bygone age. To the extent that we can introduce such changes as de-indexing Social Security and other payment flows, we will lessen the self-feeding properties of upward instability, but we will not rid ourselves of inflationary dangers, any more than our floors have rid us of the dangers of economic slumps.

The question, then, is not to exorcise the specter of inflation, but to introduce institutional changes that will limit its effects—ceilings that will restrain the extent of upward instability in the way that floors have mitigated its downward tendencies.

INSTITUTIONAL CHANGES

We have seen two general approaches to such a general anti-inflationary policy. One is what Europeans call a "social contract" or "corporatist" approach. Highly centralized trade unions, large companies (often coordinated through national employers' federations), and governments negotiate a pattern of wage increases and price behavior designed to shield the economy from an inflationary spiral. An agreement is made not to raise either wages or prices in excess of agreed-upon rates, and not to try to recoup income losses that may be imposed from exogenous shocks such as crop failures, OPEC-type cartels, and the like. This type of arrangement has been applied with some success by a number of European nations, especially Germany and Austria.

The second approach is that of the Japanese. Most employees of large companies in Japan receive a considerable fraction (about a third) of their income in the form of a bonus rather than a wage. When exogenous shocks threaten to destabilize the economy upward, bonuses can be cut, in place of a necessity to reduce negotiated wages. This makes it a great deal easier to avoid the wage–price race that has plagued the American economy.

We do not really know if such institutional arrangements can effectively prevent the recurrence of another Inflationary Decade. In a world that is increasingly interlocked in its economic and financial flows, all national schemes may come to naught if inflation fever breaks out again, whether due to exogenous shocks or whatever. But the approaches are promising *because they are essentially means of equitably sharing reductions in real income.* They are social mechanisms to prevent economic shocks from snowballing into an unmanageable political scramble. The trouble is that they require arrangements or mechanisms that the United States does not have— bonus systems, powerful, comprehensive labor and employers' federations, or well-established traditions of public–private negotiations. Lacking such institutions, we are likely to have to rely on less far-reaching, and therefore probably less successful, means of dampening a new inflationary surge, or of dealing with one if events impose another exogenous shock upon us. Let us look at three such policies.

CONTROLS

A word that keeps creeping up, when we consider how to stop inflation, is *controls.* Controls are anathema to some economists, a panacea to others. Our own view is that there is no single set of remedies called "controls," but a whole spectrum of possibilities, and that there is a lot to be said for some and a lot to be said against others.

One of the easiest and least intrusive kinds of controls is to suggest limits for wage and price increases—a kind of informal version of the European social-contract arrangements. The idea behind this policy of guidelines is clear and correct. If everyone would agree to limit his or her increase in income to, say, 2 to 3 percent, the inflation rate would promptly drop and *no one would be any worse off.* A collective decision like that would slow down the escalator, but would not change our respective positions on it.

The problem is making an informal policy stick. Unfortunately, unless everyone cooperates, the scheme will not work, and the temptations to cheat are enormous. It helps everyone see the field if all remain seated at a football game, and no one gains if all stand up. But if everyone does stay seated, the few cheaters get the best views;

whereas if everyone stands, the few law-abiders get the worst views! Voluntary controls fail for the same reason: nice guys finish last. Therefore, a number of schemes have been devised to make adherence to such programs profitable (not compulsory), as well as patriotic. Among these are TIP (Tax Incentive Plans), which would levy tax penalties against companies that gave wage settlements in excess of guideline rates. If TIP encouraged all employers to stick to their guns, wage increases would stay in line, and no union would be disadvantaged compared with any other. Hence, there is a considerable amount of interest in such plans. Their difficulties are administrative rather than economic. They require a degree of supervision and intrusion on the part of government that is certain to create bureaucracy and to generate friction. That difficulty may be worth the price, however, if other measures fail.

Alternatively, we can institute compulsory controls, such as legal ceilings on prices or administered wages. Such controls would require two attributes to be effective: (1) they would have to be permanent, or at least standby, so that they would not be on-again, off-again; and (2) they would absolutely require to be backed up by heavy taxes. Controls alone are just sandbags holding back a rising river. The necessary sluiceway to bring the river under control must be provided by taxes.

If war broke out, we could undoubtedly impose such mandatory controls and sluiceway taxes with good results—they were very successfully applied during the Korean War, for instance. This is because war provides the necessary spirit of compliance, as well as allowing the government to take whatever other measures the economy requires. If controls result in insufficient investment, for instance, a government in wartime builds or subsidizes the plant and equipment itself.

All that is much more difficult, or impossible, during peacetime. Then the attitude is not one of willing compliance, but reluctant obedience or outright evasion. In addition, controls are onerous. The Korean system required eighteen thousand inspectors. Even with modern computers, we would have to expect a similar army to enforce mandatory wage or price ceilings today.

Thus the objection to mandatory controls is twofold. They are certain to cause a great deal of public irritation: we can all imagine the headlines they will produce. And they will pose an endless series of difficult questions in deciding how this or that price or wage rate should be adjusted as the economy grows and changes and faces new challenges. On the other hand, controls have one major benefit. More effectively than any other measure, they *will* halt the inflationary spiral. The halt may be only temporary, but it will provide a breathing space in which a really effective anti-inflationary policy could be formulated, and in which the dangerous indexing and COLA arrangements could be trimmed way back. If other measures fail, therefore, and if inflation continues its threatening assault on our sense of psychological security, we may yet turn to this last remedy.

TIGHT MONEY

That brings us, of course, back to square one. If we cannot easily introduce deep institutional changes and if the use of controls promises quick relief but no permanent cure, how do we cope with the inflationary propensities that continue to lurk within modern capitalism?

The answer is very likely to be continued reliance on the one medicine that has brought inflationary fever down: tight money. As we have seen, if we are willing to tighten money ruthlessly, and to keep it tight until unions quit asking for higher wages and corporations are forced into price wars to win markets, then inflation will come to an end.

The problem with tight money is twofold. The first, obvious, problem is that the cure is so severe it threatens the health of the patient, even though it rids him of his immediate ailment. The recession that stopped inflation in the early 1980s was the worst economic catastrophe that had afflicted the capitalist world since the Great Depression itself. No one wants to go through that experience again.

The second problem is that tight money is certainly not an equitable, and likely not an effective anti-inflationary policy unless it is imposed with Draconian severity. Suppose a tight-money policy brings unemployment up to, say, 8 percent. That does not mean that every worker is laid off for 8 percent of the year. It means that some workers are unemployed for long periods of time. Over 50 percent of the total number of weeks of unemployment is typically borne by individuals who are unemployed for more than half a year. Almost half of those who suffer long spells of unemployment end up not with a job, but by withdrawing from the work force.

Thus if a relatively mild recession is the way we decide to fight inflation, we should recognize that the honor of being designated as an inflation fighter is rather selectively awarded. It does not mainly go to those whose recruitment into the brigade of the unemployed would be most effective in bringing down wage rates, namely the group of prime-age white males. Rather, enlistment in the ranks of inflation fighters is predominantly that of younger workers, age 16–24, of women, of blacks and of Hispanics. These groups share two characteristics: they tend to be relatively unskilled, and they tend to lack political clout. Thus their impact on the trend of national wage rates is small. The brigade is not only inequitably chosen, but it is ineffective. That's why unemployment rates may go up, but inflation rates may not obediently come down.

THE UNSOLVED PROBLEM

That is about all that an economist can venture to say. The basic problem is that we cannot permanently guard against inflation unless we have some ability to control individuals' money incomes. Which individuals should these be? The poor? The rich? The military? The unions? One economist will be all for helping farmers but not industrial workers, and will therefore plead for a program that encourages a free market in wheat but not in wages. Another will want controls over food prices but not over pay packets. And so it goes: economists favoring corporations, consumers, small business, the working man.

Which economist is right? There is no right. Stopping inflation can be achieved in many ways. Each will impose costs on some and yield benefits to others. The costs and benefits that appeal to one advocate will not appeal to another. Thus the solution to the problem of inflation is not to find a magic formula. It is to develop a political program that appeals to the country at large as fair and equitable, and that imposes enough restraints on enough critical elements so that the rolling juggernaut will slow down to a manageable and acceptable pace.*

We end on a more hopeful note—or rather, on a note more hopeful with regard to inflation, but not with respect to another problem. It is that inflation may be receding as the central concern of Western economies, ours included. The reason is that a new form of "inflation control" is showing up in the intensified competition of low-wage countries against high-wage countries. We noted some pages back that the real wages of unskilled labor in the United States have been falling since 1973, mainly because of competition from low-wage nations abroad: the average wage in Mexico is $1.50 per hour. These pressures exert a downward pressure on costs that may effectively offset, or at least curb, the upward pressures of wages that have been a hydraulic force for inflation in the past.

So we are a little between the devil and the deep blue sea. No one wants inflation, but at least we have some general ideas about how to fight it. But we have not yet found how live in a world of increasing international interpenetration. That will be an important object of inquiry toward the end of this book. But there is a good deal of less puzzling economics to cover first.

*To spare our readers apoplexy, we will relegate to a footnote what one such effective program might be. Inflation can certainly be curbed if we prevent households from spending more from one year to the next. Therefore, we could impose an inflation tax on all incomes, taking away, say, 95 percent of all year-to-year increases. This is tantamount to having everyone agree to a 5 percent annual wage-and-salary increase, the very recipe we often hear suggested with respect to powerful unions. No doubt there would have to be appeals boards for individuals who changed jobs, etc. But there is little doubt that the scheme would provide a tremendous barrier to inflation. The question is, how frightened of inflation would we have to be before we agreed to a national incomes policy of this kind?

THIRTEEN

Falling Behind: The Productivity Problem

One of the greatest shocks to our national ego has been the dawning realization that when it comes to standards of living, America is no longer number one. Indeed, in the world ranking of average standards of material well-being, we are probably something like number ten, and if Japan continues to catch up with us, we will soon become number eleven. In some cases, such as Saudi Arabia or Abu Dhabi, this ranking is a statistical artifact, produced by averaging together the astronomical incomes of a small ruling clique with the still abysmal living standards of the masses of the population. But that is not the case with industrialized nations such as Sweden or Switzerland or Denmark, nor will it apply if and when Japan overtakes us. The basic reason, of which we are uncomfortably aware, is that American productivity is today lower than that of a number of other advanced nations. We simply produce less per person than they do.

How could it happen that the United States, so long the envy and admiration of the world, could have fallen on such parlous times? There are two approaches to this question, one positive, one negative. The positive approach emphasizes that the loss of American leadership can better be seen as the long-overdue assertion of European and Japanese economic strength and ability. When all is said and done, a nation's productivity reflects its reservoir of skills and talents and morale, as well as its stocks of machinery and its access to resources. The nations that are now at the head of the world's parade of incomes are all there because their resources, equipment, and human capital have put them there. Swedish or German engineering, for instance, has always been as good as any in the world. The Japanese educational system is a marvel of discipline and application. Even the Saudis, benefiting from their oil, are only enjoying a claim to wealth that we too once enjoyed when the Mesabi Range or the Great Plains gave us (or still give us) a God-given advantage over everyone else.

So the positive side of the productivity story is that Europe has finally overcome the setbacks of two devastating world wars and that Japan has finally come into her own. To the extent that the world is a safer and better place as a community of equals, we can only applaud their rise to riches, even if it means that the era of cheap tourism and unchallenged American superiority is gone forever.

But there is also a negative side to the productivity issue. The newly rich have not merely claimed their rightful place in the sun. Americans have lost their own place because we have suffered a *decline* in productivity compared with our Western allies. In the 1980s, industrial productivity rose by about 2 percent per year in West Germany and by about 3 percent per year in Japan. But it rose less than 1 percent annually in the United States. During 1989–90, we not only lost out comparatively to our main competitors, but we actually ran backward! Productivity fell by 1 percent over those two years, until it finally rebounded to 2.7 percent in 1992—good, but not spectacular.

WHAT HAS HAPPENED TO PRODUCTIVITY?

What lies behind the phenomenon of "falling behind"? The ups and downs of the last few years suggest that there is a short-term process at work as well as a longer-term one. The short-term process is not particularly dangerous. It arises because measured productivity— the number of cars, or tons of steel, or ton-miles of freight produced by an average employee—rises or falls depending on whether we are in a boom or a recession. During recessions, although employers may be forced to lay off some of their working force, they try to hang on to skilled overhead personnel even if they aren't fully occupied, because employers know that when the turn comes it isn't easy to hire a knowledgeable bookkeeper, or a salesman who knows the line, or a versatile draftsman. Thus sagging output is apportioned among a working force that is somewhat larger than it could be, and the inevitable result is a fall in average output per employee. That is also why productivity bounces back quickly as soon as production picks up steam, for output can be increased without having to hire another bookkeeper, salesman, or draftsperson. Hence, in upswings, productivity data look good.

These short-term reasons caution against overreacting to newspaper headlines warning of precipitous drops in productivity. But they do not account for the continuing, year-by-year deterioration of American performance. For instance, the 1985 fall in productivity took place in a year of economic growth. Something more fundamental must have been going on.

The first place where we should direct our attention is the shift that has been going on in the allocation of America's productive effort. If we compare the 1980s with the 1950s—or with a century before that—we can see that there has been a steady streaming of labor and capital out of agriculture, first into industry and later into the service sector. To put it anecdotally, a typical worker in 1900 was a farmhand, in 1940 a factory hand, in 1990 an office worker. Put in economic terms, this has resulted in a rise in American productivity in the earlier years when the industrial sector was gaining, and a fall in recent years when the service sector has been swelling. Today about 75 percent of all employees work in some kind of service industry, whether it be a law firm, H & R Block, or the local hospital. This is a higher percentage, by far, than is found in any other industrial nation.

To be sure, the term "services" covers a very wide spread of businesses and occupations. The technical definition includes some businesses in which productivity is very high. It also embraces the field in which productivity is typically only 50 percent of the level in manufacturing. What is significant for our purpose is that certain areas within the vast service sector, marked by abnormally low productivity, are also areas in which employment has mushroomed in the last decade. Outstanding among these are personal business services, such as lawyers and accountants, health and hospital care, and education. In the last two fields, output per worker is worth far less per hour and has been growing far more slowly than elsewhere in the economy. Indeed, the 600,000 persons we now employ in our private security forces have a purely negative effect on productivity, because they add to cost but do not contribute anything to output.

This is not to say that security guards—or police—may not be necessary, or that nursing homes are a waste. On the contrary, it is likely that we have too few policemen or guards, and everyone knows that our nursing facilities are inadequate. Alas, that only demonstrates that we may have to pay the price of a somewhat lower average productivity to achieve a society that provides amenities and safety and good government. Just the same, it is one reason why our productivity has fallen.

A second reason is that a number of important industries have encountered specific productivity problems. One of these is mining, where the decline has been especially marked. Here the blame can be attributed to two very different factors. In the case of oil production (which is included in mining), it is nature that is the problem. We have simply entered a state of geological depletion in America: less oil is produced in old wells, and new wells have to be drilled deeper and yield fewer bonanzas. This is a problem that is likely to intensify, even if we learn to extract oil from shale or to recover the oil left in old rock formations.

A second part of the mining problem lies in the coal industry. Here the difficulty is not geological but social. Stricter safety and environmental measures impose higher costs on coal mining, particularly to repair the damage done by strip-mining operations. These measures add to the amount of labor needed to produce each ton of coal, and pull down our productivity as a consequence. The same is true of copper mining. As with the need for security personnel or nursing homes, we may set very high store by environmental protection, but we must also recognize that there is a price to be paid in terms of measured output per working person.

Mining is not the only industry that has slipped. So has productivity in the utility industry, partly because of very high energy costs. More interesting—because we do not really know why productivity has fallen—is the case of the construction industry. The data unmistakably point to a steady fall in the output per worker in this large area of activity. Why? Perhaps because we aren't building as many Levittowns, with their cookie-cutter designs. Perhaps because many important construction projects in nuclear energy have ground to a halt. Perhaps because construction is just more complicated than it used to be. Perhaps because the old work ethic is gone. The fact is that we do not know the answer. All we know is that productivity is off in construction, and that too pulls down the national average.

THE PRODUCTIVITY CHALLENGE

Taken together, the shift to services, the fall in mining output, and the sag in construction account for about one third of our total drop in productivity over the past few decades. Thus there are obviously other industries and other reasons behind the productivity problem. Here we are going to zero in on one and only one of these additional explanations. It is the failure of American industry to invest in enough modern capital equipment to stay abreast of its Western partners. Capital equipment alone is certainly not the secret of productivity, but it is a very important part of the problem, as we shall see.

This brings us to cars and steel. Why did these industries fare so badly, vis-à-vis their international competitors? One reason seems to concern internal management, another "external" management. Internal first. Americans are used to thinking of themselves as non-bureaucratic. But that is a self-image that simply will not stand up against an analysis of the way we organize a great deal of production. To put it bluntly, we are white-collar top-heavy. It takes many more office workers for us to produce a car than is the case with our main competitor, Japan.

It isn't just cars. During the 1980s, American firms laid off about 6 percent of their blue-collar work force. Over that same period, output rose by 30 percent, despite the decline in production-floor employees. This means that factory-floor productivity per employed worker must have risen significantly—and it did, at just under 3 percent a year. Meanwhile, however, those same firms were hiring 15 million new white-collar workers. White-collar employment rose by 33 percent—faster than the gain in output. The conclusion follows irrefutably—while blue-collar productivity was rising, white-collar productivity was falling. And since there are now almost two white-collar workers for every blue-collar worker on American payrolls, their decline in efficiency far outweighed the gain in factory-floor output per person.

Why are American firms more bureaucratic than foreign ones—including the foreign ones that have plants here, where they must abide by the same rules and regulations as American companies? No one knows. But there is a growing awareness that traditional American managerial ways must be changed if we are to hold our own in the free-for-all of world competition.

Then there is the "external" problem of management. We can illustrate it through the instances of both the steel and auto industries. Both industries made catastrophically wrong decisions that affected their ability to compete. Steel decided not to go into oxygenation and continuous casting, and the auto industry decided not to abandon the big car. Both decisions were terribly wrong, particularly because our international competition decided otherwise.

That is not quite the end of the analysis, however. *Why* did American managers make such wrong decisions? One reason seems to be a difference in the time horizon over which Americans and foreign managers have been trained to think. Americans concentrate on the "bottom line" *today*. Junking steel plants and auto-assembly lines that were still making money during the early 1970s would have required the decision to accept very poor or negative bottom lines then, in exchange for prospects of high growth and very satisfactory bottom lines five years ahead. European and Japanese managers have been trained to think in terms of long-range growth; Americans, in terms of short-period profits. The result has been extremely costly for us.

But even that is not quite the full explanation of the failure of the auto and steel industries to modernize. The changeover from existing equipment to new plant and equipment required not only an escape from the short-run bottom line mentality, but also relatively easy availability of capital. The decision to modernize steel, like the decision to "down-size" cars, required literally billions of dollars of investment. GM alone had to spend twenty billion dollars between 1974 and 1980. In Europe and Japan that capital was much more readily available than in the United States.

In part this was the case because the propensity of these nations to save is much higher than in America. We have noted that, before West Germany swallowed up East Germany, West German families saved about 15 percent of their annual incomes, and Japanese families save about 20 percent of theirs, whereas Americans typically save only 5 percent of their incomes. Even if we add corporate savings to the pot, in the United States only about one seventh of all our income is available for the replacement of old capital and the formation of new capital. In the former West Germany and Japan, the availability of total savings is about one and a half to two times as great as ours. Hence it is not surprising—although it is certainly disquieting—to learn that on a per capita basis Japan invested $2.50 in new plant and equipment in 1992 for every $1 invested in the United States.

Capital was also more readily available abroad because many foreign industrialized nations use the power of government to support—even to finance—their big, internationally oriented businesses. This is particularly the case in Japan, where the closely coordinated activities of the Japanese government, its big banks, and its largest corporations have given rise to the business-government cooperative effort we call "Japan Incorporated." The Japanese government, working closely with its banks and industrial leaders, typically chooses one or two firms to serve as the leaders in a given industry, secures large bank credits for these firms, and thus paves the way for the leaders' massive entry into the international arena, equipped with the latest technology. To some extent, this kind of government-private coordination has been used by Western nations as well. Even in Germany, where there is much less leadership by government, there has been a unified effort to make capital available when needed.

The best example is Airbus Industrie, a collective effort of the British, French, Spanish, and German governments to break into the aircraft manufacturing business. Almost twenty years and $26 billion were required, but in the end European governments created a manufacturer who has essentially driven McDonell Douglas to the Orient and who now threatens Boeing's dominant world position.

Thus another reason why American steel and auto manufacturers failed to meet the challenge from abroad was that they did not compete on even terms. Admittedly, the Americans made very costly mistakes in judging the market and in paying too much heed to immediate profits. But these mistakes also reflect the absence of a public-private structure that might have lifted sights higher and provided the wherewithal to attempt ambitious programs. In a word,

American enterprise has not learned how to organize its effort in a new setting that is global in scope, and where the traditional division between government and business is blurring. We may not like this emerging way of economic life, but it exists and must be taken into account when we inquire why we have fallen behind.

This is by no means a full analysis of the productivity puzzle. For example, we have paid no heed to the warnings of those who blame the military for our lagging productivity, claiming that too much engineering and scientific talent and too much skilled manpower go into totally unproductive armaments. Nor have we considered what the Japanese call "hard productivity"—the productivity that results from high technology and massive capital—as against "soft productivity"—the increase in output that reflects stronger morale and a genuine feeling of teamwork. How far this belated appreciation of the dignity of labor can go in the face of the imperatives of profit and the conventional wisdom of efficiency is a matter that may prove of decisive importance for the future.

But rather than continue with a long list of contributory elements, we prefer to end with two key points. The first is already apparent from our survey and would only become more evident if we continued the analysis. *It is that there is no quick fix for the problem.* There is no way of rapidly reversing the drift into the service sector. There is no way of making nature more bountiful. We may temper our environmental concerns, but it is no longer possible to ignore them. The mentality of American management will not change overnight. The savings propensities of American families will not double tomorrow. And the long-standing mutual suspicions between government and business make it very difficult to find ways of meeting the new public-private challenge from abroad. An infrastructure program will not bring productivity results for four to six years. In a word, the productivity problem will not go away quickly.

Second, *improving productivity will be painful, not agreeable.* It may mean, for instance, phasing out industries or firms that cannot hold their own in the international battle for markets. With how much enthusiasm will the American apparel trade agree to that? Under the banner of Helping American Productivity, how willingly will Chrysler's inefficient work force migrate to the sun belt, where new jobs may or may not await them in some other line of work? Raising savings requires that we cut back on our propensity to consume: "Buy now, pay later" is not compatible with "Invest now, grow later." If we are serious about raising investment, we must be serious about discouraging the national love affair with "living it up."

Thus it is not going to be easy or pleasant to reverse the trend of American productivity. There is no single great ailment to which a single great restorative effort can be applied. Everyone wants productivity to be restored—starting with the other guy's problem. Yet, if we are to compete in internaitonal markets with the Japanese and Germans, productivity *must* be raised, and raised dramatically. If we cannot find the political will to impose the necessary costs on ourselves in some fair manner, we will simply not solve the problem. Having fallen behind, we will stay behind.

III

MICROECONOMICS— THE ANATOMY OF THE MARKET SYSTEM

FOURTEEN

*How Markets Work**

It seems crazy that economics should come in two "parts"—microeconomics and macroeconomics. And it is a little crazy, for there is only one economy. Yet it is a fact that certain kinds of problems, such as those we have been looking into, reveal themselves most clearly from a macro perspective that stresses the large flows of total saving and investment and government spending, but that the same macro perspective sheds very little light on other types of economic activity, especially those having to do with the *kinds* of output we produce. Thus questions about the choices we make as producers or consumers—questions that have immense consequences for our economic life—require a different vantage point, one that highlights the activities of buyers and sellers, of consumers and businessmen. This is the vantage point of the marketplace—the grocery store, the wheat pit, the buying office—where the interaction of buyers and sellers provides the flesh-and-blood encounters we lose sight of in studying GNP.

*This chapter uses a few graphs to illustrate its points. For many people graphs make the point immediately clear, which is why economists use them a lot. For some people, they are just confusing. If you are one of the latter, just skip over the graphs. This won't affect your basic understanding of the issues.

THE PRICE SYSTEM

The micro point of view brings us immediately to look into the question of prices, a question we have entirely ignored except insofar as we talked about the level of *all* prices when we looked into inflation. But microeconomics wants to explain how particular individual prices are determined in the arena called the marketplace. Hence, microeconomics begins with a study of supply and demand, the words we hear and use all the time, without a very clear idea of what they mean.

Often we speak of supply and demand as if the phrase meant some general law of economic life, usually the "law" we have already noted, namely that "What goes up must come down." But there is no such law, and if there were, it would not be the law of supply and demand. Instead, supply and demand is a way of understanding how the clash of buyers and sellers in the marketplace brings about prices that "clear" the market—a word we will immediately investigate—or why the clash sometimes fails to bring about such prices. *Supply and demand, in other words, inform us about how markets generate a kind of order in the system,* keeping the economy together in ways we caught a glimpse of in Chapter 2 when we looked at Adam Smith's conception of the economic world.

So we shall begin by clarifying what we mean when we speak about demand. Most people think the word just means a certain volume of spending, as when we say that the demand for automobiles has fallen off or the demand for gold is high. But that is not what the economist has in mind when he defines demand as part of his explanation of markets. Demand means not just how much we are spending for a given item, but how much we are spending for that item *at its price,* and how much we would spend *if its price changed.*

Furthermore, economists make an important generalization about the behavior of our buying in the face of changing prices. It is that we tend to buy less when prices rise and more when they fall. This sounds like an awfully simple generalization, but as we shall see, a great deal can be built on it. There are two reasons why economists believe it to be true. First, as prices fall we are *able* to buy more, because our incomes stretch further. Second, as prices fall we are *willing* to buy more because at its cheaper price the commodity looks more attractive compared with other commodities.*

From this plausible reasoning, economists construct a widely used and very helpful representation of our market behavior, called a *demand curve*. The diagram below shows such a curve. Let's suppose it is designed to show how many shirts will be bought in a department store over a period of a week at different prices. If we look at the dotted lines on the graph, we can see that this (imaginary) example shows that if shirts are priced at fifty dollars, only fifty will be bought. If they are priced at twenty-five dollars, one hundred will be bought. If they are reduced to ten dollars, two hundred will be bought.

Now what about supply? As we would expect, sellers also react to price changes, but in exactly the opposite direction from buyers. The higher the price, the more sellers are able and willing to put on the market; the lower the price, the less. We're not talking about whether a manufacturer might not be able to produce more cheaply

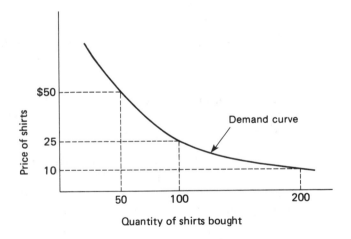

Quantity of shirts bought

*We can easily understand why our ability to buy will increase as prices fall, but why our willingness? The answer lies in what economists call the utility or pleasure we get from most goods. Generally, as we add more and more units of one good during a given period, the addition to our pleasure diminishes. One steak dinner in the week is wonderful; two are fine; three OK; seven a bore. These diminishing increments of pleasure are called diminishing marginal utility. Because each successive steak dinner brings less pleasure, we are willing to buy more of them only if their price falls. We may be willing to pay a lot for the first (and only) steak dinner of the week, but we will certainly not pay much for the seventh, unwelcome one.

at high volumes. The question, rather, is whether General Motors or the local farmer will be willing and able to offer more output to buyers *right now,* working with their existing land and equipment, if the price is high rather than low. The answer is obviously yes.

Therefore we can depict a normal supply curve as rising, instead of falling the way a demand curve does. How steeply it rises depends on how much a supplier can quickly bring to market if the price goes up. A farmer may be stuck with a given crop. General Motors may be able to jam a lot of cars through by running three shifts. Here is what a typical short-run supply curve might look like:

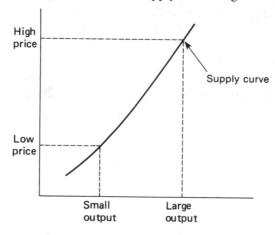

BALANCING SUPPLY AND DEMAND

We're now ready to see how the market mechanism works. Undoubtedly you have already seen the point. The fact that supply-and-demand behavior is different and opposite for buyers and sellers allows the system to find a price that will "clear" the market.

The best way to grasp the supply-and-demand mechanism is to run an imaginary example in our heads. Suppose that a store is selling blouses at $29.95. It has an inventory of a hundred dozen blouses, and it expects to sell its stock out in a month. The buyer reports that the blouses "won't move." What she means is that the demand for blouses at $29.95 isn't enough to get the merchandise into customers' hands. She cuts the price to $10.95. Now the blouses start to go. In fact, they go so fast that the buyer tries to reorder— but at a much lower price than before, so that she can continue to price them at $10.95 and still make a profit. What she finds, however, is that the manufacturer can't fill her orders at the lower price she wants. There is a lot of demand for cheap blouses, but no supply.

The question is: Is there a price that will make both the supplier and the customer happy? The answer is yes—the price that will equate the quantity of blouses demanded to the quantity supplied. We can see that in the next graph.

What we have seen so far is that markets, left to themselves, will arrive at an equilibrium price at which they will clear. But markets are rarely, if ever, left to themselves. Buyers and sellers are constantly changing their tastes or experiencing changes in their incomes and costs. As a result, they will bid for more goods at the old price, or will not be willing to buy as much as before. Sellers, too, find themselves willing and able to supply larger or smaller quantities to the market at each price. What then?

The answer, of course, is that prices change. When we are willing and able to buy more, we say that demand rises, and everyone knows that the effect of rising demand is to lift prices. We can see this in the first simple graph on page 178. The solid lines show supply and demand, and equilibrium price, *before* some change—say, higher incomes—has boosted demand. The dashed line shows what happens to demand when incomes rise, and what happens to price as a result. It goes up. Of course the mechanism works in reverse. If incomes fall, so does demand, and so does price.

Just to round the thing out, we can also show in a graph what happens when sellers are less willing to supply goods at the same quantities, perhaps due to a rise in costs. When supply decreases,

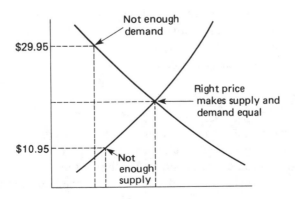

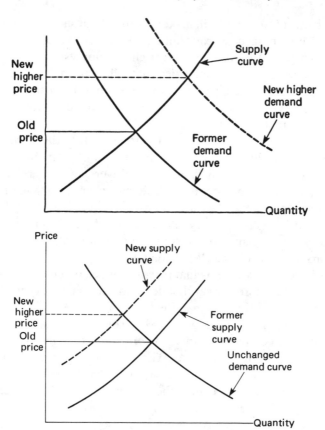

prices rise, as the second figure above makes plain. If supply increases, prices fall, as we can also see.

And of course both supply and demand can change at the same time, and often do. The outcome can be higher or lower prices, or even unchanged prices, depending on how the new balance of market forces works out.

RATIONING

Market prices interest us for many reasons, but perhaps none is so important as the *rationing* function that prices carry out.

That always comes as a surprise. We think of rationing as a formal, inflexible way of sharing goods—one ticket, one loaf of bread. This seems just the opposite of the free, unimpeded flux of the market-place. And in some ways it is indeed as different as can be. Just the same, the price mechanism performs a rationing function, exactly as do ration tickets. Indeed, there is nothing more important to grasp than this central purpose that markets serve.

Imagine a market with ten buyers, each willing and able to buy one unit of a commodity, but each having a different maximum price that is agreeable to him. Imagine ten suppliers, each also willing and able to put one unit of supply on the market, each at a different price. Such a market might look like the table following.

Price	$11	$10	$9	$8	$7	$6	$5	$4	$3	$2	$1
Number willing and able, at above price, to:											
Buy one unit	0	1	2	3	4	5	6	7	8	9	10
Sell one unit	10	9	8	7	6	5	4	3	2	1	0

As we can see, the equilibrium price will lie at six dollars, for at this price there will be five suppliers of one unit each and five purchasers of one each. But look what this shows us. All the buyers who can afford and are willing to pay the equilibrium price (or more) will get the goods they want. All those who cannot, will not. So, too, all the sellers who are willing and able to supply the commodity at its equilibrium price or less will be able to consummate sales. All those who cannot will not.

Thus the market, in establishing an equilibrium price, has in effect allocated the goods among some buyers and withheld it from others. It has permitted some sellers to do business and denied that privilege to others. Note that the market is in this way a means of excluding certain people from economic activity, namely, customers with too little money or with too weak desires or suppliers unwilling or unable to operate at a certain price.

Our view of the price system as a rationing mechanism helps to clarify the meaning of two words we often hear as a result of intervention into the market-rationing process: shortage and surplus.

When we say there is a shortage of housing for low-income groups, the everyday meaning is that people cannot find enough housing. Yet in every market there are always some buyers who are unsatisfied. We have previously noted, for instance, that in our tiny market, all buyers who could not or would not pay six dollars had to go without. Does this mean there was a shortage?

No one uses that word to describe the outcome of a normal market, even though there are always buyers and sellers who are excluded from it. Then what does "shortage" mean? We can see now that "shortage" usually refers to a situation in which some non-market agency, such as the government, fixes the price *below the equilibrium price.* As a result, some buyers who would ordinarily have been priced out of the market remain in the market, although there are not enough goods offered to satisfy their demands. The result tends to be queues in stores to buy things before they are gone, under-the-counter deals to get on a preferred list, or black or gray markets selling goods illegally at higher prices than are officially sanctioned.

The opposite takes place with a surplus. Suppose the government sets a price floor above the equilibrium price, for instance, when the government supports a crop above its free-market price.

In this situation, the quantity supplied is greater than that demanded. In a free market, the price would fall until the two quantities were equal. But if the government continues to support the commodity, then the quantity bought by private industries does not have to be as large as the quantity offered by farmers. Unsold amounts—the surplus—will be bought by government.

Thus the words "shortage" and "surplus" mean situations in which sellers and buyers remain active and unsatisfied *because the price mechanism has not eliminated them.* This is very different from a free market where buyers and sellers who cannot meet the going price are not taken into account. Most people, who have no demand for fresh caviar at eighty dollars per tin, do not complain of a caviar shortage. If the price of fresh caviar were set by government decree at one dollar a pound, there would soon be a colossal shortage.

What about the situation with low-cost housing? Essentially what we mean when we talk of a shortage of inexpensive housing is that we view the outcome of this particular market situation with non-economic eyes and pronounce the result distasteful. By the standards of the market, the poor who cannot afford to buy housing are only one more example of the rationing process that takes place in every market. When we single out certain goods or services (such as a doctor's care) as being in "short supply," we imply that we do not approve of the price mechanism as the appropriate means of allocating scarce resources in these particular instances. Our disapproval does not imply that the market is not as efficient a distributor as ever. What we do not like is the outcome of the market-rationing process. The underlying distribution (or maldistribution) of income clashes with other standards of the public interest that we value more highly than efficiency.

That word *efficiency* brings us to the last and perhaps most important aspect of how markets work. This is the ability of markets to allocate goods and services more effectively than other systems of rationing, particularly planning in one form or another.

There is no question that the market is one of the most extraordinary social inventions in human history. If we recall the attributes of the premarket societies of antiquity, we may remember that they typically suffered from two difficulties. If they were run mainly by tradition, they tended to be inert, passive, changeless. It's very hard to get things done in a traditional economy, if anything has to be done in a new way.

A command system, ancient or modern, has a different inherent problem. As we will see in Chapter 20, it is good in undertaking big projects but not in running a complex system. In addition, the presence of political power in the economic mechanism, either as a large bureaucracy or as an authority capable of sticking its nose into daily life, becomes an endless source of inefficiency.

Against these two difficulties, the price system has two great advantages: it is highly dynamic and it is self-enforcing. That is, on the one hand it provides an easy avenue for change to enter the system; on the other, it permits economic activity to take place without anyone overseeing the system.

The second (self-enforcing) attribute of the market is especially useful with regard to the rationing function. In place of ration tickets, with their almost inevitable black markets or cumbersome inspectorates or queues of customers trying to be first in line, the price system operates without any kind of visible administration apparatus

GAS RATIONING, WITH AND WITHOUT TEARS

Although we now understand that the price system is a rationing system, when we say "rationing" we usually mean a system of coupons or publicly determined priorities. If there were a permanent shortage of gasoline—meaning that at going prices, the quantity of gas sought would be larger than the quantity offered—we might ration by allowing each car owner an equal amount or by assuring that certain vehicles, such as ambulances, always had first crack at supplies.

No sooner do we begin to think about rationing by coupon or by priority than we begin to see the complexity of the problem. Clearly, the purpose of rationing is to prevent rich people from riding about in Cadillacs while poor people can't afford the gas to ride to work in their Hondas.

Imagine that you were in charge of nonprice rationing. Suppose that the number of gallons of gas expected to be available were 100 billion. Would you now determine the basic ration by dividing this number by the population, giving each person an equal allotment? That would enormously benefit a family with one car and many children, and penalize a single person who might desperately depend on his car. And what would a family do if it got its coupons but did not own a car? Would you perhaps ration supplies per car owner, rather than per person? Here, of course, the trouble is that you would be giving the same allotment to all car owners, without knowing their respective needs. Some owners would be desperate for supplies. Other owners, who hardly used their cars, would not need all their coupons.

Now suppose you issued to each adult a book of coupons entitling him to his basic allotment of gallons, and *you allowed individuals to buy or sell these coupons!* To be sure, rich citizens would be in a position to buy up coupon books, but poor citizens would not have to sell their books. If they needed their basic allotment, they would keep their coupons. If they did not need their allotment, they could supplement their income by selling it.

The point of such a plan is to use the market as a means by which individuals can determine their own economic activities according to their marginal utilities, and to combine that use with the overall fairness that a market may not attain. The ration books would insure a basically democratic sharing of one part of the national wealth, but they would permit individuals to maximize their utilities in a way that rationing alone would not.

---

or side effect. The energies that must go into planning or the frictions that come out of it are alike rendered unnecessary by the self-policing market mechanism (see box on page 182).

On the other hand, the system has the defects of its virtues. If it is efficient and dynamic, it is also devoid of values. It recognizes no valid claim to the goods and services of society except those of wealth and income. Those with income and wealth are entitled to the goods and services that the economy produces; those without income and wealth receive nothing.

This blindness of the market to any claim on society's output except wealth or income creates very serious problems. It means that those who inherit large incomes are entitled to large shares of output, even though they may have produced nothing themselves. It means that individuals who have no wealth and who cannot pro-duce—perhaps because they are ill, or simply because they cannot find work—have no way of gaining an income through the economic mechanism. To abide just by the market system of distribution, we would have to be willing to tolerate individuals starving on the street.

Therefore, every market society interferes to some extent with the outcome of the price-rationing system. It does so when an "economic problem" crosses the line to become a "social problem." In times of emergency the nation issues special permits that take precedence over money and thereby prevents the richer members of society from buying up all the supplies of scarce and costly items. In de-pressed areas, it may distribute basic food or clothing to those who have no money to buy them. Historically speaking, it has used taxes and transfers to an ever-increasing extent to redistribute the ration tickets of money in accordance with the prevailing sense of justice, rather than by the standards of efficiency. It is, in fact, in the tension between the claims of efficiency and those of justice that much of the division between conservative and liberal points of view is to be found.

FIFTEEN

Where Markets Fail

Up to this point we have been concerned with how markets work. Now we must look into two situations where they don't. One of these has to do with instances where marketers have no way of making intelligent decisions and where, therefore, the results of the market will reflect ignorance, luck, or accident rather than informed behavior. The second case involves a large category of production that we call public goods—goods that escape the ministrations of the market entirely.

THE PREVALENCE OF IGNORANCE

The whole market system is built on the assumption that individuals are *rational* as well as acquisitive—that marketers will have at least roughly accurate information about the market. A good example of the importance of information is the situation faced by the tourist in a bazaar of a country where he or she doesn't know a word of the language. Such a buyer has no way of knowing what the price of an article ought to be. That's why tourists so often return triumphantly with their bazaar trophies—only to discover that the same items were for sale in their hotel at half the price.

Without correct or adequate information marketers obviously cannot make correct decisions. But typically marketers do *not* have adequate information. Consumers guide themselves by hearsay, by casual information picked up by random sampling, or by their susceptibility to advertising. Who has time to investigate which brand of toothpaste is really best or even tastes best? Even professional buyers, such as industrial purchasing agents, cannot know every price of every product, including all substitutes.

The lack of information can be remedied, at least up to a point, but the remedy costs money or its equivalent—time. Few of us have the resources or patience to do a complete research job on every item we buy, nor would it even be necessarily rational to do so. Thus a certain amount of ignorance always remains in all markets, causing prices and quantities to differ from what they would be if we had complete information. These differences can be very great, as anyone knows who has ever discovered, with sinking heart, that he or she paid "much too much" for a given article or sold it for "much too little."

Another important cause of market failure lies in the destabilizing effect of "perverse" expectations. Suppose that a rise in prices sets off rumors that prices will rise still more. This is common experience in inflationary times, when the mounting prices of goods leads us to expect that prices will be still higher tomorrow. In this case, we do not act as ordinary demanders, curtailing our purchases as prices go up. Instead, we all rush in, with the result that prices go higher still. Meanwhile, sellers, seeing prices go up, may decide not to take advantage of good times by increasing their offerings, but to hold back, waiting for tomorrow. Thus demand goes up and supply goes down—a recipe for skyrocketing markets.

Such perverse price movements can lead to very dangerous consequences. They play a major role in the cumulative, self-sustaining processes of inflation or collapse. They can cause commodity prices to shoot to dizzying heights or plummet to the depths. At its worst, perverse behavior threatens to make an entire economy go out of control, as in the case of hyperinflations or panics. At best, it disrupts smooth, orderly markets and brings shocks and dislocations to the economy.

Can these market failures be remedied? Some can; some cannot. Ignorance can certainly be reduced by better economic reporting or by truth-in-advertising laws. Perverse behavior can be lessened by persuasive pronouncements from important public figures.

But we must recognize that there is a residue of arbitrariness even in the best-intentioned remedies. Take the matter of consumer information. We "inform" the consumer, through labels on cigarette packages, that smoking is dangerous, but we do not prohibit the advertising of cigarettes. We spread market information by having the incomprehensible contents of medications printed on their containers, but we allow the consumer to be misinformed through advertising that claims superiority of one kind of aspirin over another.

Why? There is no clear rationale in these cases. Essentially we are trying to repair omissions in the market system—injecting information so that consumers can make better choices—without becoming paternalistic. Perhaps we think it is better to allow the consumer to make some mistakes than to allow the government to make them for him.

That is perhaps as it should be. But the consequence is that the market will continue to produce less than wholly satisfactory or efficient results because a residue of ignorance or misinformation is allowed to remain—or remains despite our best efforts.

PUBLIC GOODS

Now we must turn to the range of problems that derive from the fact that certain kinds of output in our system do not have the characteristics of ordinary goods or services *because they are not sold.* That is, they never enter the market system in the first place, so it is not surprising that the market cannot allocate them. We call such outputs public goods. Since public goods are not easy to define, let us start by illustrating the properties of goods such as defense, the national weather service, or lighthouses. Such goods have three peculiar characteristics:

First, the consumption of a public good by one individual does not interfere with its consumption by another. A lighthouse is as effective for ten boats as for one. A weather service is as useful for one hundred million TV viewers as for one hundred. By way of contrast, private goods cannot be consumed in the same way. The food, clothing, or doctors' services that I use cannot also be consumed by you.

Second, no one can be excluded from the use of a public good. I can deny you the use of my car. There is no way of denying you the use of "my" national defense system.

ANOTHER REASON WHY ECONOMISTS DISAGREE

Markets "clear," equating supply and demand, without the bureaucratic problems of nonmarket allocations. No one disagrees with that. *But how long will they take to clear? How much political and social disarray will they create in the process of clearing?* There is lots of room to disagree about that. It is in fact another of the reasons that economists often fail to see eye to eye about things.

By and large, conservative economists stress the speed of market clearing and minimize the side effects that a market's dynamism creates. That's why, for example, conservative economists want to take off rent controls. They see a rapid end to housing "shortages" and a minimal degree of social distress caused by removing the ceilings. Liberal economists see things just the other way around. They see the market taking a long time, perhaps years, before it has brought supply and demand into balance. Meanwhile, they see the problems of the dislodged poor and the "unjust" profits of lucky landlords.

Which side is right? The answer is not merely one of establishing (if we could) a timetable for market movements or a count of the persons affected by its movement. It is also a matter of the importance we attach to the benefits of those whom a free market assists, versus the costs to those who are shouldered aside. There is no "right" answer to these questions, and that is why economists will continue to disagree about such things as taking off rent controls.

Last, and most important of all, public goods can be provided only by collective decisions. My private consumption depends on my individual decision to spend or not spend my income. But there is no way that I can, by myself, buy defense, weather services, or a lighthouse service.* We must not only agree to buy the public good or services, but agree how much to buy!

*Not even if I were immensely rich or an absolute monarch? In that case we would not have a market system, but a command economy catering to one person. Then indeed there would be no distinction between public and private goods.

Not all public goods are entirely "pure." Highways, education, the law courts, or sanitation services are not so universally available as lighthouse or defense. The amount of education, road space, court time, or garbage service that I consume does affect the amount left over for you. It is possible to exclude some citizens from schools or roads. But even these less-perfect examples share in the third basic attribute of public goods. They must all be produced by collective decisions, usually by the voting system of the community.

Because of their characteristics, all public goods share a common difficulty. *Their provision cannot be entrusted to the decision-making mechanism of the market.*

In the use of ordinary goods, each person can consume only as much as that person buys. Here the market works very well. By way of contrast, in the use of public goods each person will not buy an amount that he or she really wants, because each can enjoy the goods that someone else buys. Do not forget that there is no way of excluding others from the use of a pure public good (or from most not-so-pure ones). Therefore, each of us would try to get a free ride if we attempted to use the market to determine the level of output.

An example may help. Lighthouse service is a pure public good. Why couldn't we make it a private good? The answer is that no boat owner would be willing to pay what the lighthouse is actually worth to him. Why should he? So long as someone else builds a lighthouse, the boat owner can enjoy its services free!

How do we then determine the level of provision of such goods? By eschewing the useless market mechanism and availing ourselves of another means of decision making: voting. We vote for the amount of public goods we want; and because voting is a curious mechanism, sometimes we oversupply ourselves with these goods and sometimes we undersupply ourselves. One of the reasons that voting is a curious mechanism is that there is no way of doling it out in pieces, the way we spend our income. Our vote is Yes or No. As a result, we swim in defense and starve in prison reform because defense has "friends in Congress" and prisons do not.

Is there a remedy for the problem? Some economists have suggested that we should try to bring as many public goods as possible into the market system by getting rid of their public characteristics.

We could charge admission to the city's parks, so that we could produce only as much park service as people were willing to buy. We could charge tolls on all roads, even streets,, and limit the building or repair of highways to the amount of private demand for road services. We might limit the use of law courts to those who would hire the judge and jury, or ask the police to interfere on behalf of only those citizens who wore a badge attesting to their contribution to the police fund.

Such a privatization of public goods might indeed bring the level of their production up, or down, to the amount that we would consume if they were strictly private goods, like cars or movie tickets. The problems are twofold. First, there are innumerable technical difficulties in making many public goods into private ones. Imagine the problems in charging a toll for each city street!

Second, and more arresting, the idea offends our sense of justice. Suppose that we could convert defense into a private good. The defense system would then defend only those who bought its services. Presumably the more you bought, the better you would be defended. Few believers in democracy would like to see our national defense converted into a bastion for the rich. Nor would we remove from public use the law courts, the schools, the police, and so on. Unlike private goods, which we have the privilege of buying from our incomes, public goods are thought of as our rights.

There are valid arguments and clever techniques for returning some public goods into the market's fold. The main point to keep in mind that it is impossible to make all goods private; and for the ones that should remain public, the market cannot be used to establish a desirable level of output. Here the market mechanism must give way to a political method of making economic decisions.

EXTERNALITIES

Our last instance of market failure is closely connected with the attributes of public goods. It is the problem of allowing for what economists call the externalities of production; that is, for the effects of the output of private goods and services on persons other than those who are directly buying or selling or using the goods in question.

The standard example of an externality is the smoke from the local factory. The smoke imposes medical bills and cleaning bills on households that may not use any of the factory's output. Or take the noise near a jetport. That damages the eardrums—and lowers the real estate vaues—of individuals who may never benefit from the propinquity of the airport, indeed who may never fly.

Externalities bring us to one of the most vexing and sometimes dangerous problems in our economic system—controlling pollution.

What is pollution, from an economic point of view? It is the production of wastes, dirt, noise, congestion, and other things we do not want. Although we don't think of smoke, smog, traffic din, and traffic jams as part of society's production, these facts of economic life are certainly the consequences of producing things we do want. Smoke is part of the output process that also gives us steel or cement. Smog arises from the production of industrial energy and heat, among other things. Traffic is a by-product of transportation. In current jargon, economists call these unwanted by-products "bads," to stress their relation to things we call "goods."

The basic reason that externalities exist is technological: we do not know how to produce many goods cleanly; i.e., without wastes and noxious by-products. But there is also an economic aspect to the problem. Even when we do know how to produce cleanly, externalities can exist because it is the cheapest way to do many things, some having to do with producing goods, some with consuming them. It is cheaper to litter than to buy waste cans (and less trouble, too); cheaper to pour wastes into a river than to clean them up. That is, it is cheaper for the individual or the firm, but it may not be cheaper for the community. A firm may dump its wastes in a river "for free," but people living downstream will suffer the costs of having to cope with polluted water.

Finally, we should note that some externalities are not "bads," but "goods." A new office building may increase the property value of a neighborhood. Here is a positive externality. The benefit gained by others results from the new building but is not paid to the owners of that building. Such externalities give some private goods the partial attributes of public goods.

Faced with the ugly view of smoke belching from a factory chimney, sludge pouring from a mill into a lake, automobiles choking a city, or persons being injured by contaminants, most ecologically concerned persons cry for regulation: "Pass a law to forbid smoky chimneys or sulfurous coal. Pass a law to make mills dispose of their wastes elsewhere or purify them. Pass a law against automobiles in the central city."

What are the economic effects of regulation? Essentially, the idea behind passing laws is to internalize a previous externality. That is, a regulation seeks to impose a cost on an activity that was previously free for the individual or firm—although not free, as we have seen, for society. This means that individuals or firms must stop the polluting activity entirely or bear the cost of whatever penalty is imposed by law, or else find ways of carrying out their activities without giving rise to pollution.

Is regulation a good way to reduce pollution? Let us take the case of a firm that pollutes the environment in the course of producing goods or services. Suppose a regulation is passed, enjoining that firm to install antipollution devices—smoke scrubbers or waste-treatment facilities. Who bears this cost?

The answer seems obvious at first look: The firm must bear it. But if the firm passes its higher costs along in higher selling prices, we arrive at a different answer. Now a little economic analysis will show us that the cost is in fact borne by three groups, not just by the firm. First, the firm will bear some of the cost because at the higher price, it will sell less output. How much less depends on the price sensitivity of demand for its product. But unless demand is totally insensitive, its sales and income must contract.

Two other groups also bear part of the cost. One group is the factors of production—labor and the owners of physical resources. Fewer factors will be employed because output has fallen. Their loss of income is therefore also a part of the economic cost of antipollution regulation. Last, of course, is the consumer. Prices will rise so that the consumer must also bear some share of the cost of regulation.

Offsetting all these costs is the fact that each of these three groups and the general public now have a better environment. There is no reason, however, why each of these three groups, singly or collectively, should think that its benefit outweighs its costs. Most of the benefit is likely to go to the general public, rather than to the individuals actually involved in the production or consumption of the polluting good or service.

Thus a regulation forcing car manufacturers to make cleaner engines will cost the manufacturers some lost sales, will cost the consumer added expense for a car, and will cost lost income for whatever land, labor, and capital is no longer employed at higher production costs. As part of the public, all three groups will benefit from cleaner air, but each is likely to feel its specific loss more keenly than its general gain.

Is regulation useful? Regulations are good or bad, *mainly depending on their ease of enforcement.* Compare the effectiveness of speed limits, which attempt to lessen the externality of accidents, and of regulations against littering. It is difficult enough to enforce speed laws, but it is almost impossible to enforce antilittering laws. On the other hand, regulation of the disposal of radioactive wastes is simpler to enforce because the polluters are few and easily supervised.

This in turn is largely a matter of cost. If we were prepared to have traffic policemen posted on every mile of highway or every city block, regulation could be just as effective for speed violations or littering as for radioactive waste disposal. Obviously the cost would be horrendous, and so would most people's reaction to being overpoliced.

A second way to cope with pollution is to tax it. When a government decides to tax pollution (often called effluent charges), it is essentially creating a price system for disposal processes. If an individual company found that it could clean up its own pollutants more cheaply than paying the tax, it would do so, thereby avoiding the tax. If the company could not clean up its own pollutants more cheaply than the tax cost, which is often the case, it would pay the necessary tax and look to the state to clean up the environment.

The effluent charge looks like, but is not, a license to pollute. It is a license that allows you to produce some pollutants for a price.

As a result of effluent charges, an activity that was formerly costless is no longer so. Thus, in terms of their economic impacts, these charges are just like government regulations. In fact, they *are* a type of government regulation. The difference is that each producer can decide whether it pays to install clean-up equipment and not pay the tax, or to pollute and pay whatever tax costs are imposed.

Which is better, regulation or taxation? Practical considerations are likely to decide. For example, taxation on effluents discharged into streams is likely to be more practical than taxation on smoke coming from chimneys. The state can install a sewage tratment plant, but it cannot clean up air that is contaminated by producers who find it cheaper to pay a pollution tax than to install smoke-suppressing equipment. Moreover, to be effective, a pollution tax should vary with the amout of pollution; a paper mill or a utility plant would pay more taxes if it increased its output of waste or smoke. One of the problems with taxation is that of installing monitoring equipment. It is difficult to make accurate measurements of pollution or to allow for differences in environmental harm caused by the same amount of smoke coming from two factories located in different areas.

The third way of dealing with pollution is to subsidize polluters to stop polluting. In this case the government actually pays the offending parties to clean up the damage they have caused or to stop causing it. For example, a township might lessen the taxes on a firm that agreed to install filters on its stacks. This is, of course, paying the firm to stop polluting.

There are cases when subsidies may be the easiest way to avoid pollution. For example, it might be more effective to pay home-owners to turn in old cans and bottles than to try to regulate their garbage-disposal habits or to tax them for each bottle or can thrown away. Subsidies may therefore sometimes be expedient means of achieving a desired end, even if they may not be the most desirable means from other points of view.

THE MARKET IN REVIEW

In one way, the problem of externalities differs markedly from the problem of public goods. The difference is that it is possible to allow the market system itself to handle the otherwise hidden costs of pollution by using the various techniques we have examined. There is no way of using the market to determine the output or consumption of, say, the system of justice.

Therefore, in offsetting externalities in the production of private goods, we avoid some of the arbitrariness that troubles us in the provision of public goods. We can internalize the costs of pollution in a way that we cannot privatize the costs or benefits of public goods.

Nonetheless, we must keep in mind one theme of this chapter. It is that a market system has weak spots or ineffective areas peculiar to its institutional nature. The remedy requires political intervention of one kind or another—regulation, taxation, or subsidy—for there is no recourse other than political action when the self-regulating economic mechanism fails.

This is not a conclusion that should be interpreted as a kind of general plea for more government. Many economists who severely criticize the market want less government—certainly less bureaucratic, nonparticipatory, nondemocratic government. The point, however, is to recognize that the existence and causes of market malfunction make *some* government intervention inescapable. We can then seek to use government power to repair individual market failures in order to strengthen the operation of the system as a whole.

After so much criticism of the market system, perhaps it is well to conclude by recalling its strengths. Basically they are two. *First, the market encourages individuals to exert energies, skills, ambition, and risk taking in the economic pursuits of life. This gives to market systems a high degree of flexibility, vitality, inventiveness, changefulness.* For all their failures, the market economies have displayed astonishing growth, and the source of that growth lies ultimately in the activities of their marketers.

Second, the system minimizes the need for government supervision, although for reasons we now understand it cannot dispense with it. It would be a mistake to suppose that every instance of government intervention is an abridgement of freedom, or that every area of market activity is an exemplar of liberty. The truth is that government and market are equally capable of promoting liberty or giving rise to oppression. Nonetheless, in a world in which concentration of government power has been one of the greatest scourges of mankind, there is clearly something to be said for the existence of a mechanism capable of handling the basic economic tasks of society with but a minimal dependence on political authority.

SIXTEEN

A Look at Big Business

Monopoly—and nowadays oligopoly—are bad words to most people, just as competition is a good word, although not everyone can specify exactly what is good or bad about them.* Often we get the impression that the aims of the monopolist are evil and grasping, while those of the competitor are wholesome and altruistic. Therefore the essential difference between a world of pure competition and one of very impure competition seems to be one of motives and drives—of well-meaning competitors and ill-intended monopolists.

The truth is that exactly the same economic motives drive the monopoly and the competitive firm. Both seek to maximize their profits. Indeed, the competitive firm, faced with the necessity of watching costs and revenues in order to survive, is apt to be, if anything, more penny-pinching and more intensely profit-oriented

---

*Monopoly in its pure form is a rarity. Most big corporations operate in a market structure of oligopoly rather than monopoly. In an oligopolistic market situation, a few sellers divide the bulk of the market. Sometimes there is a long tail of smaller competitors who share the leftovers.

The soap industry is a typical oligopoly. In 1982 there were over 642 makers of soaps and detergents, but the top 4 in that industry accounted for 60 percent of the market. In tires and tubes, 108 companies made up the industry, but the top 4 cornered about two thirds of all sales. In automobiles and car bodies, the top 4 manufacturers out of 284 had 92 percent of the domestically produced sales. (Imports have now taken 25 percent of the total market.)

than the monopolist, who (as we shall see) can afford to take a less hungry attitude toward profits. Bad motives have nothing to do with the problem of less-than-perfect competition.

Then what is so good about competition? In theory, the answer is very clear. In a purely competitive market, the consumer is king. Indeed, the rationale of such a market is often described as *consumer sovereignty.*

The term means two things. First, in a purely competitive market the consumer determines the allocation of resources by virtue of his or her demand. The public calls the tune to which the businessman dances. Second, the consumer enjoys goods that are sold as cheaply and produced as abundantly as possible. In a purely competitive market, each firm is producing the goods consumers want, in the largest quantity and at the lowest cost possible.

In an imperfectly competitive market the consumer loses much of this sovereignty. Firms have *strategies,* including the strategy of influencing consumer demand: the advertising firm tries to get the consumer to dance to its jingle. Goods are not sold as cheaply as possible, but with a "monopolistic" profit; and because prices are not rock-bottom, the volume of goods sold to the public is not as high as it could be.

THE COSTS OF IMPERFECT COMPETITION

No one contests these general theoretical conclusions. How important are they, however, in actuality? Here the problem becomes muddier.

Take the question of consumer demand. In 1867 we spent an estimated $50 million to persuade consumers to buy products. In 1900, advertising expenditures were $500 million. In 1990 they were $20 billion—roughly one tenth as much as we spend on primary and secondary education. Indeed, advertising expenditures can be considered as a vast campaign to educate individuals to be good consumers.

To what extent does advertising infringe on consumer sovereignty? The question is perplexing. For one thing, it is no longer possible to think of consumers as having "natural" tastes, once we go beyond a subsistence economy. For that reason, much advertising has a genuine informational purpose. People do have to be made aware that it is possible (and imaginable) for, say, a factory worker to take a vacation by airplane rather than in the family car.

Moreover, numerous efforts to create tastes have failed. In the mid 1950s the Ford Motor Company poured a quarter of a billion dollars into a new car, the Edsel, and spent prodigious amounts on advertising to make the American public like it. The public did not, and the car had to be discontinued. So, too, consumers spontaneously decided to buy small sports cars, beginning in the 1950s; and after valiant efforts to turn the tide, American manufacturers capitulated and admitted that American car buyers do want small cars.

Yet it is obvious that all advertising is not informational, and that consumers' tastes are manipulated to a considerable (although not clearly measurable) degree. We are mainly creatures of brand preference, not because we have sampled all the choices and made up our minds, but as a result of advertising exposure. It is difficult to contemplate the battles of aspirin, soap (up to 10 percent of the price of soap is selling expense), cars, and beer without recognizing that much of this is a sheer waste of resources and talents. Worst of all is the effect of advertising in making the consumer a mere target of opportunity, shamelessly manipulating his or her image of life through little dramas of sparkling kitchen floors and gleaming hair.

Product differentiation—making one brand of toothpaste recognizably different from another—is also an ambiguous case. Few would deny that the proliferation of brands is often carried to the point of absurdity and, more important, to the point of substantial economic waste.

Yet, as with advertising, the question is where to draw the line. Where product differentiation results in variations in the actual product and not merely in its image, one must ask whether an affluent society should aim to produce the largest possible quantity of standardized product at the least possible cost or to offer an array of different products that please our palates, admittedly at somewhat higher cost. Few consumers in a rich society would prefer an inexpensive uniform to more expensive, individualized clothes. From this point of view, even the wasteful parade of car styles has a certain rationale.

Thus, as with advertising, *some* production differentiation plays a useful and utility-increasing function. The question is, how much? It is difficult to form a purely objective judgment. No doubt there is a real pleasure in variety, although one doubts that it would take the form of a yearning for "this year's model" without a good deal of external stimulation. The proliferation of brands is in part an effort to maximize the public's utilities (or pleasures); in part an effort to *create* those utilities to maximize the producer's profits.

What about the second main attribute of consumer sovereignty—the ability to buy goods as cheaply as possible? To what extent does oligopoly introduce inefficiency into the system?

Once again the evidence in fact is murkier than in theory. For one thing, we tend to leap to the conclusion that a competitive firm is also an efficient one. Is this really so? Suppose that the competitive firm cannot afford the equipment that might lead to economies of large-scale production. Suppose it cannot afford large expenditure on research and development. Suppose its workers suffer from low morale and therefore do not produce as much as they might.

These are not wild suppositions. There is good evidence that many large firms are more efficient, in terms of productivity per man-hour, than small firms, although of course some large, monopolistic firms tolerate highly inefficient practices simply because of the lack of competition. Big businesses generate higher rates of technical progress than small, competitive firms, and may well justify their short-run monopoly profits by long-run technical progress.

Once again, however, we must consider the other side. Profits in monopolistic industries as a whole are 50 to 100 percent higher than those in competitive industries. In certain fields, such as prescription medicines, there is evidence that consumers are sometimes badly exploited. Over-the-counter brand-name aspirins sell for up to three times the cost of nonbrand versions of the identical product. Certain medicines, such as antibiotics and the like, have enjoyed enormous profits—which is to say, have forced consumers to pay far more than they would have had to pay were the rate of profit a competitive one.

To turn the coin over once more, a further complication is introduced by virtue of the fact that oligopolies have often provided more agreeable working conditions, more handsome offices, and safer plants than have small competitive firms. Thus some of the loss of consumers' well-being is regained in the form of workers' well-being. Needless to say, this is not solely the result of a kindlier attitude on the part of big producers, but reflects their sheltered position against the harsh pressures of competition. Nonetheless, the gains in work conditions and morale are real and must be counted in the balance.

BUSINESS AND POWER

Thus the economic balance sheet is by no means simple to draw up. The advantages are not all on one side, the disadvantages on the other. Although we take the model of pure competition as a baseline for efficiency and economic "virtue," we find in fact that the world is more complicated than that.

There is, however, one final consideration. It concerns power. Economists do not speak much about power because in the competitive situation which is taken as the norm, power disappears. At the core of the idea of consumer sovereignty is the idea that the firm does not have power, that business cannot impose its will either on those it hires or on those it serves.

Clearly this is not true in the real world of imperfect competition. That is why the issue of how to control power becomes of increasing consequence—not just in the sphere of government, where it has always been a central concern of philosophers and political thinkers, but in the private spheres of business and labor. The question takes on even larger significance when we recognize that the field in which corporations exert their power is more and more the entire globe, not just one country. The multinational corporation, drawing its supplies from one part of the world, locating its production facilities in another, selling its products in a third, is a new dimension to business whose implications we still do not fully grasp. We shall devote a chapter to it later in the book.

In the meantime, however, the question remains: what to do about the big corporations within their national boundaries? Here are some of the suggested answers:

Do Nothing

The first suggestion is most prominently associated with the name of Milton Friedman, the philosophic conservative whose monetarist views we have already encountered in Chapter 11. Friedman's response to the question of what a corporation should do to discharge its social responsibility is very simple: Make money.

The function of a business organization in society, argues Friedman, is to serve as an efficient agent of production, not as a locus of social improvement. It serves that productive function best by striving after profit—conforming, while doing so, to the basic rules and legal norms of society. It is not up to business to "do good"; and it is up to government to prevent it from doing bad.

Moreover, says Friedman, as soon as a businessman tries to apply any rules other than moneymaking, he takes into his own hands powers that rightfully belong to others, such as political authorities. Friedman would even forbid corporations to give money to charities or universities. Their business, their responsibility to society, he insists, is production. Let the dividend receivers give away the money the corporations pay them, but do not let corporations become the active social-welfare agencies of society.

Ask Corporations to Be Professionally Responsible

It is interesting to note that few corporate heads espouse Friedman's position. They take the view that the corporation, by virtue of its immense size and strength, has power thrust upon it, whether it wishes to have it or not. The solution to this problem, as these men see it, is for corporate executives to act professionally in using this power, doing their best to judge fairly among the claims of the many groups to whom they are responsible: labor, stockholders, customers, and the public at large.

There is no doubt that many top corporate executives think of themselves as the referees among contending groups, and no doubt many of them use caution and forethought in exercising the power of decision. But the weaknesses of this argument are also not difficult to see. There are no criteria for qualifying as a responsible corporate executive. Nor is there any clear guideline, even for the most scrupulous executive, defining the correct manner in which to exercise responsibility. Should an executive's concern for the prevention of pollution take precedence over concern for turning in a good profit statement at the end of the year? Or for giving wage increases? Or for reducing the price of the product? Is the company's contribution to charity or education supposed to represent the executive's preferences or those of customers or workers? Has Mobil a right to help the cause of public broadcasting; the makers of firearms to help support the National Rifle Association?

These questions begin to indicate the complexity of the issue of social responsibility and the problems implicit in allowing important social decisions to be made by private individuals who are not publicly accountable for their actions.

Break Up the Big Firms

A third approach to the problem of responsibility takes yet another track. It suggests that the power of big business be curbed by dividing large corporations into several much smaller units. A number of studies have shown that the largest plant size needed for industrial efficiency is far smaller (in terms of financial assets) than the giant firms typical of the *Fortune* list of the top five hundred industrial corporations (or for that matter, of the next five hundred). Hence a number of economists have suggested that a very strict application of antitrust legislation should be applied, not only to prohibit mergers, but to separate a huge enterprise such as General Motors into its natural constituent units: a Buick Company, an Oldsmobile Company, a Chevrolet Company, and so on.

Only a few decades ago, there was virtually unanimous agreement among economists that a strict application of antitrust laws was one of the most effective remedies for the problems of oligopoly. Today this view is on the wane. One reason is that economists have come to recognize that an industry with one or two giant firms and a tail of small firms does not operate very differently—if at all—than does an industry with five or six leading members. Even the breakup of the aluminum industry from a near-monopoly under the domination of Alcoa to an industry in which four firms have big shares of the market does not appear to have changed aluminum prices or aluminum pricing policies. The breakup of Ma Bell has raised, not lowered, local phone bills.

Defenders of antitrust legislation do not seriously question the above views. It is not really imaginable that General Motors, for example, will ever be broken into a thousand firms each with a capitalization of over $60 million, even though GM is big enough to yield that many pieces. In all likelihood, trust-busting GM would result in the formation of three or four giant firms, each worth over $15 billion or so and each still possessing enormous market power.

Economists have also begun to pay more attention to the fact that industries dominated by big firms have the ability to create technical advances. Over time, many competitive industries have remained technologically static, whereas the oligopolistic industries—with some exceptions—have been innovators. A third consideration is the tremendous time lag involved in major antitrust cases. A big antitrust case may go on for twenty or thirty years before it is finally resolved. One may ask whether the eventual savings are worth the huge legal costs.

Finally, the zeal of the trustbusters has been dampened by increasing evidence that competition exists today on an international, not merely national scale. Recent experience has taught us that even giants like GM can be severely mauled by Japanese and German and other foreign companies. One of the strengths of these foreign firms is the government support they enjoy. Against these massive public-private competitors, fragmentation by antitrust action seems less attractive than in the days before this kind of state enterprise existed. We will look into this again when we get to the multinationals in Chapter 20.

Regulate the Giants

Regulation has been a long-standing American response to the problem of corporate power. Regulation has sought to influence or prohibit corporate actions in many fields: pricing, advertising, designing products, dealing with unions or minority groups, and still other areas. Given the variety of ways in which corporations are regulated, it is hardly surprising that the effectiveness of the regulatory process is very uneven. Yet we can discern two general attributes that affect most regulatory agencies.

First, economic events tend to change faster than the regulations governing them. City building codes that were perfectly appropriate when adopted become obsolete and then retard the use of new techniques and materials that would be more efficient and just as safe. Why are not regulations kept abreast of events? Partly because the political process is simply slower than the economic process; partly because any regulation soon creates its own defenders. Vested interests, formed around existing codes, fight to prevent changes in the regulations. The plumber who installs the copper pipes required by law might not be the plumber who would install the plastic pipes if they were allowed.

Second, regulatory commissions often take on the view of the very industry they are supposed to regulate, because they must turn to that industry for the expertise to staff their own agencies. Thus it is common for a regulatory body to become the captive of its own agencies. Thus it is common for a regulatory body to become the captive of its own ward. The Interstate Commerce Commission, established in 1887 to regulate the railroads, is a prime example of this reversal of roles. When the ICC was established, the railroads were a monopoly that badly needed public supervision. Autos and trucks had not yet come into existence, so there were few alternative means of bulk transportation in many areas.

By the end of the first quarter of the twentieth century, however, the railway industry was no longer without effective substitutes. Cars, trucks, buses, planes, pipelines—all provided effective competition. At this point, the ICC became interested in protecting the railroads against competition rather than in curbing abuses. One by one, these alternative modes of transport fell under its aegis (or under that of other regulatory agencies), and quasi-monopoly prices were set, as little empires were established for each form of transportation.

There was much enthusiasm a few years ago for using the mechanism of the marketplace itself to restore a higher level of competition. Where regulation had created fat, comfortable semimonopolies, it was hoped that deregulation would produce lean, aggressive competitors. In some cases—the deregulation of AT&T—this was spectacularly successful (see box on page 204). In others—the scandalous disregard of reckless behavior on the part of the deregulated Savings and Loan banks—it was a national disaster. In the airline industry it was a mixed blessing. Today opinion is pragmatic. Deregulation has its place—but so does regulation. Each industry must be studied and appraised to ascertain what is best for it, and for the economy as a whole.

THE DIFFERENCE THAT COMPETITION CAN MAKE

A drama of monopoly versus competition concerns the fates of The American Telephone and Telegraph Comapny (AT&T) and International Business Machines Corporation (IBM), long among the most respected names in American firmdom. Until a few years ago, both were regarded as impregnable fortresses of technology and managerial skills. In the case of AT&T, the fortress aspect resulted from the recognition of the firm as a kind of protected monopoly, under the supervision of the public utility authorities of the states in which it operated. IBM was not so recognized, but its immense prestige and worldwide status made it tower above its pygmy competitors.

Both companies prided themselves on their far-reaching and integrated operations. Ma Bell ran a nationwide telephone system that extended from the manufacture of phones and equipment, through their installation and service, to the pursuit of both short-range and long-range scientific research. Big Blue (IBM) dominated the mainframe computer business—the high-powered computers, housed in rows of steel cabinets, that seemed, until perhaps ten years ago, the vital center of the computer industry.

Then fate entered, in the shape of two antitrust suits initiated by the Justice Department in the 1970s. To the consternation of both companies, the United States government decided to seek their breakup under the Sherman Antitrust Act, originally passed to foil the business-grabbing tactics of the nineteenth-century robber barons. To the further consternation of business leaders generally, in January 1982 the breakup of AT&T was agreed on, whereas the integrity of IBM was preserved by the government's decision to drop the case against Big Blue. At that point AT&T consisted solely of two former companies, the Bell Labs and the Western Electric Company, plus its own long-distance service. All other business was transferred to seven entirely independent regional companies—NYNEX, US West, Southwestern Bell, Pacific Telesis, Bell Atlantic, BellSouth, and Ameritech.

Here is what has happened since. The regional companies

are doing fine, still operating under the scrutiny of local public utility regulation. But Ma Bell, now free to enter new business areas, has discovered a new life. Its long-distance business is not flourishing, under competition from MCI and Sprint, but AT&T has aggressively entered new areas, including the computer field once dominated by IBM. Big Blue, on the other hand, remained locked into its chosen area—mainframe computers—for which there has been a steadily decreasing demand. Although free to expand into any field, it placed its chips on one square only.

It was the wrong square. IBM's losses in 1992 were almost $5 billion. It has had to reorganize its business from top to bottom because smaller companies, such as Microsoft, simply nibbled away at the base of the great monolith until one day it collapsed.

Moral: there is something to be said for competition.

. . .

All these difficulties make it clear that the problem of social responsibility will not be easy to solve (or for that matter, even to define), no matter what step we choose, from do-nothing laissez-faire to outright nationalization. *And for each of these problems with the corporation, we could easily construct counterparts that have to do with the control over labor unions or over the government itself.*

What, then, is to be done? A number of other lines of action suggest themselves. One is the widening of the legal responsibility of the corporation to include areas of activity for which it now has little or no accountability. Environmental damage is one of these. Consumer protection is another.

A second step would be increased public accountability through disclosure, the so-called fishbowl method of regulation. Corporations could be required to report to public agencies to make known corporate expenditures for pollution control, political lobbying, and so on. Corporate tax returns could be opened to public scrutiny. Unions and corporations both could be required to make public disclosure of their practices with regard to hiring, admission, advancement, and rates of pay for minorities.

Still another course of action would be to appoint public members to boards of directors of large companies or to executive organs of large unions and to charge these members with protecting the consumers' interest and with reporting behavior that seemed contrary to the public interest. Worker-members of boards of directors might also serve such a useful purpose (there are such members in Germany and a movement toward "workers' codetermination" in a number of other European nations).

Finally, there is the corrective action of dedicated private individuals such as Ralph Nader, who rose to fame on his exposé of the safety practices of the auto industry, and who has since turned his guns on pollution, other irresponsibilities of big business, and on poor performance in the federal bureaucracy. Such public pressure is necessarily sporadic and usually short-lived, but it has been a powerful source of social change.

But it would be a mistake to conclude this recital with the implication that corporate (or union or government) power can be easily brought under control through a few legal remedies or by the power of public opinion. Certainly many abuses can be curbed, and much better levels of social performance achieved.

Yet mass organizations seem an inescapable concomitant of our age of high technology and increasing social interdependence. Here we should note that, depending on our interests, we stress different aspects of this universal phenomenon. *To some, who fear the continued growth of very large scale business, the most significant aspect is that we have not managed to control business power. To others, concerned over the emergence of large labor unions, it is labor power that most dangerously eludes effective control. And to still others who are most worried by the growth of big government, it is the growth of public power that is the main problem.*

Thus the question of economic power remains, at best, only partially resolved. Many years ago A. A. Berle wrote: "Some of these corporations can be thought of only in somewhat the same way we have heretofore thought of nations." Unlike nations, however, their power has not been rationalized in law, fully tested in practice, or well defined in philosophy. Unquestionably, the political and social influence and the economic power of the great centers of production pose problems with which capitalism—indeed, all industrialized societies—will have to cope for many years to come.

SEVENTEEN

Rich and Poor

If you ask most people why one person's income is larger than another's, they will probably answer—assuming that the person in question isn't the recipient of a large inheritance or the victim of circumstances—that people "earn" the incomes they get. What they mean is that individuals are generally believed to get back from society some rough equivalent of what they give to it.

Economists often make the same claim, in more sophisticated language. They assert that incomes by and large reflect the "marginal productivities" of different contributors to the economic process, which is only a more complicated way of saying that individuals tend to receive incomes that approximate the value of the work they perform for others or for themselves.

Does this explanation help us understand the actual distribution of incomes we find in society? The answer, as many times before, is yes and no. It throws some light on matters because in many cases a person's productivity obviously bears on his or her income: skilled workers make more money than unskilled ones. But the importance of productivity has only slight relevance in understanding the top and bottom layers of the American income cake, where explanation is most needed.

POVERTY AND PROPERTY

In the box on page 50 we have already looked at a profile of "typical" poor families. The profile raises as many questions as it answers: there is obviously a heavy incidence of poverty among black families and families headed by women.

How do economists explain that? They don't. They turn to historians and sociologists. Clearly, when we want to explain most poverty, marginal productivity theory will not serve us well. People are not poor mainly because they are unproductive. Often they are unproductive because they are handicapped in ways that also make them poor.

What about the other end of the income scale, the top 5 percent of households enjoying incomes over $105,000 per year, or the topmost echelon of millionaires? Can marginal productivity help us explain high incomes?

It must be clear that the productivity of an individual has no connection whatsoever with the *inherited* property income that the individual receives. But what about millionaires who have earned their fortunes? Can we explain their wealth by their productive contribution to society?

Not very well. Conventional economic theory explains the accumulation of wealth by saving. Undoubtedly some persons do accumulate modest sums by refraining from consumption, but they do not accumulate fortunes. If you start with $100,000 and if you invest the sum at 10 percent, paying income tax on your interest, it would take a long time to pile up $1 million.

Very few millions are put together this way. The goal of riches seems to have two approaches. One is via the road of inheritance, the source of approximately half of today's fortunes. The other is via the road of instant riches, the main source of new fortunes and in most cases the original source of the old fortunes as well.

How does someone become rich overnight? Luck is helpful— once, anyway. People who make a fortune in one endeavor rarely go on to make as great a gain in another. Financial institutions, which employ the best expertise available, actually do not fare any better with their investments than the average performance of the stock market.

If luck seems to play a crucial role in selecting the winner, another element establishes the size of the winnings. Suppose that an inventor figures it will cost $1 million to build and equip a plant to make a newly patented product. The product should sell at a price that will bring a profit of $300,000. A bank puts up the money.

The plant is built and the expected $300,000 profit is realized. Now comes the instant fortune. To the nation's capital markets, the actual cost of the plant is of no consequence. *What counts is the rate of return on investments of the same degree of risk.* If that rate is 10 percent, the inventor's plant is suddenly worth $3 million, for this is the sum that will yield $300,000 at a 10 percent return. The inventor is now worth $2 million, over and above what he owes to the bank. He will have risen to the status of an instant millionaire because the financial markets will have capitalized his earnings into capital gains and not because his marginal productivity—or his saving—has made him rich.

PRODUCTIVITY ENTERS

When we move from property income to earned income, the explanatory power of productivity obviously becomes more relevant. There is clearly some connection between the incomes of top-earning lawyers and pilots and artists and TV newscasters, and the contribution they make to output. (We may not *like* that contribution, or we may think that it's a shame that society values the output of rock stars so highly, but that's not to deny that by market criteria their contribution to society is large.)

Yet even here there is a problem. Some of these very large earned incomes are large because hurdles have been placed in the way of acquiring these productive abilities. Of course not everyone can be a rock star, but many could be lawyers or surgeons or simply high-paid technicians if it were not for difficulties of entering the field. In other words, there exist *barriers* of race or wealth, of patents or initiation fees, of expensive training or social custom, that give rise to shelters behind which some individuals can receive incomes higher than their productivities would warrant in a wide-open market.

The other side of this story is that barriers also constitute sources of discrimination which lower the incomes of those who are prevented from earning the incomes that a free market would otherwise make available to them. The most obvious instance has to do with blacks. In virtually every field, black earnings are less than white earnings in the same jobs. In itself, of course, such facts do not prove that discrimination exists. An apologist for the differentials in wages could claim that there is a real difference in productivity of whites and blacks. In that case the question is whether there has been discrimination at a more basic level; for instance, in the access to education and training.

Only a few years ago, it would have been simple to demonstrate that blacks *were* systematically prevented from acquiring equal skills or gaining access to jobs on equal terms. Their output was lower because they were forced into the bottom jobs of society, unable to gain admission into many colleges, kept out of the high-wage trades, and simply condemned by their own past poverty to be unable to accumulate the money needed to buy an education that would allow them to compete.

This picture is now changing in some important respects. Average earnings of blacks are closer to those of whites than in the past, especially among younger workers. Among black women aged twenty-five to forty-four they are even higher than whites. This change is the result of substantial lowering of barriers against blacks entering many professions and occupations.

A second major area of discrimination militates against women. The table on page 212 compares women's pay (on a full-time, year-round basis) to that of men. As the table shows, women typically earn substantially less than men in all occupations. A portion of this differential may stem from women withdrawing from the labor force to have children and to nurture them in their early years, but there is no doubt that these "productivity" reasons for pay differentials do not begin to account for the full differences we observe.

Statistics comparing men and women at age thirty-five show that the average single woman will be on her job another thirty-one years—longer than her male counterpart will work—and the average married woman will work another twenty-four years. Second, the facts show that married women are less likely to leave one employer for another than men are. Finally, U.S. Public Health data reveal that on the average, women are absent from work slightly fewer days than are men.

In recent years we have seen a good deal of stirring for equal rights for women, and we get the impression that discrimination

PUERTO RICANS, CHICANOS, INDIANS, OTHERS

Blacks are the racial minority that attracts most attention, because of our responsibility for their "starting point"—slavery.

In point of fact, however, blacks are not the most disprivileged minority in the nation. That unhappy distinction belongs to a small group of native Americans, about whom there is not much economic information and even less concern. These are the American Indians who, according to reports from about half the Indian reservations, received incomes that were on the order of *one third* those of white families.

Another much disadvantaged group are the Hispanic minorities. We use the plural because there are in fact two such groups. One of them consists of Spanish-speaking families who are legally in residence in the United States. Their family incomes are roughly two thirds as large as white incomes, a little better than average black performance. A second group of Hispanics are illegal entrants, such as "wetback" laborers. We have no statistics about this group, but anecdotal information indicates that they are very poorly paid.

Now, a more cheerful word. If we look at income data of all ethnic groups, we find only three major groups with incomes below the national average: blacks, those of Hispanic heritage, and Indians. Of one hundred million Americans who claim ethnic backgrounds, eighty million have incomes *higher* than those of Americans who consider themselves to be ethnically native. In 1972 the ethnic groups with the highest average family income were Russians, then Poles, then Italians. Asian-Americans do very well too.

against women is disappearing. The statistics do not support this. Since 1939 the ratio of female to male earnings (for full-time, year-round workers) has risen from 59 percent only to about 65 percent.

Will it change? The Women's Liberation movement has won court battles to establish the right of equal pay for equal work, as well as

MALE AND FEMALE EARNINGS, 1990 FULL-TIME, FULL-YEAR WORKERS

Occupation	Women	Men
Professional, management	27,282	40,832
Engineers, salaried	38,626	45,224
Sales workers	16,986	29,852
Craft	18,737	26,506
Clerical	18,473	26,192
Operatives	14,606	21,986
Service workers	12,139	18,550
Nonfarm laborers	13,650	18,420

equal rights to jobs, regardless of sex. Perhaps this will begin to alter our prevailing sexist patterns.

The United States has been very slow to admit women to a full range of professional and occupational opportunities. Only about 10 percent of our doctors are women, for example, whereas in West Germany 20 percent and in Russia 70 percent are women. Perhaps even more surprising, in Sweden some years ago, most overhead crane operators were women, an occupation virtually unknown to women in the U.S. These percentages at both ends of the social scale leave little doubt that women could earn a great deal more than they do, if the barriers of discrimination were removed.

CHANGING INCOME DISTRIBUTION

Can we change the distribution of income? Of course we can. Should we? That is a more difficult question. When we speak of deliberately trying to change the distribution of income, our purpose is usually to make it fairer. By fairer, we generally mean more equal, although not always. Sometimes we say it is not fair that certain groups, such as schoolteachers, do not get higher incomes, even though they are already receiving incomes that are above the median for the society. In the discussion that follows, we will largely be concerned with ways of making income distribution fairer by making it more equal. At the end of this chapter we will take a careful look at the problems that a bias toward equality brings with it. (Meanwhile, see the box on page 214.)

Assuming that low productivity is an important reason—if not the only reason—for low incomes, someone who wants to change income distribution would do well to begin by boosting the productivity of the least skilled and trained. How? By and large, by giving education, a generalized skill, or training, a specialized skill, to those who lack them.

A glance at the following table makes it clear that there is a strong relationship between education and lifetime earnings. We must be careful not to jump to the conclusion that education is the direct cause of these earnings, however. For example, 30 percent of white high-school graduates will end up making more money than the average college graduate, and 20 percent of college graduates will make less than the average high-school graduate. Clearly there is no guarantee that education will pay off for everyone. Taking all factors into account, probably the cost of a college education gives its recipient a lifetime return of about 7 to 10 percent on that investment, hardly a bonanza.

A quite different way of going about the task of changing the income distribution is to intervene on the demand side of the market. The most widespread current intervention is that of minimum wages, whether imposed by law or unions. Minimum wages have two impacts. They raise earnings for those who are employed, but may cause other people to lose their jobs. The size of the group that is helped and the group that is hurt depends on the structure of the demand for labor and will vary from case to case. For instance, high minimum or union wages may cause many garment workers to lose jobs because their employers may move to Hong Kong. High wages

MALE EDUCATION AND AVERAGE EARNINGS, 1991

Elementary School	
8 years or less	14,023
High school	
1–3 years	15,589
4 years	22,663
College	
1–3 years	24,075
4 years or more	29,793
Graduate school	44,169

for migrant farmers may cause some pickers to lose jobs, if their employers can switch to machinery. High wages for hospital orderlies may cause little loss of jobs, because there is no way of moving the hospital or automating the job. In other words, the direct impact of enforced higher wages varies from one case to the next, and is very hard to generalize about.

A third means of altering income distribution is to tax high incomes and to subsidize low ones. Taxes and subsidies (transfers) are used by all governments to redistribute incomes. The tax system is more or less proportional—that is, it applies with an unchanging bite—on all income brackets above the lowest and below the very highest. Between twenty thousand and seventy thousand dollars, taxpayers pay about the same portion of their incomes to the government.

If we look at inheritance taxes—which hit wealth, not income—we see a system that appears to be progressive, i.e., to tax high incomes proportionately more than low ones. Maximum tax rates on estates reach as high as 30 percent. But the loopholes to avoid these estate taxes are so numerous that inheritance-tax collections have amounted to an annual wealth tax of less than 0.2 percent. Obviously, these taxes cannot have much impact on the distribution of wealth.

TOWARD A WORKING DEFINITION OF FAIRNESS

Can we specify with certainty what a fair income distribution would look like? Of course not. Can we specify a distribution of income that would accord with what most people think is fair? Here we put the question in such a way that we could test the results, for example by an opinion poll.

If we took such a poll, most persons in the United States would probably agree that existing income is not fairly distributed. They consider it unfair that some people are as poor as they are and others are as rich as they are.

Suppose we asked whether the public would approve of an income distribution that had the same shape as that for one group in which the more obvious advantages and disadvantages of the real world were minimized. *That group consists of white adult males who work full-time and full-year.* It ranges from surgeons to street sweepers. In general, these workers suffer minimally or not at all from the handicaps of race, sex, age, personal deficiencies, or bad economic policies. By examining their earnings rather than their incomes we can eliminate the effects of inherited wealth. Might not such a standard appeal to many people as constituting an operational definition of a just income distribution?

Since the poll has never been taken, we cannot answer the question. But we can examine what income distribution would look like under such a dispensation. The results are shown in the table based on 1980 data. It is interesting to note that this standard of fairness, if applied, would reduce the dispersion of income by 40 percent.

Annual earnings ($000s)	Distribution of income in accordance with "fairness" standard	Actual distribution of income, 1980
$ 0 – 4	2.7%	25.8%
4 – 8.5	8.0	19.2
8.5–12.5	15.3	16.3
12.5–17.5	20.1	14.1
17.5–25	26.9	13.5
25 –35	17.0	7.2
35 –50	6.3	2.5
50 –75	2.6	1.1
75 and over	1.1	0.4

Although taxes do not have much impact on the distribution of income, transfer payments do. If we look at the families in the bottom 20 percent of the population, we find that over 60 percent of their income comes in the form of transfer payments. Without such payments, their share of total income would be less than half of what it is now.

At the same time, existing income-transfer programs are not well coordinated. Some poor people receive a lot of benefits; other poor people receive none. Some programs provide benefits for people who, on a lifetime basis, will not be poor. Programs are often locally administered, leading to benefit levels that differ greatly from state to state. To overcome these problems, Presidents of both parties— Nixon, Ford, and Carter—have recommended the establishment of a negative income tax—an automatic payment of enough income to all families designated as poor to lift them above the poverty line.

There are two problems with these proposals. The first is that they are expensive. The second is that they are politically unpopular. Essentially they ask the better-off to shoulder the burden of aiding the not-so-well off. That may accord with our Sunday morality, but not with our workday morality. So far, the Negative Income Tax has remained an idea whose time has not yet come.

EQUITY AND EQUALITY

One last problem remains to be faced. Sooner or later, in all discussions of income distribution, the idea of equity—fairness—raises its head. Often it takes the form of bitterly opposed views on equality as the ideal form of equity. Then people become violently polarized—some claim that when all is said and done the only fair income distribution is one that aims at equality; others maintain with equal fervor that equality of incomes is as foolish (and as unattainable) as equality of talent or physique or whatever else.

The issue of equality is indeed a vexing question but it is not beyond some degree of thoughtful analysis. Let's start with the fact that most Americans—indeed, most people in the modern world—admit to an underlying bias in favor of equality in their social values. We hear of policies in every nation that seek to diminish the differences between rich and poor. We hear of very few policies that openly advocate greater inequality. Even policies that support greater inequality—for example, tax breaks for millionaires—are justified in terms of their ultimate effect in raising the incomes of all, presumably lessening poverty.

Starting with this bias in favor of equality, we need some understanding of the kind of exceptions we may make to the general rule. That is, we need to know and to look carefully at the arguments in favor of *inequality*. There are four of them.

1. We agree that inequality is justified if everyone has a fair chance to get ahead.
Most of us do not object to inequality of outcome—in fact, we generally favor it—if we are convinced that the race was run under fair conditions, with no one handicapped at the start.

What are fair conditions? That is where the argument becomes complex. Are large inheritances fair? Most Americans agree that some inheritance is fair, but that taxes should prevent the full passage of wealth from generation to generation. What about inheritances of talent? No one is much concerned about this. Inheritances of culture? For some time we have been getting exercised over the handicaps that are inherited by persons born in the slums or to nonwhite parents.

2. We agree to inequality when it is the outcome of individual preferences.
If the outcome of the economic game results in unequal incomes, we justify these inequalities when they accord with different personal desires. One person works harder than another, so he deserves a larger income. One chooses to enter the law and make a fortune; the other chooses to enter the ministry and make do with a small income. We acquiesce in these inequalities to the degree that they appear to mirror individual preferences.

3. We abide by inequality when it reflects merit.
Merit is not quite the same as fairness or personal preference. It has to do with our belief in the propriety of higher rewards when they are justified by a larger contribution to output. We do not object to people receiving different remunerations in the market when we can show that each person contributes a different amount in total output.

This is, of course, only a value judgment. Suppose there are two workers side by side on the assembly line. One is young, strong, unmarried, and very productive. The other is older, married, has a large family and many expenses—and is less productive. Should the first be compensated more highly than the second? We find ourselves in a conflict of values here. Our bias toward equality tells us no. Our exception for merit tells us yes. There is no correct solution for this or any other problem involving value judgments. Once again, social values prevail, sometimes paying the younger person more than the older, sometimes both the same, sometimes the older more.

4. Finally, we agree on violating the spirit of equality when we are convinced that inequality is for the common good.

The common good is often translated into practical terms of gross national product. Thus we may agree to allow unequal rewards because we are convinced (or persuaded) that this inequality will ultimately benefit us all by raising all incomes as well as the incomes of those who are favored. This is an argument often adduced to defend high incomes because they will lead to saving and thus enrich us all via investment.

There is an easy and a difficult question here. The easy question is to reply that there may be other ways of attaining the same end, without yielding to inequality. For instance, we can finance public investment through taxation rather than private investment through saving.

The more difficult question involves the definition of "common good." Is public investment part of the common good? There are obviously many ways of defining what we mean by that term. All incorporate value judgments. Even the common good of survival, which might justify giving a larger reward to those who must be entrusted with survival, is a value judgment. Do all societies deserve to survive? Was Nazi Germany justified in seeking survival at all costs?

These general principles do not describe the way we *should* think about inequality. They are an attempt to describe the way we *do* think about it—the arguments we commonly hear or raise ourselves to defend an unequal distribution of goods and services or of wealth.

Each of these arguments, as we can see, poses its own tangled problems. And there is every reason that they *should* be tangled, for the distribution of incomes poses the most perplexing of all economic problems to any society. At one extreme, it criticizes all the privileges and inequalilties that every society displays, forcing us to explain to ourselves why one person should enjoy an income larger than he or she can spend, while another suffers from an income too small to permit him or her a decent livelihood. At the other extreme, it forces us to examine the complications and contradictions of a society of absolutely equal incomes, where each individual (or family?) receives the same amount as every other, regardless of differences in physical capacity, life situation, and potential contribution to society.

Usually we have to compromise, to find reasons to support income distributions that are neither completely equal or completely unequal. Here is where we lean partly on our actual knowledge of the effects of income distribution on work and output, and partly on our value systems, which define allowable exceptions to our basic rule that societies should seek equality as their goal. As our values change—and we are now living in a period when values seem to be changing rapidly—we accord different weights to the various arguments by which we traditionally justify unequal incomes.*

*Here are two real-world cases to which you might wish to apply the criteria above:

1. The U.S. ratio of the pay of CEOs (chief executive officers) to that of the lowest full-time worker in their company is 125 to 1. In Europe and Japan it is 25 or 30 to 1. Could this inequality bear on the problem of national differences in productivity?

2. During the decade of the 1980s, real GNP rose by thirty percent. The real income of the bottom 60 percent of the nation remained the same. All income gains went to the top 40 percent. The basic explanation: Social Security taxes rose; income taxes fell. Is this fair?

IV

THE REST OF THE WORLD

EIGHTEEN

Pricing the Dollar

Foreign trade and international finance used to be subjects that Americans could afford to be ignorant about. In nearly all college textbooks, for examples, they were relegated to a special section at the end, and it was generally understood that if an instructor had to sacrifice any part of the course because of insufficient time, international economics was the part to go.

That has changed, and changed dramatically, within the last few years. For one thing, international trade has permeated our economy to an unprecedented degree. Imports and exports used to amount to no more than a twentieth of our GNP. Nowadays they are about a fifth. Multinational corporations have become household words—Honda and Toyota are as familiar to us as GM and Ford. For another thing, the American dollar, once the Rock of Gibraltar in a stormy world, took a terrible battering in the 1980s. Millions of Americans who always thought the dollar was as good as gold learned that it was not. The days of indifference to the world of international economics are gone forever.

THE PRICE OF A DOLLAR

In this chapter and the next we will learn something about these new realities of life. A good place to start is the vagaries of the dollar. But there is a problem here: Should we discuss the problems of a high dollar, which made headlines in Germany or France in the early 1980s, or the problems of a low dollar, which made headlines in the United States in the late 1980s? It would be tedious to go back and forth, as at a tennis match, looking at both sides of the problem. Therefore, we will zero in mainly on the particular events and characteristics of a low dollar, which has been our most recent trouble. As we will see, however, it is not at all difficult to look into a mirror and see the problems posed by a high dollar, and from time to time we will remind ourselves that there are two sides to the story. If we understand one side, the other will be easy to grasp.

Let us begin by going back to the years just before 1985, when headlines told us that the dollar was soaring. Sometimes the headlines said that the yen or mark or pound had hit new lows. All these phrases meant the same ting—but what was that thing?

When the dollar is high on the international money markets, it does not mean that a dollar will buy more *American* goods. That is a very important point to bear in mind. Our dollars are "high" in domestic purchasing power only to the extent that domestic prices fall, and they are low (or falling) in domestic purchasing power only insofar as inflation is rampant or worsening. But the purchasing power of the dollar at home does not have a direct link to its purchasing power abroad.

When we speak of a "high" dollar in international finance, we mean only one thing: A dollar will buy a lot of German marks, Swedish kronor, French francs, or whatever. As a result, it becomes cheaper to buy *foreign* goods or services. And by way of turnabout, if the dollar is "low" in the international world, it means that dollars buy few units of foreign currency, so that foreign goods become expensive.

Suppose, for example, that you enjoy French wine. French wine is sold by its producers for francs, the currency in which French producers pay their bills and want their receipts. Let us suppose that they price their wine at 20 francs the bottle.

How much would twenty-franc wine cost in America? The answer depends on the rate at which we can exchange dollars for francs— that is, it depends on the price of francs. We discover this price by going to banks, who are the main dealers in foreign currencies of all kinds, and inquiring what the dollar-franc *exchange rate* is. In the early 1980s we got up to ten francs for a dollar. To buy a bottle of French wine in those days (ignoring transportation, insurance and other such costs) would have cost us two dollars (20 francs ÷ 10 = $2).

Then in 1986 the dollar "fell." This meant that the dollar became cheaper on the market for foreign money. It followed, of course, that the franc became dearer in terms of dollars. In point of fact, when we changed a dollar into francs we no longer got 10 of them but only five. Suppose that the price of wine in France hadn't changed—that it still cost twenty francs. Because of the fall in the exchange rate, it now cost us twice as much, because we needed four dollars, not two, to buy those twenty francs.

A falling dollar therefore raises the price of foreign goods in terms of American money. Conversely, a rising, or high exchange rate, such as we experienced in 1984, cheapens them. Imagine that we were contemplating a trip to Germany in those days. We inquire into the prices of German hotels, German meals, and the like, and we are told that we can do it comfortably for (let us say) three hundred marks per day. "How much is that in American money?" we ask. The answer depends, of course, on the exchange rate. Suppose the rate is three marks to the dollar. Then three hundred marks would be the same as one hundred dollars a day. But if the dollar happens to be rising, we will be in for a pleasant surprise. Perhaps by the time we are ready to leave, it will have risen to four marks to the dollar. It still costs three hundred marks a day to travel in Germany, but we can now buy three hundred marks for only seventy-five dollars.

We must remember, however, that international economics must always be viewed from both sides of the ocean. When the dollar rises, foreign goods or services become less expensive for us. But for a German, just the opposite is true. A German tourist coming to America might be told that he should allow one hundred dollars a day for expenses. "How much will that cost me in marks?" he asks his bank. The answer, again, hangs on the exchange rate. If it costs only three marks to buy a dollar, it will obviously be cheaper for the German tourist than if it costs four marks. Notice that this is exactly the opposite of the American tourist's position.

International economics entered our consciousness with a vengeance in the mid 1980s, at a time when the falling dollar was making headlines—at least in American newspapers. (In Germany, they talked about the rising mark, in Japan about the rising yen.) We now know that this means that the price of dollars, on the market for foreign currencies, was dropping—not perhaps vis-à-vis *every* currency, but against those in which we conduct most of our business.

Why was the dollar high in the early '80s, low in the mid '80s, high again in the early '90s? As with all price changes, the first task is to look at the supply-and-demand situation. And that requires us to investigate the nature of the market for dollars and other currencies.

Here we can best begin by mentally grouping all the kinds of dealings in which dollars and other currencies change hands into two basic markets. One is the market for currencies to carry on current transactions. The other is the market for currencies to carry on capital transactions. You will have no trouble following the story if you bear these two markets in mind.

THE MARKET FOR CURRENT TRANSACTIONS

The first market in which currencies are bought and sold is that in which the current transactions between firms, individuals, or governments are carried out. Here the demand for dollars comes from such groups as foreigners who want to import U.S. goods and services, and who must acquire dollars to purchase them; or from foreign tourists who need dollars to travel in the U.S.; or from foreign governments who must buy dollars to maintain embassies or consulates in America; or from firms abroad (American or foreign) that want to send dividends or profits to the United States in dollars. All these kinds of transactions require that holders of marks or francs or yen buy U.S. dollars on the market for foreign exchange, the international money market. By and large, you can do that at most big banks.

And, of course, there are similar groups of Americans who supply dollars to the foreign exchange market for exactly the opposite reasons. Here we find American importers who want to bring in Japanese cameras and must offer dollars in order to acquire the yen to make their purchases; American or foreign firms that are sending dividends or profits earned in the U.S. to a foreign branch or headquarters; Americans or foreign residents who sell dollars in order to buy lire or drachmas or kronor to send money to friends or relatives abroad; or the American government, which uses dollars to buy foreign currencies to pay diplomatic living expenses or to make military expenditures abroad.

Taken all together, these supplies and demands for dollars establish what we call our *balance on current account.* Until 1971, the United States regularly ran a small positive balance on this account, meaning that year in and year out we sold more goods and services to foreigners than we bought from them. Then, starting in the early 1970s we began to show irregular *negative* balances on current account—buying more abroad than we were selling. Finally, in 1983 the irregular negative balances became regular and massive, until by 1986 we were running negative balances of $140 billion a year.

What happened to turn the balance from black to red? The answer in part is the OPEC oil crisis, which resulted in a sharp rise in the number of dollars we had to supply to buy oil abroad. In 1972 our oil bill was $5 billion. In 1974 it was $27 billion. By 1980 it had grown to $83 billion.

But oil shock was not the only reason for the falling merchandise balance. As we have seen, we have experienced a long gradual decline in our competitive position vis-à-vis the other industrial nations of the West, a decline attributable in considerable part to laggard American productivity. In addition, a number of other developments have tilted the merchandise balance away from America—the international agricultural situation, the respective inflation rates of the U.S. and its main competitors, and still other factors.

This is one major reason why the supply of dollars, needed for imports, came to exceed the demand for dollars, needed by foreigners to purchase American exports. When the quantity of any commodity supplied exceeds the quantity demanded, its price drops. The dollar was no exception. It fell.

During the '90s, our trade balance slowly and painfully improved. In 1987 we imported $115 billion more than we exported; by 1990 that was down to $31 billion. In 1991 we actually balanced the account, but in fluky ways: partly because of payments we received from the rest of the world for fighting the Persian Gulf war, partly because we had a recession, and accordingly cut our imports. Our structural problems with the rest of the world have not yet been solved: we still import more than we export, although nowhere near as much more as ten years ago.

THE MARKET FOR CAPITAL TRANSACTIONS

But what falls can rise again. For the market for current transactions is not the only arena in which the supply and demand for dollars establish a price for dollars against other currencies. A second, quite separate market arises to accommodate the need for dollars and other currencies to finance capital transactions, not current ones. Here are such items as building or buying plants and equipment in another country, or buying the bonds or stocks issued within another nation.

The first of these capital flows is called direct investment. It arises from the efforts of American firms (mainly multinationals) to expand their ownership of plants and equipment abroad, and from the corresponding efforts of foreign companies to do the same thing here. The second part of the capital market is made up of American or foreign individuals or firms who want to add to their overseas portfolio investments of stocks and bonds. Here we have Americans who buy stock in a Swedish firm or who buy German government bonds, and foreign investors who buy General Motors stock or U.S. Treasury bonds.

Adding direct and portfolio investment to the balance on current account, we get a big reversal in the overall flow of foreign exchange. During the 1970s, U.S. corporations were expanding their overseas production facilities at record rates. This gave rise to an American demand for foreign currencies on capital account that offset, to some extent, the net demand for American dollars on current account. Then in the early 1980s, the capital flow did a remarkable flip-flop. In part this was the result of a petering out of the American expansion drive abroad, and the rise of a European and Japanese expansion drive into the United States. But in still greater degree it resulted from an unprecedented flow of foreign portfolio money into the United States. The tight-money policy initiated by the Federal Reserve in the early 1980s drove interest rates on three-month Treasury bills to over 14 percent. At the same time, the inflation rate began to fall. The result was a kind of international suction machine that drew unprecedented quantities of foreign funds into U.S. Treasury and other bonds and investments to take advantage of the irresistible combination of high interest rates, falling inflation, and political security.

The result of this vast capital inflow was to prevent what would otherwise have been a self-correcting tendency in the foreign-exchange markets. The poor showing of American exports and the success of foreign imports should have resulted in a steady pressure *against* the dollar. This would have lowered the price of the dollar in marks and yen and other foreign currencies, thereby cheapening our exports abroad and making foreign goods more expensive at home. After a time we would have expected our exports to pick up and our imports to subside, until the one-sided balance on current account evened out, or at least showed a considerable improvement.

But the suction machine prevented that. Instead of falling, the dollar rose—and rose to such heights that the balance on current account worsened to the point at which our international economic position was no longer sustainable. There was a genuine fear that the United States was hopelessly priced out of its former markets, not just because of considerations of productivity, but because of the stratospheric dollar. By 1985 the dollar crisis had achieved such importance that a financial summit was convened among the leading Western nations to bring the dollar down. This meant that the big central banks of Europe and Japan agreed to drive down the value of the dollar on the international currency markets, even though this meant acting against the interests of their nations' exporters.

As we write these words, the shoe is again on the other foot. The dollar came down precipitously, to about 30 percent below its peak, but in the early 1990s, it was rising again. When it fell one heard groans of pain from foreigners who saw the price of their goods going up in terms of dollars; and as it rose one heard the same groans from American manufacturers who saw the price of their goods going up in terms of yen or marks or whatever. No rate of exchange satisfies everybody. Every movement, up or down, hurts some and helps others.

PROBLEMS OF HIGH AND LOW DOLLARS

So let us consider the question of foreign exchange, not as Americans but as economists. Is there such a thing as a "right" price for the dollar, or for any other currency?

Like so many economic questions, this has a political answer. For the exchange value of a currency affects different individuals or groups or regions in different ways. Suppose that the dollar is cheap. Obviously this is good for anyone who wants to buy a U.S. good or service, using foreign money. It makes travel in the U.S. inexpensive for foreigners. It makes American exports attractive. It makes American stocks or physical plant tempting to foreign investors. All this redounds to the benefit of U.S. exporters or hotel keepers or stockholders or owners who want to sell to foreigners.

On the other hand, a cheap dollar penalizes other groups. An American traveling abroad finds prices terribly high. An American importer finds that foreign wines, cameras, cars, sweaters are expensive—and so do his customers. American firms thinking of investing abroad are deterred by the high price of foreign exchange. All this is bad for American tourists, consumers, and investors.

Is there any reason for giving preference to those groups who benefit from the cheap dollar over other groups who benefit from expensive dollars? From the point of view of our national well-being, there is no particular reason to favor one over another. Is it better for a million consumers to buy cameras cheap, or for one hundred thousand steel workers to have higher incomes? There is no cut-and-dried answer, only a contest of wills.

How, then, does a nation determine the right rate for its exchange when cheap rates help some groups and expensive rates help others? The answer is that a nation tries to discover the rate that will roughly balance out all the supplies and all the demands for its currency, so that it has a stable, "equilibrium" relationship between its own currency and those of other nations.

What happens if a country does not have such an equilibrium relationship? If the rate is too high, there will be a stimulus for the country to buy imports and a deterrent to its exports. The result will be unemployment in its export industries and, as a consequence, unemployment elsewhere. Perhaps the most famous case of an overvalued currency was that of England following World War I, when

Winston Churchill, then Chancellor of the Exchequer, tried to establish an exchange rate of £1 = $5. At that rate the demand for pounds was far less than the supply, and English exports went into a tailspin, dragging the economy down with them. England suffered a severe depression until its exchange rate was finally reduced to about $4.

An undervalued exchange rate also brings problems. Now there is an incentive for foreigners to buy the cheap exports or assets of the undervalued country. Foreign money will flow into its banks, raising the money supply. As the money supply increases, inflationary pressures also increase. The country will suffer from rising prices.

Thus we can present the problem of exchange rates that are too high or too low in this fashion:

Overvalued (too high) exchange rates lead to unemployment.

Undervalued (too low) exchange rates lead to inflation.

Finding the right price for the dollar, then, means finding an exchange rate that will roughly balance our total supplies and demands for foreign exchange for transactions purposes and capital flows. When the dollar falls, it means that we have not yet found such a rate. The verdict of the marketplace is that the dollar is too high. We know this is the verdict because the demand for dollars vis-à-vis marks and francs and other strong currency has been steadily less than its supplies.

What happens when the dollar falls? Clearly, we move from the dangers of an overvalued currency toward those of an undervalued one. That is, a falling dollar spurs our exports and helps employment. It also makes imports more expensive. Alas, in our inflation-prone economy, this results not just in fewer imports, but in another fillip to the price level. Oil prices go up because of the falling exchange rate, along with the price of Hondas and TV sets, coffee and tea.

The net effect of a falling dollar is therefore measured, in part, by the benefit we ascribe to expanding employment minus the cost we assign to higher inflation. As we have seen so often, most people place a higher priority on inflation than on unemployment. We welcome the boost to exports but put more emphasis on the boost to the cost of living.

Now what about a rising dollar? Here we are at the tennis match. The ball is in the other court. A rising dollar means that going abroad is cheaper, but selling American goods abroad is harder. It makes Japanese and German goods cheaper, and thereby tends to force some American workers out of jobs. So a rising dollar imposes costs, just as does a falling dollar. It also distributes benefits—but to different groups of people, different regions, industries, interests. It helps reduce inflation (cheaper imports) and helps swell unemployment (more foreign goods). Should we therefore defend the dollar against rising? We begin to see the difficulty of the problem.

WHAT CAN BE DONE

We'll come back to the question of whether or not we should defend a falling dollar or worry about a rising dollar. First it's necessary to understand how we can go about altering the exchange value of a currency. Once again, we shall begin with the case when the currency falls, because that always seems much more alarming than when a currency is rising. When our dollar falls, we say it is weak; when it rises, we call it strong. What can we do about a weak dollar?

One measure is simplicity itself: Prevent the flow of imports from rising. Anything that will turn the balance of merchandise payments in our favor will unquestionably alter the supply-demand situation and help the dollar go up.

Is this a sound policy? It will come as no surprise when we say that the answer is a political, not just an economic, judgment. To be sure, there are certain kinds of imports that we would like to diminish not merely to defend the dollar, but to strengthen the nation. For instance, if we can substitute domestic energy (such as solar or coal) for imported oil, or if we can cut down on oil imports by conservation measures, the United States gains a much-needed measure of strategic independence as well as helping the dollar.

If, however, we cut down imports by blocking cheap shoes, textiles, or steel from abroad, we are simply protecting inefficient industries at home and penalizing American households and businesses by depriving them of the right to buy shoes, textiles, or steel as cheaply as they otherwise might. We can sharpen the point by imagining that our tariff wall was sky-high. Then no goods would come into the United States. Would that be good for America?

On the other hand, imports cost jobs. Even if we compensate the workers in threatened industries, or help relocate them, or retrain them, some will not make the transition and will remain unemployed. There is a real human cost to competition—from abroad or home—that should not be lost to sight. We have already let something like a half million steel and auto and computer workers go down the drain to get cheaper steel, autos, and PCs from abroad. Is this a good exchange? Is the North American Free Trade Agreement (NAFTA) with Mexico warranted in terms of the undoubted benefits it will yield to consumers or unwarranted because of the undoubted erosion it will inflict on U.S. job opportunities?

These are tough questions because they cannot be answered in a void. If we had strong systems of worker retraining, coupled with effective government assistance for industrial conversion, the NAFTA agreements would take on a much more attractive face than they do in their absence. (The same is true for the pace of cutting back our arms industry.) Perhaps the Clinton administration will provide these public reinforcements. They are to be found in almost all other industrial countries, but are sadly lacking here. Once again, the success or failure of the private economy hinges more intimately than we tend to think on the support system provided by government.

Many economists would say that in the end, the benefits to the economy of having cheaper foreign goods, plus the benefits of moving our own resources and labor away from inefficient uses, outweigh the costs of unemployment. It would be interesting to see if they would come to the same conclusion if we were to import cheaper economists from abroad, asking our domestic practitioners to find another way of making a living. But even if we accept the conventional wisdom, we can see that there is a real conflict of interest involved in defending the dollar through restricting imports. That is, of course, the political nub of the matter, and it is this political issue—Who is to gain? Who is to lose?—that must be satisfactorily resolved before we can really address ourselves to the economics of the question.

What about helping our exports? Many countries have tried to help *their* exports by giving subsidies of various kinds to their producers, so that they could sell their wares abroad cheaply. We have also subsidized some exports by underwriting our merchant marine, by arranging for special deals on U.S. arms sales to foreign nations, and by foreign-aid policies that have permitted us to sell large amounts of farm products abroad.

As with imports, it is not possible to give black-and-white answers about the wisdom of defending the dollar by export assistance. It may be in the national interest to sell $1 billion of arms on easy terms, or to export $1 billion of foodstuffs to the underdeveloped nations, but these policies should be judged on their own merits. The fact that they help defend the dollar is not, and should not be, a controlling consideration.

Policies to help exports or to hinder imports affect the balance of payments on current account. But there is also the market for foreign exchange for capital purposes. Can we defend—or can we assist—the dollar by intervening in that market?

We recall that there are two basic kinds of transactions in the capital market—direct investment, which purchases plant and equipment and other physical assets abroad, and portfolio investment, which buys stocks and bonds or simply parks money in bank accounts. One way of defending the dollar is simply to pass a law preventing United States companies from acquiring foreign assets; and the opposite side of the coin is to support the dollar by forbidding foreign companies to buy or build plants in America.

There is a great deal of immediate appeal to "keeping foreigners out"—an appeal that finds as much response among the Japanese who don't want U.S. computer companies in their own backyards as it does among Americans who don't want Japanese manufacturers in *their* backyards. In both cases, the economist urges caution. Foreign investment makes for *domestic* employment, a consideration that is very important when we are considering whether or not to let foreigners in. And foreign investment leads to profits that come back to domestic countries, a consideration that must be taken into account in judging the effects of letting U.S. corporations build plants abroad. Such reasons lie behind the general economic consensus that a fairly free flow of international investment is probably the best way to raise productivity and encourage economic growth, even though one nation may gain a little on another in the short run.

Note "fairly free." There are considerations of strategy and power at stake in the world of international economic dealings, not just profit and employment. Politics often asserts its priority over economics when considerations of investment are at stake. This is particularly the case when investment flows bring capital from the developed to the underdeveloped world, a problem of great political and economic complexity about which it is difficult to make hard-and-fast generalizations. Hence, as with international trade, the position toward which we incline is one of overall support for the pushes and pulls generated by the market, accompanied by a willingness to intervene against the market, or at least to cushion its blows, when serious social and political considerations so dictate. That is far from a precise formula, but in an imperfect world it is the best we can come up with as a general guide for public policy.

THREE PROBLEMS, NOT ONE

How can we wrap up this complicated problem? Economist Robert Blecker has a useful way of disentangling its complexities.* He suggests that the United States faces three problems in the world of international trade and production, each calling for a different approach.

The first of these is unquestionably our competitive standing vis-à-vis Germany and Japan, our two main industrial competitors. Here the central problem is the lag in U.S. productivity, much aggravated in the case of Japan by its well-known reluctance to open its markets to U.S. exports. The latter problem, although extremely aggravating, has a relatively simple remedy: we can impose surcharges on Japanese imports unless Japan permits our goods to reach its consumers on the same terms that we allow Japanese goods access to ours.

The productivity problem is not so easily remedied. In the case of both Germany and Japan, their edge is not merely traceable to

*Robert Blecker, *Beyond the Twin Deficits*, (Armonk, New York; M. E. Sharp, 1992).

superior technological skills and strategies, but to a range of social policies that greatly enhance the overall levels of efficiency in their nations. Japan and Germany both far outperform the United States in the education of their youngsters, the training they accord their non-college graduates, and the active cooperation that marks the relations betwen industry and government generally. In addition, the "social contract" that we have mentioned earlier permits a degree of union-management cooperation that is visibly missing in our country, to the detriment of our economic performance.

That means that a balance in our European competitors will have to be won, product by product, and year by year, through an effort aimed at a long-term elevation of the performance of the U.S. industrial economy as a whole. That cannot be accomplished overnight. Nonetheless, the situation is far from black. The United States is now running a trade surplus with the European Community, aside from Germany; and German superiority has been greatly hampered by the huge problems of merging its backward eastern "half" with its modern Western "half." So we have a breathing space in which to catch up, socially as well as economically, with our European competitors, who have stolen a march on us that we must now try to make up.

The second main problem concerns the relation between the United States and the Newly Industrializing Countries (NICs). Here the difficulty lies at first glance entirely in the striking difference between their wage rates and ours. As we can see in the table on page 237, workers' compensation in these countries is a quarter or less than that of their U.S. counterparts. These low wages are only in part the consequence of a difference in productivity. They result, in considerable part, from repressive (anti-union) wage policies by the firms and governments of the NICs themselves.

But the problem is more complex than that. It is that low-paid workers are combined with industrial equipment and techniques that are in many cases comparable, or nearly comparable, to our own. Beyond that near-unbeatable combination, the wage-cost advantage is further maintained by foreign exchange policies that keep their NIC currencies low, compared with the dollar.

Here Blecker suggests a different strategy for the United States. It is to encourage the NICs to allow their wages to rise to the levels

HOURLY COMPENSATION COSTS FOR MANUFACTURING PRODUCTION WORKERS

	Percent of U.S. 1989
United States	100
Mexico	16
Brazil	12
Hong Kong	19
Singapore	22
South Korea	25
Taiwan	25
Sri Lanka	2

Source: Blecker, op. cit., p. 101 (U.S. Bureau of Labor Statistics).

justified by their productivity and to relax exchange policies that have artifically depressed their currencies. The NICs would undoubtedly retain a price advantage for many of their exported industrial goods, but it would not be a differential that made it utterly impossible even for the most productive U.S. producers to compete. As with the first problem, the threat of imposing an equalizing surtax on imports could be used to bring about a more "level" playing field.

The last of the three problem overlaps to some degree with the second, insofar as it concerns the enormous problem of international indebtedness that mainly weighs down underdeveloped countries. Many of these countries must use much, or all, of their hard-won export earnings to pay interest on their debts, mainly to United States banks, rather than to buy the exports of U.S. producers. Latin America, for instance, was actually a net exporter of capital during the 1980s, as a consequence of having to pay interest to U.S. creditors.

What is needed, many economists agree, is forgiveness of a burden of indebtedness that now penalizes debtor and creditor alike. Some substantial portion of the existing debt, or some limitation of debt service (payment of interest), or yet alternatively some purchase of the debt, at reduced prices, by an international agency will be needed to get the international economy back on an even keel.

All these proposals will be difficult to achieve, but as we have said before, difficult is not the same as impossible. They help us see that the international position of the United States is not beyond repair, although repair will not be easy. They also show us that much of the current difficulties stems from foolish United States policies of the past—allowing our productivity to fall; ignoring the needs of our public household; carelessly lending money abroad, without a thought to the realistic chances of its repayment.* To some extent the United States is to blame for its own disadvantaged position today. That does not make unraveling its problems any easier, but it helps us recognize that we have a certain responsibility for our present uncomfortable plight. This is an attitude that will be helpful if we are to attend to our international future as seriously as we should.

---

*As we write these pages, the Latin American debt crisis seems finally to be easing, partly because some of the steps mentioned above have been taken, partly because a slow improvement in their economic condition makes it possible to try reforms that were impossible while their economies were dead in the water. Meanwhile, similar debt problems have appeared in many countries of Eastern Europe, which are struggling to finance debts that were in many cases shoved down their throats by American banks only too eager to lend money at high rates for hopeless projects to corrupt governments. Does it make sense for us to require that the struggling governments of Eastern Europe repay the debts incurred by their communist precessors? Probably not.

NINETEEN

The Multinational Corporation

The problem of big business is one of old standing, dating back to the period just after the Civil War. But recently that problem has been given a new twist by the appearance of enormous corporations whose business empires literally straddle the globe—the multinational corporations. Take PepsiCo, for example. PepsiCo does not ship its famous product around the world from bottling plants in the United States. It produces Pepsi Cola in more than five hundred plants in over one hundred countries. When you buy a Pepsi in Mexico or the Philippines, Israel, or Denmark, you are buying an American product that was manufactured in that country.

PepsiCo is a far-flung, but not a particularly large, multinational. In 1992 it was the 17th-largest U.S. company, ranked by sales. Compare it with the Ford Motor Company, a multinational that consists of a network of 60 subsidiary corporations, 40 of them foreign-based. Of the corporation's profits in recent years, one third have come from abroad. And if we studied the corporate structures of GM or IBM or the great oil companies, we would find that they too are multinational companies, with substantial portions of their total wealth invested in productive facilities outside the United States.

If we broaden our view to include the top one hundred American firms, we find that at least two thirds have such far-flung production facilities. Moreover, the value of output that is produced overseas by the largest corporations by far exceeds the value of the goods they still export from the United States. In 1985, for example, sales of the 150 largest multinationals from their foreign branches amounted to over $415 billion. In that same year, our total exports of merchandise from all U.S. firms came to only $207 billion—half the value of the overseas production of the 150 top U.S. multinationals.

Another way of establishing the spectacular rise of international production is to trace the increase in the value of U.S. foreign direct investment; that is, the value of foreign-located, U.S.-owned plant and equipment (not U.S.-owned foreign bonds and stocks). In 1950 the value of U.S. foreign direct investment was $11 billion. Forty years later, it is in excess of $400 billion. Moreover, this figure too needs an upward adjustment, because it includes only the value of American dollars invested abroad and not the additional value of foreign capital that may be controlled by those dollars. For example, if a U.S. company has invested $10 million in a foreign enterprise whose total net worth is $20 million, the U.S. official figures for our foreign investment take note only of the $10 million of American equity and not of the $20 million wealth that our equity actually controls. In general, something between a quarter and a half of the real assets of our biggest corporations are abroad. Effectively, American big business is today world big business.

The movement toward the internationalization of production is not, however, a strictly American phenomenon. If the American multinationals are today the most imposing (of the world's biggest five hundred corporations, over three hundred are American), they are closely challenged by non-American multinationals. Philips Lamp Works, for example, is a huge Dutch multinational company with operations in sixty-eight countries. Of its 225,000 employees, 167,00 work in nations other than the Netherlands. Royal Dutch/Shell is another vast multinational, whose home is somewhere between the Netherlands and the United Kingdom (it is jointly owned by nationals of both countries). Another is Nestlé Chocolate, a Swiss firm, 97 percent of whose revenues originate outside Switzerland. Measured by the size of the Swedish capital invested there, São Paulo is Sweden's second biggest industrial city! Recently the United Nations surveyed the size of the world of the multinationals. Gerard Piel reports on their findings: "The 350 largest [multinationals] had a combined turnover of $2,700 billion in 1985. That was 30 percent of the entire GNP of the world market economy and larger by several hundreds of billions of dollars than the combined GNP of all the preindustrial economies, China included."*

Thus, there is today an international economy that literally envelops the economies of the 150-odd nations that constitute the political world. It is doubtful that the international economy would last a month, were the major nation-states to disappear overnight; but it is an open question how long the present political map will reflect the realities of world power if the global economy continues to grow in strength. We have noted in Chapter 11 that it is increasingly difficult for the Federal Reserve, and by extension, any central bank, to regulate the money supply of its own nation because of the globalization of money itself: $1 trillion worth of foreign exchange business is transacted *daily* around the world. It remains to be seen how modern industrial states, such as our own, will mesh their domestic economies into or insulate them from the flows of the international economy.

Two cautionary thoughts should be borne in mind as we take stock of this very large and still very ill-understood problem. The first is that the multinationals are not to be thought of only as foreign enterprises seeking to invade someone else's market. They also include enterprises that have located branches abroad to invade *their own* markets. For example, much of the influx of automotive and other manufactures from Mexico into the United States arises from U.S. subsidiaries that have gone south to take advantage of low wage costs there. Thus, the real challenge of the MNCs (multinational corporations) is their ability to move technology around the world. How does a country hold on to a technological edge if its own companies are transferring that technology to their foreign sites? The question this raises is a new one for political economy: "Who is 'us'?"

A second cautionary thought alerts us to the nature of the multinational problem itself. It is not, at bottom, a question of a competitive struggle among national economies, although interfirm rivalry is certainly an important driving force behind the multina-

---

*Gerard Piel, *Only One World*, (New York: W. H. Freeman & Co., 1992), p. 246.

tionals' behavior. But the underlying issue is different. It is a struggle for a redefinition of national sovereignty itself. The real challenge posed by the multinationals is that the world's economic map does not neatly coincide with its political map. This raises the question of how national sovereignty will be protected as the reach of international finance and production widens and deepens. Here, the means by which sovereignty will be defended—tariffs, quotas, regional trading blocs, new international organization—cannot be foreseen. But it is helpful to recognize that the issue is not merely how the world's markets will be divided up, but the ways in which sovereignty itself will be expressed in the twenty-first century.

THE ECONOMICS OF MULTINATIONAL PRODUCTION

What drives a firm to produce overseas rather than just sell overseas? One possible answer is straightforward. A firm is successful at home. Its technology and organizational skills give it an edge on foreign competition. It begins to export its product. The foreign market grows. At some point, the firm begins to calculate whether it would be more profitable to organize an overseas production operation. By doing so, it would save transportation costs. It may be able to evade a tariff by producing goods behind a tariff wall. A very important consideration is that it may be able to take advantage of lower wage rates. And so, gradually, it ceases shipping goods abroad and instead exports capital, technology, and management—and becomes a multinational.

Calculations may be more complex. By degrees, a successful company may change its point of view. First it thinks of itself as a domestic company, perhaps with a small export market. Then it builds up its exports and thinks of itself as an international company with a substantial interest in exports. Finally its perspective changes to that of a multinational, considering the world (or substantial portions of it) to be its market. In that case, it may locate plants abroad before the market is fully developed, in order to be firmly established abroad ahead of its competition.

More and more of the great corporations of the world have come to consider their "natural" markets to be the globe, not just their home countries. The struggle in automobiles, in computers, in telecommunications, in steel, is for shares of a world market. That is why we find companies such as IBM or General Motors considering the entire globe as their oyster, not only with regard to the "sourcing" of raw materials, but to the location of plants, and finally the direction of sales effort. With modern rapid jet transportation, instant global data retrieval, and highly organized systems of production and distribution, the manufacture of commodities is more and more easily moved to whatever country produces them most cheaply, whereas their sale is focused on the countries that represent the richest markets. Thus we have a transistor radio whose parts have been made in Hong Kong or South Korea or Singapore, assembled in Mexico, and sold in the United States—by a Japanese manufacturer!

THE IMPACT OF THE MULTINATIONALS

Whether or not the multinational boom continues at its past rate, the startling rise of multinationals has already changed the face of international economic relationships. One major effect has been a dramatic shift in the geographic location and the technological character of international economic activity.

The shift away from exports to international production has introduced two changes into the international economic scene. One change is a movement of foreign investment away from its original concentration in the underdeveloped areas of the world toward the richer markets of the developed areas. A century ago, in the era of high imperialism, most of the capital leaving one country for another flowed from rich to poor lands. Thus foreign investment in the late nineteenth and early twentieth centuries was largely associated with the creation of vast plantations, the building of railways through jungles, and the development of mineral resources.

But the growth of the multinational enterprise has coincided with a decisive shift away from investment in the underdeveloped world to investment in the industrial world. In 1897, 59 percent of American foreign direct investment was in agriculture, mining, or railways, mainly in the underdeveloped world. By the end of the 1970s our investment in agriculture, mining, and railways, as a proportion of our total overseas assets, had fallen to about 20 percent. More striking, almost three quarters of our huge rise in direct investment was in the developed world; and the vast bulk of it was in manufacturing (and oil) rather than in plantations, railroads, or ores. Thus the multinational companies have been investing in each others' territories rather than invading the territories of the underdeveloped world. In recent years there has been a highly visible thrust of multinational investment in manufacturing facilities in a few poorer nations—big factory investments in Mexico, Hong Kong, Taiwan, Singapore, Korea, most recently, in parts of China. Nonetheless, these investments are still much smaller than the multinationals' investments in the developed countries.

The second economic change is really implicit in the first. It is a shift away from heavy technology to high-technology industries—away from enterprises in which vast sums of capital were associated with large, unskilled labor forces as in the building of railways or plantations—toward industries in which capital is perhaps less strategic than research and development, skilled technical manpower, and sophisticated management techniques typical of the computer, petrochemical, and other new industries. Our table sums up the overall shift.

Size and Distribution of U.S. Foreign Direct Investment

Total (millions)	1929	1989
	$7,528	$373,436
Distribution by market (%)		
Canada	27	19
Europe	18	47
Latin America	47	14
Asia, Africa, Near East	8	20
Distribution by sector (%)		
Manufacturing	24	38
Petroleum	15	10
Transport and utilities	21	10
Mining	15	*
Trade	5	6
Agriculture	12	*
Other (finance, insurance, etc.)	8	36

*Negligible.

Note the dramatic shift away from Latin America into Europe and away from transport, mining, and agriculture into manufacturing, a shift that would be even more accentuated if it were not still dependent on oil as a major source of the world's energy. If solar energy or the fuel cell displaces oil within the next decades, we can expect a still more rapid decine in investment in the backward areas (especially in the Near East), and a proportionately still-larger concentration of foreign direct investment in manufacturing.

MULTINATIONAL PROBLEMS

Multinationals have not only changed the face of international economic activity, but also have added considerably to the problem of controlling domestic economies. Assume that a country wants to slow down its economy through monetary policies designed to reduce plant and equipment spending. A restrictive monetary policy at home may be vitiated by the ability of a multinational to borrow abroad in order to finance investment at home. Conversely, a monetary policy designed to stimulate the home economy may end up in loans that increase production in someone else's economy. Thus the effectiveness of national economic policymaking is weakened. Moreover, it is not easy to suggest that monetary policies should be coordinated among countries, since the economic needs of different countries may not be the same: what is right for one country at a given time may be wrong for another.

More important, the jealous claims of nation-states that seek to retain national control over productive activity within their own borders and the powerful thrust of transnational corporations for new markets in foreign territories introduce profound tensions into the international world. On the one hand, the multinational is in a position to win hard bargains from the host country into which it seeks to enter because the corporation is the main bearer of new technologies and management techniques that every nation seeks. On the other hand, the power is by no means entirely one-sided, for once a multinational *has* entered a foreign nation, it becomes a *hostage* of the host country. It is now bound by the laws of that country and may find itself forced to undertake activities that are "foreign." In Japan, for example, it is an unwritten law that workers engaged by giant corporations are never fired, but become permanent employees. Japan has been extremely reluctant to allow foreign capital to establish manufacturing operations on Japanese soil, to the great annoyance of foreign companies. But if, as now seems likely, Japan is opened to American and European capital, we can be sure that American or European corporations will be expected to behave in the Japanese way with their employees. This will not be an easy course to follow, since these corporations are not likely to receive the special support that the Japanese government gives to its own big firms.

Or take the problem of a multinational that is forced by a fall in demand to cut back the volume of its output. A decision made along strictly economic lines would lead it to close its least profitable plant. But this may bring very serious economic repercussions in the particular nation in which that plant is located—so serious that the government will threaten to take action if the plant is closed. What dictates shall the multinational then follow—those of standard business accounting or those of political accounting?

THE UNDERDEVELOPED WORLD

All these problems take on a special significance in the relation between the multinationals and the underdeveloped world. For the multinationals are now the main conduit between the dynamic, expansive thrust of Western capitalism and the restive, but still passive, periphery of Asia and Africa and Latin America. This raises problems of great difficulty. As former Under Secretary of State George Ball has candidly asked: "How can a national government make an economic plan with any confidence if a board of directors meeting five thousand miles away can, in altering its pattern of purchasing and production, affect in a major way the country's economic life?"

For these and other reasons there is a great deal of suspicion and unease surrounding the attitude toward the multinationals on the part of the less-developed countries. And for good reason. There is something profoundly disturbing in the spectacle of breakfast foods and Coca-Cola displacing native diets, often to the detriment of people living at the edge of nutritional safety; of transistor radios and plastic ornaments pushing aside native entertainments and adornments; of Hilton hotels towering over squalid tenements; of ugly and monotonous factory labor driving out peasant and artisan skills and crafts. Anyone who has traveled in the underdeveloped world cannot help but be struck by the careless violence with which the multinationals have uprooted established ways, exposing untrained and unreadied people to the hurricane winds of modern technology and modern values—and all in the name of profit, certainly not in that of human development.

And yet it is too easy to wax indignant before we have thought the matter over. The societies that are being torn apart by the multinationals have indeed great traditions of solidarity and stability—if they did not, they would have perished long ago—but they have achieved their endurance by harsh and exploitative ways of their own, keeping their lower castes and classes, and their women, in conditions of severe oppression and ignorance. From this perspective, the multinationals, for all their ruthless exploitation of naive appetites and docile labor, are also carriers of social relationships and technical abilities without which the underdeveloped world would remain hopelessly subordinate to the invincible material and organizational capabilities of the West.

But are there not alternatives to the hegemony of the multinationals—more effective ways of transferring technologies and social skills to the peoples of Africa and Southeast Asia, China and Latin America? The question really raises for examination the complex relationship between the core of capitalist nations and the periphery of the regions into which capitalism has partly penetrated. This relationship, historically of great importance for capitalism, is now in a period of stress and strain as the underdeveloped world, hopelessly in debt to the West, seeks to loosen its dependency on the West.

To explore this problem in depth would take us far beyond the scope of our book. Moreover, whatever that relationship has been, over the near-term future there seems to be no workable alternative to the present tension-ridden mutual dependence of core and periphery. Socialist governments in all the underdeveloped regions have tried to institute the process of economic and social development without recourse to the conduits of capitalist enterprise, but the results have been disappointing at best and catastrophic at worst. However inadequate or lopsided the development process may be when it occurs through the channels of the multinationals, so far it has been superior to the development that can be conjured up from scratch, or to the technology and organization that have come from regimes such as the former Soviet Union. The disrupting effects and the social deformations that result from connections with IBM or Exxon may be easier to deal with, in the end, than those of Ministries of Computer Technology or of Energy.

The multinationals will therefore occupy a strategic position in world economic affairs for a long time. Yet in the end, it seems doubtful that the world will be made in their image of hierarchical efficiency. There are may things that the multinationals can do which the emerging nations cannot, but there is one central thing an emerging nation can do that the multinationals cannot. This is to command the devotion of huge masses of people. Men and women will die for the image of their nation, but they will not die for the profits of a company.

Finally, it may be that the world will move defensively toward "managed trade" among regional trading blocs. That would mean that trade among members of a bloc—such as the European Community or (if it is finally approved) NAFTA, the North American Free Trade Association—would be relatively unhindered by tariffs and quotas, whereas trade between blocs would have to abide by rules and regulations negotiated by governing entities representing those blocs.

So the overall prospect is mixed, challenging, difficult to foresee. Perhaps little can be said other than that both nation-states and huge corporations are necessary. They seem to be the only ways in which we can organize mankind to perform the arduous and sustained labor without which humanity itself would rapidly perish. Perhaps after the long age of capital accumulation has finally come to an end and sufficient capital is available to all peoples, we may be able to think seriously about dismantling the giant enterprise and the nation-state, both of which overpower the individual with their massive organized strength. However desirable that ultimate goal may be, in our time both state and corporation promise to be with us, and the tension between them will be part of the evolutionary drama of our time.

TWENTY

Where Are We Headed?

And so at the end of our book we come back to the theme of the beginning—the trajectory of economic history. In fact, we now face for the first time those commanding but obscure questions that we touched on in our opening pages: Where is capitalism headed? What are the signs and omens for the future of our kind of society? What, if anything, can be hazarded about the years ahead?

These are questions that go far beyond the competence of economists. In the end it will be considerations of political morale and belief, of social cohesion, of ideology and conviction that determine the future of the United States or Japan or France or Sweden just as much as, or more than, their common economic mechanisms. Nevertheless, there are some things that an economist can say about the future, for there are a few lessons that we have learned about the workings of capitalism and of socialism that bear on, even if they do not determine, the shape of things to come.

THE SOVIET DISASTER

What are the *economic*—not the political or social—plusses and minuses of socialism? The question may seem irrelevant in light of the extraordinary collapse of the Soviet system and its satellites. But there are two reasons to think otherwise. First, a few countries, such as China, still retain some of the old Soviet-type system, and other nations, particularly in the underdeveloped world, may well turn to centralized planning for a takeoff, if their economic situation becomes desperate enough. Second, the Soviet collapse was one of the great economic events of history. We should know something about what happened.

Centralized planning, as the Russians tried it, differed from capitalism in two vital particulars. First, it outlawed the private ownership of the means of production—land, factories, etc.—although not of personal belongings or even personal savings accounts. Second, it organized the flow of both production and distribution by the issuance of orders from a central planning bureau, not by the activities of individuals seeking to make a profit in an open market. Thus, the managers of Soviet factories did not produce what they wanted, but what the plan wanted; could not shop around for materials; could not pick and choose customers; could not hire or fire labor without authorization; could not even go out to buy an unauthorized light bulb if one blew out. Everything was arranged from above: the kind and volume of production, the suppliers from whom each factory or store would receive shipments, the factories or warehouses to which output would be sent, the inventories that were expected to be kept on hand, from raw materials to light bulbs.

Centralized socialism therefore resembled an immense jigsaw in which the location and size of each piece, and the designation of the other pieces into which it would fit, were first figured out at the planning headquarters, and thereafter sent to the managers of the collective farms and ministry-owned factories in which the pieces of the puzzle were produced. In retrospect, the final collapse of the system was not to be marveled at so much as the fact that it lasted as long it did.

The reason it did last is that in the beginning the system very much resembled a military operation. After the Russian Revolution in 1917, Lenin confronted an almost totally disorganized society, and tried at first to build a "socialism" that was partly capitalist— private farming and private small enterprise—and partly socialist, in the form of state-owned banks and large centers of production. Russia staggered along under this mixed system for a few years, without either great success or great failure, but after Lenin's death in 1927, Stalin took command and rapidly instituted the highly centralized system we have sketched in.

Stalin's methods were ferocious and bloody, but they were successful in bringing about an immense accumulation of wealth, much as did the ruthless ways of ancient pharaohs of Egypt and emperors of Rome or China. The difference was that whereas the latter built palaces and cities, Stalin built factories, steel mills, hydroelectric plants, and railway systems—the ingredients of an industrial economy. The fact that Stalin's Russia was strong enough to resist Hitler's armies—and efficient enough, after its reconstruction following World War II, to impress the world with its industrial and military capabilities—shows that Soviet central planning was by no means a failure in its initial years. That is why "military socialism" may yet be a model for development efforts in the future. China is today a semi-military socialism which appears to be successfully negotiating the early stages of industrialization, much aided by a carefully supervised free market sector attached to the planned core. Hence the collapse of the Soviet system should not lead us to the snap judgment that centralized socialism is no longer on the agenda of the coming century. That is indeed likely to be the case with the North, but it is not a foregone conclusion in the troubled countries of the South.

THE COLLAPSE

But we are ahead of ourselves. After so successful a beginning, why did Soviet socialism finally break down? The answer is that it is a great deal easier to design and assemble the skeleton of a mighty economy than to run it. Building a steel plant requires good industrial draftmanship, but running a steel plant requires good industrial management. Management, in turn, depends on the ability to adapt flows of production to ever-changing conditions—the unforeseen contingencies, mistakes, mismatches, shortages, and overruns that are inescapable in any complex undertaking.

In a market system, these mistakes are repaired and remedied as soon as possible because they cost the factory or store money. Hence suppliers are told to hurry up, or to hold back on shipments, unprofitable items are canceled and profitable ones run overtime, the Yellow Pages are searched for last-minute necessities. None of this can happen in a society planned from top to bottom. When mistakes are made, they bring about a kind of gridlock in the flow of production, so that the pace of Soviet economic life production was a never-ending sequence of feast or famine, too much or too little, with no way of remedying the errors other than recasting next year's plan or seeking the semi-illegal channels of "tolkachi"—fixers.

The increasingly arthritic condition of the Russian economy had already become apparent by the early 1980s, when firsthand reports, and the calculations of the CIA, agreed that the Soviet economy was increasingly inefficient, save in the production of military and scientific goods, where producers were given first priority on whatever they needed. We tend to forget that it was the Soviets, not the Americans, who launched the first human being into space. But in the sectors that catered to everyday life, no such red carpet arrangements existed. Warehouses were full of shoes that Russian consumers wouldn't buy because they were so badly made; there were recurrent shortages of diapers, toilet paper, and other everyday items; the level of medical care declined until the Soviet Union became the first industrial nation in the world to experience a diminution in life expectancy during peacetime.*

We do not know how long this slow deterioration might have continued under the aging and increasingly incompetent tutelage of Communist Party leaders. In actual fact, the collapse seems to have been set in motion by the advent to power of Mikhail Gorbachev in 1985. Whatever judgment history may finally pass on this remarkable man, he will certainly be remembered as the starting point for the final downfall of the Soviet system—not because he plotted it, which he certainly did not, or because he wanted it, which he equally certainly did not. Gorbachev is the key figure because he launched a new era of *glasnost* coupled with *perestroika*—openness combined with reform—that undermined and eventually undid the communist monolith.

Glasnost meant that for the first time dissent and dissatisfaction could be openly voiced. Once public criticism could be openly voiced, long-dormant dissatisfactions quickly surfaced. Once in the open, they had to be heeded, and *perestroika* led to plan after plan to break up the detested centralized system. The plans ranged from

---

*For a vivid close-up view of the failures of central planning, see the account by two Soviet economists, Nikolai Shmelev and Vladimir Popov, *The Turning Point,* (New York: Doubleday, 1989).

cautious introductions of small private enterprises, such as restaurants and hair salons, to ambitious blueprints for "privatizing" the whole system at one fell swoop. The little plans produced negligible results; the big ones died in blueprint because they were too audacious to attempt. The net result was that the existing planned system was instructed to produce on a much less supervised but by no means wholly free basis.

This was a change that only further disorganized the workings of the economy. One instance sheds a good deal of light on the problem. Under central planning, many crops were gathered by transfers of labor from factories to the land when the moment for harvesting arrived. When the potatoes were ready, for example, the heads of collective farms telephoned the heads of nearby plants to send over their workers for a few days to get the crop in from the field. The plant managers agreed because they would be bawled out by the regional planning authority if they did not, and because the "loan" of the work force had been allowed for their in respective plans.

After *perestroika,* that rough-and-ready accommodation was no longer possible. As individual factories were gradually cut free from the planning system, their managers refused to send workers to the farms, because they were needed in the plant. Often there was no longer a regional boss for the collective farm manager to telephone. Hence, potatoes rotted in the field and the food lines in Moscow grew longer.

The rest can be summed up in a few quick strokes. With astonishing speed, the interlocks that kept the economy together came apart. It was not just potatoes that did not move to consumers, but cotton that did not become cloth, iron ore that failed to become steel girders. By the beginning of the '90s, economic chaos was producing political chaos. People simply lost fiath in the system. Gorbachev was displaced by Boris Yeltsin; the political monopoly of the Communist Party was legally ended. In 1991 the USSR itself was officially declared to be at an end. Soviet socialism, the proud child of the future, died of old age in its historical infancy.

LOOKING INTO THE FUTURE

But why did a market system not spring up to fill the void? The answer is that markets are not just places where buyers and sellers meet and bargain, as in a village square. The market is only the outer shell of a complex social order called capitalism. And the reality of moving from a planned system to a market system is likely to be very different from the dream of leaping from an economy of lines and empty shelves to stores bulging with merchandise and pockets bulging with cash. Workers may find themselves discharged from inefficient enterprises and told to fend for themselves—nothing like that ever happened under socialism, they complain. Managers and bureaucrats find that they have to take risks and chances that may cost them their jobs—nothing like *that* ever happened under socialism, they exclaim. Pensioners discover that their incomes may not even suffice for subsistence, as the old state subsidies are taken away and prices rise; many people find themselves exposed to the confusion that comes from having not one, but two or ten viewpoints on what is wrong and how to fix it.

Thus the great transformation is by no means easy, agreeable, or guaranteed of success. It took some three centuries for feudalism to evolve (and finally to explode) into capitalism. It would be foolish to presume that communism will evolve, or explode into capitalism within a matter of a few months or even years. In all likehood the transition will be stretched out over decades, perhaps even over generations.

During the time of transformation, we will probably see many outcomes with many different economic configurations for the formerly communist states. All will doubtless encourage private undertakings, such as small stores, cafés, personal services, repair shops, and the like; many may experiment with cooperatives, perhaps in light manufacturing, like the early kibbutzes in Israel. There will be a surge of new professions—bankers, accountants, lawyers, and other such skills without which a market system cannot function. But it will not be an easy matter to create a new working economic order in societies that are not used to the ways of the market, that do not have a well-established framework of private ownership, that lack the hard currency to buy modern industrial equipment or the know-how to maintain it. That is why aid from the outside world will be needed. We can also expect that many countries will retain a core of central planning for essential goods, or that efforts to "privatize" large enterprises, like steel plants, may be stymied for lack of sheer managerial skills as well as by the complex problems of deciding who will be given, or who will have the right to buy, shares in these newly created businesses.

So it is entirely possible that some of these post-communist economies will fail to make the leap into capitalism, and will drift—or explode—into some form of authoritarian political and "planified" economic system or into gangsterism. Others may succeed well enough so that in ten or twenty years they achieve the levels of economic well-being of, say, Portugal or Turkey or Greece. One or two may find a prosperous place for themselves attached to the burgeoning economies of transnational Europe. No one can say with confidence which nations will end up where in this huge historical free-for-all. Right now China seems the most promising candidate among the ex-socialist nations; and some economists speak of the emergence of a high-tech, low-wage, politically stable Chinese system as a major player on the economic scene in the twenty-first century. But there are too many imponderables to make that a sure bet. We will have to wait and see.

CAPITALISM TODAY

What does that panorama of outcomes portend for the question that lies at the center of our book—the prospect for the social order in which we live? Here we turn back to problems we have encountered before, except that we now place them in a wider historic context. There are three such problems that will affect, for better or worse, the operation of all capitalist economies:

First, the market is an inefficient instrument for provisioning societies—even rich societies—with those goods and services for which no price tag exists, such as education or local government services or public health facilities.

A market society buys such public goods by allocating a certain amount of taxes for these purposes. Its citizens, however, tend to feel these taxes as an exaction in contrast with the items they voluntarily buy. Too easily, therefore, a market society underallocates resources to education, city government, public health, or recreation, since it has no means of bidding funds into these areas, in competition with the powerful means of bidding them into autos or clothes or personal insurance. Thus private opulence and public squalor: New York, the city of the richest people in the world, lacks the money to keep its streets clean or safe.

A second and perhaps even deeper-seated failing of the market system is its application of a strictly economic calculus to the satisfaction of human wants and needs. The market is an assiduous servant of the wealthy, but an indifferent servant of the poor. It presents us with the anomaly of a surplus of luxury housing existing side by side with a shortage of inexpensive housing, although the social need for the latter is incontestably greater than the former. Or it pours energy and resources into the multiplication of luxuries for which the wealthier classes offer a market, while allowing more basic needs of the poor to go unheeded and unmet.

This is not just an economic failure. It is a moral failure. Market systems promote amorality. We count as gains the increases in GNP that result from the market system, but we do not give much heed to the commercialism, the trivialization, the psychological frustration and dissatisfaction that also accompany so much market activity.

This recital of the failings of the market system ends with a third failure—the micro and macro ills that spring up as a consequence of its operations. We know the severity and extent of some of these maladies, having just finished an examination of micro and macro economics. But it is well to remember that inflation and unemployment, poverty and pollution, are all to some degree the products of the hugely vital but careless and even dangerous momentum that the market imparts to the social process. We must be aware of linking every social ill with the economic system in which it appears, but it would be equally foolish to ignore the linkage that often binds the one with the other.

A TIME OF CHANGE FOR CAPITALISM?

These general remarks bring us closer to our target. What is the outlook for our own capitalism—the capitalism embodied in the institutions of the United States?

Here we must begin by reviewing very rapidly the sorry story of America's position in the world economy over the last half century. We came out of World War II war in a position of unrivaled military, economic, and political leadership. With only 6 percent of the world's population we produced half the world's output. We were the leader—the lowest in cost, the highest in quality, the most advanced in technology—in every kind of commodity—agriculture, steel, automobiles, airplanes, ships, machine tools, electronics, or ladies' fashions. America was the powerhouse of the economic world, and the conventional wisdom thought it would always remain so. Japan's future appeared to lie in the export of inexpensive Christmas tree decorations, Europe's in the encouragement of tourism to its quaint towns and villages.

Do we have to recount the extraordinary events that followed—events not so catastrophic, but almost as surprising as the fall of the Soviet economy? One by one we lost leadership in steel, automobiles, ships, machine tools, electronics, and ladies' fashions. By the 1990s the only major area in which American economic preeminence was still widely acknowledged was in the production of airplanes—mainly the famous Boeings—and that was already being seriously challenged by the European Airbus.

Along with the decline in economic power came a gradual but cumulative loss of political leadership. From the 1950s through the 1970s, the United States was the world's hegemon—its undisputed political center. As such, the dollar was always considered "as good as gold" simply because it was the money of the hegemonic power. By the 1990s, the precipitous fall of the dollar and the huge foreign debt entanglements of the United States economy made that hegemonic position very dubious. America was still the most powerful military power in the world, but its political clout in the East was not much greater than that of Japan, if indeed greater at all; and with the fall of the Soviet system, its political cloud in Europe all but disappeared.

How did this astonishing fall come about? We already know the answer, but it is worth repeating. Both Europe and Japan laid in the basis for a new kind of more economically flexible, and more socially resilient capitalism, whereas we stood idly by. Both Europe and Japan established social security and health systems that took away much of the anxiety that had weakened the mass support for capitalism before the war. Alone among the rich nations of the world, we failed to create a national health insurance scheme. They built strong infrastructures of roads, high-speed railroads, public housing, research and development centers; we cut our infrastructure expenditures by 30 to 50 percent. They established world-leadership public-education systems; we allowed our high schools to graduate students who regularly came in last or next to last in international rankings, especially in the sciences and math. They encouraged small family firms to combine into larger modern managerial units, and looked with favor on interbusiness cooperative ventures when the prospective market exceeded the reach of any single firm alone; we look on business amalgamations as targets for antitrust violations, not as potential sources for economic growth. They encouraged their banks to work closely with big industrial customers to finance long-term undertakings; we allowed our banks to get involved in one of the most destructive—and self-destructive—orgies of finance in the history of American business. Many countries in Europe worked out arrangements for trade union representation on corporate boards of directors, and for generous government unemployment benefits and retraining arrangements, paving the way for union agreement on noninflationary wage pacts. We presided over an era of anti-unionism on the part of government as well as managment.

And so at the end of thirty years America was seriously behind its competitors in organizational flexibility, economic know-how, managerial sophistication, labor skills, and national morale. That is the reason—not "unfair trade practices" or uneven playing fields— that we have fallen from the unchallengeable champion among the leading nations of the world's economy to its least up-to-date member in hardly more than a generation.

LOOKING AHEAD

The key to the American future lies in changing our mind about the role of government in the economy. For almost two decades our view of that role has been negative. We have seen nothing constructive in government's role—only waste or inefficiency. We have imagined that the public sector in twenty-first-century capitalism would play a smaller role than in the twentiety century!

That strikes us as a view that flies in the face of history and that ignores the clear lessons of the present. Our policy of negativism toward government overlooks the decisive role that government played in building the transcontinental railways, the Manhattan Project, the Interstate Highway System. It looks suspiciously at the way in which government and business have worked together abroad to build the Airbus or the Japanese automobile industry, but the thought never seems to enter our heads that we could do the same, perhaps even better. We are shocked and dismayed to discover that 96 percent of all Japanese high school students graduate, compared with 71 percent of ours, but we do not go further to consider the consequences of this disparity for our economic future or how we could use government's financial assistance in bringing our educational system up to Japanese or German or Dutch or Swedish levels.

This certainly does not mean that the United States could or should try to copy the institutions of other countries. It does mean that we must recognize that there are many ways of organizing twenty-first-century capitalism, and that our defensive, anti–public sector way shows no signs of being a winner. It need hardly be said, after the Russian fiasco, that this is no call for central planning! It is, rather, a call for a return to American pragmatism in economic policy. As we have said earlier, this means undertaking a long-overdue investment program in infrastructure, including education. It means using government finance to help private enterprise achieve research and development objectives that are beyond purely private industries that may become the "Airbuses" of the future. To repeat what we have said before, it means using government to represent the interests of the future to the present.

In a word, we look forward to a twenty-first-century capitalism in which the public sector will be boldly used to support and strengthen the private sector. The dynamism, the choice of inventive technologies, the business acumen and managerial skills that drive the capitalist locomotive will always be the crucial element in determining the system's performance. But we have learned painfully that the private locomotive cannot gather much speed when the public embankment is crumbing or weak. In our view the success of American capitalism in the coming century depends first and foremost on learning how to use the two sectors as one—private enterprise providing the driving energy, public capital the strong foundation for an economy that strives to be, both at home and abroad, the world model that it ought to be.

Should the authors of a book on explaining economics be so outspoken in their views? Better to be outspoken, we think, than to pretend to a neutrality that we do not feel. And then there is another consideration. This book is titled *Economics Explained*, but one lesson should be clear from its pages. It is that the real challenge does not lie in our economic problems, but in the political and moral values that *always* enter into our economic determinations. Economics is the language we use to talk about the workings and options of our system, but it is not the language in which we appraise the value of the system or decide what elements in it to preserve or change. Politics and morality—our collective wills and our private value systems—remain the bedrock of society. The outcome of the crisis of our times will reflect the strength of that will and the quality of those values.

APPENDIX

How the Banking System Works

Banking is a business that inspires both jokes and awe. Perhaps both attest to our uneasy feeling that we don't understand how banks work, and whether or not banks can "create" money. Here is an explanation of these questions. The explanation poses no particular difficulties, but it should be read through slowly to grasp the process. (Note: there is no law saying that you *have* to understand how the banking system works. Lots of bankers don't. But if you are curious, here is the answer.)

We begin by introducing two basic elements of business accounting: *assets* and *liabilities*. Every student at some time or another has seen the balance sheet of a firm, and many have wondered how total assets always equal total liabilities. The reason is very simple. Assets are all the things or claims a business owns: its cash, accounts receivable, plant and equipment, etc. Liabilities are claims against those assets—some of them the claims of creditors, some the claims of owners (called the *net worth* of the business). Since assets show everything that a business owns, and since liabilities show how claims against these selfsame things are divided between creditors and owners, it is obvious that the two sides of the balance sheet must always come to exactly the same total. The total of assets and the total of liabilities are an identity.

Businesses show their financial condition on a *balance sheet* on which all items on the left side represent assets and all those on the right side represent liabilities. By using a simple two-column balance sheet, we can follow very clearly what happens to our bank as we deposit money in it or as it makes loans or investments.

We start off with the following example in which we open a brand-new bank with $1 million in cash and checks on other banks. Hence, our first entry in the balance sheet shows the two sides of this transaction. Notice that our bank has gained an asset of $1 million, the cash and checks it now owns, and that it has simultaneously gained $1 million in liabilities, the deposits it *owes* to its depositors (who can withdraw their money).

ORIGINAL BANK

Assets	Liabilities
$1,000,000 (cash and checks)	$1,000,000 (money owed to depositors)
Total $1,000,000	*Total $1,000,000*

As we know, however, our bank will not keep all its newly gained cash and checks in the till. It may hang on to some of the cash, but it will send all the checks it has received, plus any currency that it feels it does not need, to the Fed for deposit in its account there.

ORIGINAL BANK

Assets		Liabilities	
Vault Cash	$100,000	Deposits	$1,000,000
Deposit at Fed	900,000		
Total	*$1,000,000*	*Total*	*$1,000,000*

This is how the balance sheet looks after checks have cleared through the Federal Reserve. If you will examine any bank's balance sheets, you will see these items listed as "Cash and due from banks." This means, of course, cash in their own vaults plus their balance at the Federal Reserve.

Banks are money-making businesses. Therefore our bank does not want to remain in this very liquid, but very unprofitable, position. According to the law, it must retain only a certain percentage of its deposits in cash or at the Federal Reserve—20 percent in our hypothetical example. All the rest it is free to lend or invest. As things now stand, however, it has $1 million in reserves—$800,000 more than it needs. Hence, let us suppose that it decides to put these *excess reserves* to work by lending that amount to a sound business risk. (Note that banks do not lend the excess reserves themselves. These reserves, cash, and deposits at the Fed remain right where they are. Their function is to tell the banks how much they may loan or invest.)

Assume now that the Smith Corporation, a well-known firm, comes in for a loan of $800,000. Our bank is happy to lend them that amount. But making a loan does not mean that the bank now pays the company in cash out of its vaults. Rather, *it makes a loan by opening a new checking account for the firm* and by crediting that account with $800,000. (Or if, as is likely, the Smith firm already has an account with the bank, it will simply credit the proceeds of the loan to that account.)

Our new balance sheet shows some interesting changes:

ORIGINAL BANK

Assets		Liabilities	
Cash and at Fed	$1,000,000	Original deposits	$1,000,000
Loan (Smith Corp.)	800,000	New deposit	
		(Smith Corp.)	800,000
Total	$1,800,000	Total	$1,800,000

There are several things to note about this transaction. First, our bank's reserves (its cash and deposit at the Federal Reserve) have not yet changed. The $1 million in reserves are still there.

Second, notice that the Smith Corporation loan counts as a new asset for the bank because the bank now has a legal claim against the company for that amount. (The interest on the loan is not shown in the balance sheet; but when it is paid, it will show up as an addition to the bank's cash.)

Third, deposits have increased by $800,000. Note, however, that this $800,000 was not paid to the Smith firm out of anyone else's account in the bank. It is a new checking account, one that did not exist before. As a result, the supply of money is also up! More about this shortly.

Was it safe to open this new account for the company? Well, we might see whether our reserves are now sufficient to cover the Smith Corporation's account as well as the original deposit accounts. A glance reveals that all is well. We still have $1 million in reserves against $1.8 million in deposits. Our reserve ratio is much higher than the 20 percent required by law.

It is so much higher, in fact, that we might be tempted to make another loan to the next customer who requests one, and in that way further increase our earning capacity. But the experienced banker shakes his head. "The Smith Corporation did not take out a loan and agree to pay interest on it just for the pleasure of letting that money sit with you," he explains. "Very shortly, the company will be writing checks on its balance to pay for goods or services; and when it does, you will need every penny of the reserve you now have."

That, indeed, is the case. Within a few days we find that our bank's account at the Federal Reserve Bank has been charged with a check for $800,000 written by the Smith Corporation in favor of the Jones Corporation, which carries its account at another bank. Now we find that our balance sheet has changed dramatically, as we can see below:

ORIGINAL BANK

Assets		Liabilities	
Cash and at Fed	$200,000	Original deposits	$1,000,000
Loan (Smith Corp.)	800,000	Smith Corp. deposits	0
Total	*$1,000,000*	*Total*	*$1,000,000*

The borrower uses the loan, reducing its deposits to zero.

Let us see exactly what has happened. First, the Smith Corporation's check has been charged against our account at the Fed and has reduced it from $900,000 to $100,000. Together with the $100,000 cash in our vault, this gives us $200,000 in reserves.

Second, the Smith Corporation's deposit is entirely gone, although its loan agreement remains with us as an asset.

Now if we refigure our reserves, we find that they are just right.

We are required to have $200,000 in vault cash or in our Federal Reserve account against our $1 million in deposits. That is exactly the amount we have left. Our bank is now fully "loaned up."

But the banking *system* is not yet fully loaned up. So far, we have traced what happened only to our bank when the Smith Corporation spent the money in its deposit account. Now we must trace the effect of this action on the deposits and reserves of other banks.

We begin with the bank in which the Jones Corporation deposits the check it has just received from the Smith Corporation. A look below will show you that the Jones Corporation's bank now finds itself in exactly the same position as our bank was when we opened it with $1 million in new deposits, except that the addition to this second-generation bank is smaller than the addition to the first-generation bank.

SECOND BANK

Assets		Liabilities	
Cash and at Fed	$800,000	Deposits (Jones Corp.)	$800,000
Total	*$800,000*	*Total*	*$800,000*

The assets of a new (second-generation) bank have risen.

As we can see, our second-generation bank has gained $800,000 in cash and in deposits. Since it needs only 20 percent of this for required reserves, it finds itself with $640,000 excess reserves, which it is now free to use to make loans and investments. Suppose that it extends a loan to the Brown Company and that the Brown Company shortly thereafter spends the proceeds of that loan at the Black Company, which banks at yet a third bank. The balance sheet below show how the total deposits will now be affected.

SECOND BANK (AFTER BROWN CO. SPENDS THE PROCEEDS OF ITS LOAN)

Assets		Liabilities	
Cash and at Fed	$160,000	Deposits (Jones Corp.)	$800,000
Loan (to Brown Co.)	640,000	Deposits (Brown Co.)	0
Total	*$800,000*	*Total*	*$800,000*

THIRD BANK (AFTER BLACK CO. GETS THE CHECK OF BROWN CO.)

Assets		Liabilities	
Cash and at Fed	$640,000	Deposits (Black Co.)	$640,000
Total	*$640,000*	*Total*	*$640,000*

Here is a repetition of the same process, as the Second Bank uses its lending capacity to finance Brown Co.

As the next diagram makes clear, the process will not stop here, but can continue from one bank to the next as long as any lending power remains. Notice however that this lending power gets smaller and smaller and will eventually reach zero.

EXPANSION OF THE MONEY SUPPLY*

If we now look at the bottom of this last diagram, we will see something very important. *Every time any bank in this chain of*

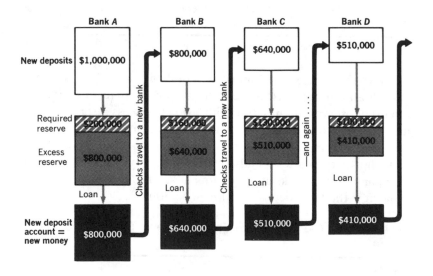

*We have followed how increases in bank lending can lead to a rise in the money supply. The same process can take place if a bank uses its excess reserves to buy investments, such as government bonds, instead of lending its money. For simplicity's sake we have omitted the investment process here.

transactions has opened an account for a new borrower, the supply of money has increased. Remember that the supply of money is the sum of currency outside the banking system (i.e., in our own pockets) plus the total of demand deposits. As our chain of banks kept opening new accounts, it was simultaneously expanding the total check-writing capacity of the economy. Thus, money has materialized, seemingly out of thin air.

Now how can this be? If we tell any banker in the chain that he has "created" money, he will protest vehemently. The loans he made, he will insist, were backed at the time he made them by excess reserves as large as the loan itself. Just as we had $800,000 in excess reserves when we made our initial loan to the Smith Corporation, so every subsequent loan was always backed 100 percent by unused reserves when it was made.

Our bankers are perfectly correct when they tell us that they never, never lend a penny more than they have. Money is not created in the lending process because a banker lends money he doesn't have. Money is created because you and I generally pay each other by checks that give us claims against each other's bank. If we constantly cashed the checks we exchanged, no new money would be created. But we do not. We deposit each other's checks in our own bank accounts; and in doing so, we give our banks more reserves than they need against the deposits we have just made. These new excess reserves make it possible for our banks to lend or invest, and thereby to open still more deposit accounts, which in turn lead to new reserves.

This all sounds a little frightening. Does it mean that the money supply can go on expanding indefinitely from a single new deposit? Wouldn't that be extremely dangerous?

It would of course be very dangerous, but there is no possibility that it can happen. For having understood how the supply of money can expand from an original increase in deposits, we may now understand equally well what keeps an expansion within bounds.

1. Not every loan generates an increase in bank deposits.
If our bank had opened a loan account for the Smith Corporation at the same time that another firm had paid off a similar loan, there would have been no original expansion in bank deposits. In that case, the addition of $800,000 to the Smith account would have been

MONEY AND DEBT

All this gives us a fresh insight into the question of what money is. We said before that it is whatever we use to make payments. But what do we use? The answer is a surprising one. We use *debts*—specifically, the debts of commercial banks. Deposits are, after all, nothing but the liabilities that banks owe their customers. Furthermore, we can see that one purpose of the banking system is to buy debts from other units in the economy, such as businesses or governments, in exchange for its own debts (which are money). For when a bank opens an account for a business to which it has granted a loan or when it buys a government bond, what else is it doing but accepting a debt that is *not* usable as money, in exchange for its deposit liabilities that *are* usable as money? And why is it that banks create money when they make loans, but you or I do not, when we lend money? Because we all accept bank liabilities (deposits) as money, but we do not accept personal or business IOU's to make payments with. You cannot buy groceries with a General Motors IOU, but you can with a Chase Manhattan IOU—a check drawn on your account there.

---

exactly balanced by a decline of $800,000 in someone else's account. Even if that decline would have taken place in a different bank, it would still mean that the nation's total of bank deposits would not have risen, and therefore no new money would have been created. Thus, only net additions to loans have an expansionary effect. Such a net addition arises when the Fed buys U.S. securities. (See page 125.)

2. There is a limit to the rise in money supply from a single increase in deposits.

As our figure shows, in the chain of deposit expansion each successive bank has a smaller increase in deposits, because each bank has to keep some of its newly gained cash or checks as reserve. Hence the amount of *excess* reserves, against which loans can be made, steadily falls.

Further, we can see that the amount of the total monetary expansion from an original net increase in deposits is governed by the size of the fraction that has to be kept aside each time as reserve. If each bank must keep one fifth of its increased deposits as reserves, then the cumulative effect of an original increase in deposits, when it has expanded through the system, is five times the original increase. If reserves are one fourth, the expansion is limited to four times the original increase, and so on.

3. The monetary expansion process can work in reverse.

Suppose that the banking system as a whole suffers a net loss of deposits. Instead of putting $1 million into a bank, the public takes it out in cash. The bank will now have too few reserves and it will have to cut down its loans or sell its investments to gain the reserves it needs. In turn, as borrowers pay off their loans, or as bond buyers pay for their securities, cash will drain from other banks, who will now find *their* reserves too small in relation to their deposits. In turn, they will therefore have to sell more investments or curtail still other loans, and this again will squeeze still other banks and reduce their reserves, with the same consequences.

Thus, just as an original expansion in deposits can lead to a multiple expansion, so an original contraction in deposits can lead to a multiple contraction. The size of this contraction is also limited by the size of the reserve fraction. If banks have to hold a 25 percent reserve, then an original fall of $100,000 in deposits will lead to a total fall of $400,000, assuming that the system was fully loaned up to begin with. If they had to hold a 20 percent reserve, a fall of $100,000 could pyramid to $500,000.

4. The expansion process may not be fully carried through.

We have assumed that each bank in the chain always lends out an amount equal to its excess reserve, but this may not be the case. The third or fifth bank along the way may have trouble finding a credit-worthy customer and may decide—for the moment, anyway—to sit on its excess reserves. Or borrowers along the chain may take out cash from some of their new deposits and thereby reduce the banks' reserves and their lending powers. Thus the potential expansion may be only partially realized.

5. *The expansion process takes time.*

Like the investment multiplier process, the expansion of the money supply encounters many frictions in real life. Banks do not instantly expand loans when their reserves rise; bank customers do not instantly expand the proceeds of bank loans. The time lags in banking are too variable to allow us to predict exactly how long it will take for an initial increase in new deposits to work its way through the system, but the time period is surely a matter of months for two or three "rounds."

Understanding the mechanics of the expansion of the money suply now enables us to understand better the role of the Federal Reserve. The Fed, we recall, has three means of exerting its authority: raising or lowering the amount of required reserves; changing the bank borrowing rate (discount rate); and buying or selling U.S. bonds (open-market operations). All of these have the same end result. They increase or decrease the excess reserves of banks. As a consequence, they allow the expansion process—or the contraction process—to start on its course.

And that's how the banking system works!

Index